ACQUITTAL

ACQUITTAL

AN INSIDER REVEALS THE STORIES AND STRATEGIES
BEHIND TODAY'S MOST INFAMOUS VERDICTS

RICHARD GABRIEL

BERKLEY BOOKS, NEW YORK

THE BERKLEY PUBLISHING GROUP
Published by the Penguin Group
Penguin Group (USA) LLC
375 Hudson Street, New York, New York 10014

USA • Canada • UK • Ireland • Australia • New Zealand • India • South Africa • China

penguin.com

A Penguin Random House Company

This book is an original publication of The Berkley Publishing Group.

Library of Congress Cataloging-in-Publication Data

Gabriel, Richard K., author.
Acquittal : an insider reveals the stories and strategies behind today's most
infamous verdicts / Richard Gabriel.
pages cm
ISBN 978-0-425-26971-8 (hardback)
1. Trials—United States.   2. Defense (Criminal procedure)—United States—Case studies.   I. Title.
KF220.G33 2014
345.73'07—dc23   2014004157.

FIRST EDITION: June 2014

PRINTED IN THE UNITED STATES OF AMERICA

10   9   8   7   6   5   4   3   2   1

Jacket photography of O. J. Simpson © Getty Images; Heidi Fleiss ©
Dan Groshong/Getty Images; Phil Spector Retrial ©
Pool/Getty Images; Casey Anthony Acquitted © Pool/Getty Images.
Jacket design by Danielle Abbiate.
Interior text design by Laura K. Corless.

Contents

Acknowledgments

To my remarkable wife, Kay, and the three beauties Lily, Imogen, and Emma for their patience, love, support, and taking care of all creatures great and small. To my mother for her inspiration, unending kindness, and noodging. To my father for teaching me how to push, question, and challenge. To my brothers for their calm reassurance. To Sharon Gross, gone too soon, for all of her guidance and insight. To Suzy Hoyt, Michelle Ward, and especially Jonathan Ross for their commitment to excellence, critical eyes, and responding to late-night emails. To Whitney Bowens and Marilyn Orozco for all of their help in research. To Paul Lisnek, Ted Donner, Rich Matthews, and Frank Wolfe for their friendship and brilliance. To Brian Lipson for his perseverance and confidence. To Don Winslow for his encouragement, creativity, and sick humor. To Linda Kenney Baden, Michael Baden, Roger Rosen, Rex Shelby, Ed Tomko, Jason Ross, Shawn Holley, Tony Brooklier, Tom Dawson, Howard Asher, Nancy Haydt, Tom Henze, and Pat McGroder for the work, the stories, and the memories. To Jim Robie, also gone too soon, for his integrity and his laugh. To Larry Scarborough, Steve Lamar, and Isaiah Fields for the war stories and the battle scars. To Rebecca Kourlis, Judy Chirlin, and Barry Scheck for the difference they are making. To Bill Cloke, Peter Sawaya, Pat Cady, Leslie Reidel, Jewel Walker, and Sandy Robbins for teaching me how to learn. To the Detroit Team for making a lasting difference in their city. Finally, to all of the attorneys and judges whom

I have worked with over the years for teaching me, encouraging me, challenging me, and demanding more. Your dedication to your clients and the principles of justice are what make the justice system a cornerstone of our democracy.

ACQUITTAL

Introduction

| | | | | | | | | | | | | | | | | **RICHARD GABRIEL** | | | | | | | | | | | | | | | | | | | |

When I was fourteen years old, I remember biking down to a little bungalow in Santa Monica that contained the California Superior courtroom of my mother, the judge. She was conducting a sentencing hearing in which a seventeen-year-old kid had shot and killed a neighbor in his apartment. The kid had claimed self-defense, but the decedent did not have a weapon, and the jury convicted the young man of manslaughter. I watched as my mother carefully questioned the attorneys from the bench, probing their arguments about aggravating and mitigating factors that would determine his sentence.

Later, she brought an armful of accordion and manila file folders home that contained all of the case documents. Poring over them at the breakfast table she talked to my brother and me about the case and her dilemma. Although the evidence and his past record called for a sentence on the upper end of the prescribed term, she thought he was generally a good kid at the wrong place at the wrong time. She didn't want his life to be over by institutionalizing him and possibly creating a career violent offender. She sentenced him to a middle term, but I watched her struggle with the decision, knowing that her sentence would have a very real impact on his life.

That same year, I traveled with my father up to San Francisco to watch him give a paper before the American Psychological Association. He was presenting a new theory of clinical psychotherapy, and I didn't understand a word of it. However, I distinctly remember a host of attendees first questioning him, then standing, then yelling at him about his therapeutic approach. He calmly answered their questions and then questioned them back, challenging them. They grew more furious until the session finally ended.

Later he looked like he could not have been more pleased. This puzzled me. He said that to create change in his clients, he had to interrupt their habituated behavior. This usually makes them angry, but then they could learn. He said that psychologists were no different.

Needless to say, growing up with a mother as a judge and a father as a psychologist, I rarely won an argument or snuck one by my parents. My mother's family escaped the Russian pogroms, and my father's mother, Grandma Jolie, escaped Hungary before the rise of Hitler, losing most of her family to the Nazis. I was raised in the long shadows of the Holocaust and the civil rights movement. Both of my parents arm-wrestled Joe McCarthy and the House Un-American Activities Committee in the 1950s, the ghosts of Stalin and Hitler pulling at their shoulders. My father, a World War II flight navigator, was black-listed from working for the Veterans Administration for refusing to sign a loyalty oath. My mother was refused admittance to the California State Bar for reasons of "moral turpitude"—McCarthy-speak for people who had certain kinds of friends, attended certain kinds of parties, and subscribed to certain types of publications. But my mother, fresh from law school, hired a lawyer, made an argument to McCarthy's committee, and was admitted to the Bar. However, since law firms didn't hire women lawyers at the time, she hung out her own shingle and saw clients at the house so she could take care of my brother and me. I was raised with a healthy skepticism of authority and an appreciation of outcasts and iconoclasts.

I graduated a year early from high school and worked in construction for a year so I could earn enough money to travel in the summer before I went to college. I had planned to go to Europe with a friend of mine from my neighborhood, Brian Dean. He was finishing up high school, and I was helping his family remodel a room in his house, a block away from mine.

One morning my mother woke me up and told me that Brian had been killed. After walking home from school, he and his sister had surprised burglars that were robbing their home. They had both been bound and gagged, Brian's sister was sexually assaulted, and then they were both bludgeoned and stabbed to death. Brian's parents never went back to that house.

I had been playing pool with Brian in his family room and planning our trip to Europe the day before his murder. And then my world changed the next day. While before I had lived in a safe and sleepy sepia-toned beach town filled with surfers and retirees, I now lived in a darker, more dangerous place. I had nightmares. I couldn't drive up that street, imagining the moment when Brian and his sister had first walked in that house. In a just world, how could a good and sweet family be devastated in such a hideous manner? Were these murderers evil monsters or sick psychos? Was this horror due to bad timing, bad luck, and unseen coincidence? In a fair world, on a sunny street in *my* neighborhood, how could this happen? For me, the world was now a worse place, people were unpredictable and mostly bad.

I went to Europe by myself that summer, scared to death but determined to do the trip that Brian and I had planned. To somehow bring him with me. I visited an old school friend who was living in Israel, and we went on an expedition down into the Sinai, within mortar shell range of Jordan. We camped at the base of the mountain, and awoke at four in the morning to climb the carefully carved stairs to the top of Mount Sinai. At the top were thirty-four priests that had traveled from all over the world to hold Mass on top of the mountain where

Moses had received the Ten Commandments. They started the service by singing Bob Dylan's "Blowin' in the Wind" in Italian as the sun rose. And something lifted in me.

When I came home, despite my parents' strong suggestions that I attend law school or a PhD program, I opted to train for a life in the theater—a sure cause of *tsuris* for them. *Tsuris* is a combination of Jewish anxiety, aggravation, and heartburn. As the reality of acting-induced poverty set in, I went back to school to complete my master's work in communication. I was fascinated with linguistics and the inherent theatricality of trials. But, when I started to observe actual cases in court, I was struck by the tedium of testimony, wondering how jurors ever made sense of complex cases, legal instructions, and verdict forms.

Over the last three decades, I became a kind of legal Forrest Gump, finding my way into numerous high-profile trials, more out of curiosity, fascination, and luck than a desire for notoriety. I became president of the American Society of Trial Consultants and president of the American Society of Trial Consultants Foundation, where our mission is to create a more efficient and effective justice system by better understanding the psychology of decisions and the principles of communication in litigation.

In almost thirty years, I have worked on more than a thousand trials. I have listened to tens of thousands of jurors and trained hundreds of lawyers. I have studied everything I could about how individuals and groups make decisions. I have learned it is important to dig deep into the archaeology of a case: the motivations of defendants; the biases of the attorneys, judges, and witnesses; the emotional issues; the values and public opinions in the community of the trial; the attitudes and experiences of jurors; their cultural interpretations and unconscious rules; the media's coverage of a case; the personalities and communication preferences of everyone in the courtroom. If you dig deep enough and decipher the hieroglyphics, you will discover a vivid and abundant world.

As you will see in the book, I am a big fan of William Shakespeare. He wrote all thirty-seven of his plays in the late sixteenth and early seventeenth centuries, before there was a formal study of psychology. Yet he understood the richness and complexity of human emotion and behavior. In 1791, when the Sixth Amendment was added to our Bill of Rights, I believe our founders had written their own homage to democratic principles in iambic pentameter by implementing our jury system. Even though they could not have anticipated the scope and global reach of laws affecting every aspect of our lives; even if they could not foresee television, the Internet, or the instantaneous access to information we now take for granted, they still built a system based on core values of the democracy: freedom, choice, and human judgment.

If I have learned anything over the past three decades, it is that our justice system is a living, breathing, dynamic system that deals daily with the hopes and heartaches of thousands of citizens. By understanding how political and personal desires pull at judges, juries, lawyers, defendants, and witnesses in our judicial system, we can better dispense justice. By knowing our psychology, our biases, and ourselves, we can make better decisions. I have written the first chapter of this book to try to give you a view of this dynamic system that the public rarely sees. After that, hopefully you will have a better understanding of how I worked on these extraordinary cases.

This book is intended to reflect my observations and my opinions only and not the views of the attorneys and clients I have worked for. As I believe that jurors are the unsung heroes of our justice system, I am only using the jurors' first names and last initials. They have given their time and extraordinary effort to these cases, and deserve their privacy. Many of the juror quotes in the book come from Internet or newspaper articles and some of the quotes in the O. J. Simpson chapter came from two books jurors published after the verdict in the case.

I have used numerous research papers and social science studies when discussing some of the psychological principles in the book. Some of the cited public opinion surveys come from news outlets or professional polling organizations such as Pew Research Center or Gallup, Inc. And of course, much of the background of the trials comes from my personal experience, actual transcripts of the trials, or from news stories for which I am forever grateful to the media for their diligence and fastidiousness.

Big-Top Justice
and Three-Ring Theater

| | | | | | | | | | | | | **TRIALS AND STAGECRAFT** | | | | | | | | | | | | |

When law can do no right,
Let it be lawful that law bar no wrong:
Law cannot give my child his kingdom here,
For he that holds his kingdom holds the law.
—*King John*, William Shakespeare

There is no such *thing* as justice. Justice is not a noun. It is an adjective, a description uttered with satisfaction or dismay by weeping victims' families, head-shaking cops, stunned defendants, righteous journalists, and pontificating pundits. Judges and lawyers don't use the word very much. For those involved in the legal system, justice is the grinding process of research, motions, argument, and waiting. Mostly waiting. Waiting for coroner's reports, for disclosures, for a court date, for a judge's rulings. It is haunted by the ghosts of prior cases, sometimes determined by what one judge decided a hundred years ago in a court thousands of miles away.

America has four separate justice systems. The first is Capital-J Justice. It exists in history books, law school lectures, and philosophical debates. It lives in our Constitution, our Bill of Rights, and in the tumultuous history of our country. It is an aspirational goal and, most importantly, the working engine of our democracy. The Capital-J Justice system dictates the laws of our land—it is the Big Rule Book by which we all must play. If we break certain rules, we are criminals. If we break other rules, we have to pay money. This system places an important level of compliant fear in us as we live our everyday lives. "I don't want to go to jail" is supposed to keep us from cheating on our taxes or drinking too much before getting in a car. "I don't want to be sued" keeps us from making inappropriate comments or gestures to employees, or from selling products that we know are dangerous.

Capital-J Justice was developed by our founders as a reaction to the British monarchy, a response to imperious authority and unchecked power: the power to take someone's life or property without reason. Capital-J Justice exists in legislation, lobbying, backroom deals, and the oily political passing of laws such as death penalty legislation, three strikes laws, and tort reform measures. This system is debated in town halls, state capitals, mahogany-paneled conference rooms, and voted on in curtained booths from Anchorage to Baton Rouge. Capital-J Justice is used in campaign propaganda, uttered in righteous tones, and painted in bold colors. It is an atonal chorus sung by a choir of nine robes in Washington, DC, when they rule that gun rights are inviolable, that gay people have a right to marry, and that corporate campaign contributions are free speech.

Capital-J Justice does not just derive from our Bill of Rights but has roots growing in a field in Runnymede, England, as far back as 1215. In that year, King John signed the Magna Carta near Windsor Castle, planting the seeds of Western democracy. Ironically, the much-revered Magna Carta was a political ploy by barons to usurp the monarchy of the incompetent King John. The king wanted more money and more men to fight wars in France. The barons did not mind as long as the king was winning the wars, but a string of defeats and his excommunication by Pope Innocent left the king with few friends and few options. The Magna Carta was a legislative attempt by the barons to keep from paying more taxes and to gain more power over the throne. It was an abject failure, and ten weeks later, civil war engulfed England.

Our founders Jefferson, Adams, Madison, and Hamilton understood that any distribution of power, be it democratic or monarchic, involved feudalism and political deal making. However, they established an aspirational and idealized set of principles as a barricade against the inevitable corruption and self-dealing that is inherent in any justice system.

The second justice system is lowercase justice, the machinery by which the *process* of justice occurs. These are the mines where thousands of lawyers, judges, paralegals, clerks, bailiffs, messengers, copying services, and court reporters toil every day. The creaky, unwieldy, but still-working machinery by which Big Rule Book violations are determined. It is a messy, infuriating process, marked by clenched jaw admonitions of judges, the indignant bellows of righteous barristers, and spoken in the whispered prayers of defendants sitting in their holding cells, waiting for their day in court.

Lowercase justice is rife with pervasive bias and moral ambiguity. It occurs when a defendant confesses his crime to his lawyer and then tells him to plead not guilty. Lowercase justice occurs when a prosecutor promises a cooperating witness a favorable plea deal in exchange for incriminating testimony. Mostly, lowercase justice occurs in dimly lit rooms where lawyers, paralegals, and clerks spend hundreds of hours reviewing books, boxes, and reams of evidence and case law, the voices of soon-to-be ex-wives and ex-husbands calling, "When are you coming to bed?" echoing faintly in their ears. It is a two-hundred-billion-dollar machine in the United States, counting police protection, legal services, and corrections. In California alone, the prison-worker unions are the second most powerful union in the state, behind teachers, making education and punishment two of California's greatest expenses and values.

The third system is the JUSTICE! system that is featured on *48 Hours*, *CSI*, *Dateline*, *Law & Order*, CNN, HLN, and Investigation Discovery. It is a blend of news, entertainment, and commentary streamed into our homes, workplaces, and pockets through television, tablets, smartphones, and personal computers. We watch detectives solve mysteries and catch killers in an hour, lawyers prosecute criminals, news reporters tell us about the shocking testimony in the latest scandalous trials, and experts tell us what it all means. They are all usually good-looking. We can see this "entertainews" in restaurants, hotel lobbies, elevators, and airport departure gates. On one screen we can watch the game of the night on ESPN and then the latest crime or trial story on CNN. Both are sporting events. Both are real. Both seem important. They must be important if they are up there on the screen, being watched by millions of people.

When you sit in the television studio, they powder you to take the shine off your face, fit you with an earpiece, and make you count to ten to get a sound check. Gloria Allred is in the next room, getting in makeup. Alan Dershowitz, Jeffrey Toobin, and the blond, beautiful body-language expert are all talking about the latest case du jour. You hope you have your talking points ready because you only have a two-minute segment, and you better have a pithy eight-second comment to sound intelligent and insightful. Like the courtroom, the questions revolve around the adversarial polemic in the trial you are discussing or the social issues that the media decides are the touchstone topics in the case: race in Zimmerman, parenting in Anthony, mental illness in Holmes. The audience at home wants it because in a connected society, we see a little part of us in every case. As we gaze into that courtroom mirror, we need that aberrant behavior to be explained. And we get instant interpretation through the experts' editorials on our smartphones, laptops, and televisions.

This information conduit is as old as the printing press and as new as fiber-optic cable streaming 24/7 news, images, and 140-character tweets. Where people were previously content to get their news once a day, sitting down at the breakfast table with a newspaper or watching the 6:30 p.m. news, they now demand information constantly. Two and a half billion worldwide users are voraciously hungry and demand to be fed every day, every hour, and every minute.

The fourth and most important justice system is a work of imagination. It exists in the individual and collective minds of jurors as they work to interpret the evidence in a case and arrive at a verdict. It is a constructed reality, cobbled together by shifting memories of witnesses, attorney arguments, legal instructions, personal experiences, and beliefs of jurors. This type of justice occurs in the minds of postal workers, teachers, middle managers, engineers, and retired plumbers as they listen to evidence and pore over the testimony and evidence they have seen. This type of justice occurs in an Orlando courtroom when jurors react to testimony by Casey Anthony's father or in a Los Angeles courtroom when jurors listen to detectives in the O. J. Simpson case describe their discovery of evidence and their use of the n-word. This justice happens slowly, cumulatively as jurors gather various pieces of a jigsaw puzzle they will use to ultimately come up with their own picture of "what really happened." It happens in the minds of judges as they pore over the precedent, reflect on the weighed merits of the case, and make their rulings. The heart of this system is human judgment. This is the real justice system and where we will spend most of the time in this book.

Ultimately, Capital-J Justice and lowercase justice are conceived in policy, statutes, rules, and rationality. JUSTICE! is driven by entertainment, journalism, public interest, and commerce. But the fourth system is a rich world composed of jury and judicial decision making. Indeed, all judgment is fallibly human, wrought in long-held beliefs, emotional reactions, and personal experience. In fact, jurors are instructed in the law that tells them to *not* abandon their common sense, and to scrutinize witnesses for their demeanor, two instructions that are notably subjective. In capital cases, jurors weigh aggravating versus mitigating circumstances of the crime, including highly emotional victim impact statements and testimony about the abusive background of the defendant, to come up with a highly personal formula to decide on the death penalty for a defendant.

All of these systems coincide and collide with one another, both working with and against each other. Capital-J Justice demands that jurors be fair and impartial, yet lowercase justice employs ridiculously antiquated ways of finding out if and how they can be. The system of advocacy and argument also demands that the lawyers try to use their powers of persuasion to influence a systematic and logical evaluation of evidence and law. The JUSTICE! system seeks to inform the public about a case, while in lowercase justice jurors struggle to separate the evidence they have heard from the witness stand from the media stories they saw before being sworn as jurors.

Additionally, lowercase justice involves the practical reality of continuous negotiation and deal making. In this justice system, a majority of criminal defendants are presumed to be guilty by both prosecutors and defense attorneys. Even if they are not, juries convict criminal defendants in 85–95 percent of trials. These odds make it too great a risk for most defendants to go to trial. The risk of longer prison terms with a criminal conviction prompts many to take a plea deal, even if those defendants believe they are innocent and want their day in court.

In this justice system, criminal defense lawyers and prosecutors rely on their relationships as part of the normal plea bartering process. But the white-hot spotlight of publicity also acts as a magnifying glass, enhancing and exaggerating the personalities of all who fall within its beacon.

In a high-profile case, those involved in the lowercase justice system operate under the same rules as they would normally. And yet the omniscient eye of 24/7 news coverage challenges and contradicts the normal procedural rules and principles of due process. The home jury presumes that the defendant is guilty and must prove his or her own innocence. It is also presumed that they should testify on their own behalf. If they don't, they have something to hide. In these expectations, the Fifth and Sixth Amendments of the United States Constitution are counterintuitive.

Which of these four systems represents real justice? And who is the real jury? Those that are sworn in court or those of us opening our bags of chips and settling down to hear recitations from doyenne Nancy Grace and the multitude of pundits and experts? Should we have a jury system or just a text vote or Internet poll about guilt or innocence? Where does justice really exist?

THE ATTORNEYS

There are only two things going on in front of a jury. I'm going to tell you a story, and you're going to believe mine. And he is going to tell you a story, or she's going to tell you a story, and you're going to believe hers. Whichever one you choose, whatever it be, the defendant will be guilty or innocent whosever story you decide is the truth. So it's all a form of performance. It's all a form of narrative. The idea that it's somehow a search for the truth is a wonderful idea. It just isn't true.

—Attributed to Gerry Spence, noted author and
attorney who obtained acquittals for Filipino
First Lady Imelda Marcos and Randy Weaver
in the Ruby Ridge incident

While we think of the Clarence Darrows and Johnnie Cochrans of the world as great oratorical advocates, bending the will of judges and juries with their powerful rhetoric and even more powerful personalities, great attorneys have a series of personal characteristics that go beyond their charisma or linguistic skill.

One of the first characteristics of highly successful attorneys is a voracious competitiveness, a hunger to win, and a will to dominate the case. While we normally associate these traits with loud, pulpit-pounding zeal, I have seen these same characteristics in quiet, methodical, and meticulous attorneys. The will to win is manifested in an excellent advocate's ability to control the focus of the case from the very beginning, to assert their essential perspective so that the judge and the jury are already looking at the issues in the case from their viewpoint. From pretrial motions through to the verdict, excellent advocates are constantly and subliminally shifting and refocusing the fact finder toward their worldview so that the judge and jury are already seeing the case from their frame of reference.

Part of this comes from an innate ability of great lawyers to know what is important to their audience and the ability to adapt both their case and their message to the expectations and sensibilities of their jury. When you look at the craft behind a Steven Spielberg movie, it is not just his ability to tell a good story; he is also his own best audience. That is, he has the ability to know what an audience needs at any point in his movie to slowly build the dramatic tension and further the arc of the story toward its inevitable conclusion.

Great trial lawyers are great storytellers, knowing how to craft a compelling, consistent, and credible case by developing vivid characters, understandable actions, and believable environments in which their clients live and breathe. These attorneys can organize and simplify complex issues so the jury can easily grasp and embrace the nuances of DNA, agonal breaths, and bullet trajectories.

Great attorneys are great communicators. While competent lawyers present evidence to a jury, excellent advocates have the ability to convey the emotion in the case, eliciting that same emotion in their audience. Through either learned or innate talent, they combine a variety of vocal and nonverbal gestures as well as visual images to accompany the rhetorical design of their message. Words have power, but they are notes on a sheet of music unless you have the instruments to play the piece. Attorney arguments are words in a script, a very real script about very real people. And with all great players, whether they are performing music or a play, the best attorneys know the tempo, tone, and the dynamics of the piece. They know how to bring out the varied emotional colors in the composition. Because whether it is a concert, play, or death penalty case, it is all just notes, words, and evidence until it has meaning. And it is the musician, the actor, or the lawyer who gives it meaning.

Unlike a musician or actor, an attorney doesn't have to just tell a good story, they have to tell the best story. They know their audience, the jury, is also listening to another story and will vote on which story wins. As a result, being a great lawyer/performer also means being a great strategist and tactician, anticipating the other side's moves and adapting their case to actually turn the opposing side's theories and themes into support for their own position. So they look at the other side's case and reframe their arguments to essentially show the jury, "Look how *their* evidence demonstrates *our* case." The attorneys with the greatest will to win don't want a fifty-fifty proposition—an equal contest of opposing parties. They want only one true case—their case—to be before the jury.

THE JUDGES

The judiciary has done a stellar job of convincing the general public and the legal profession that they are essentially rational robots, databases of legal knowledge that follow mathematical algorithms to decide issues based on the rules of evidence and law. This misconception has been compounded by Chief Justice John Roberts's simplified and wrongheaded quote in his confirmation hearing to the Supreme Court, "My job is to call balls and strikes and not to pitch or bat." It has been further compounded by the heated rhetoric about "activist judges" and "originalist intent" as if a judge reads only the Dead Sea Scrolls or deciphers sage Talmudic wisdom passed down by others instead of actually interpreting and applying the law.

The static interpretations of judging do not take into account that judges are people that have personal experiences, beliefs, and biases like the rest of us. Everyone has biases. Judges deny like hell that they do, but that is what people who don't understand their biases do. Honest (and insightful) people know they are biased. To be human is to be biased. Biases are preferences and beliefs driven by life experiences, personality constructs, and personal values. Judges have all of these and call more than "balls and strikes." They decide what kind of pitches are thrown, who bats, how many fielders play, where the bases and foul lines are, and how many innings the game will last.

In fact, many attorneys decide whether they forfeit the game based on these "balls and strikes" calls that judges make. In many trials, the case is decided in rulings that a judge makes about which evidence he or she will or will not allow. In Phillip Spector's trial, Judge Larry Paul Fidler's decision to allow five women to testify about his prior gunplay virtually assured an eventual conviction. Judge Lance Ito's allowing of impeachment testimony about Detective Mark Fuhrman's past racial remarks certainly allowed the O. J. Simpson team to persuasively argue that Fuhrman had motivation to plant evidence to incriminate Simpson.

While we spend a lot of time discussing how evidence will affect the ultimate verdict in the case, one factor alone is the most determinative of case outcome: the judge. The ability of the judge to not only include or exclude evidence makes them the writer, producer, and director of the play. Some judges just let all the evidence in, and the trial becomes an epic saga. Some judges want a minimalist drama with few characters and limited action. How they cut the material profoundly shapes how the audience, in this case the jury, views the case.

Richard Posner, a Seventh Circuit Appellate judge and prominent legal theorist, writes in his book, *How Judges Think*, that there are eight ways in which judges make decisions: attitudinal, strategic, psychological, economic, organizational, pragmatic, phenomenological, and legalist. Simplified, this theory says that judges are affected by their political beliefs, are outcome oriented, try to cope with legal uncertainty in big cases, are self-interested, try to operate within organizational rules, are aware of the impact of their decisions, and yes, also conform their decisions to the law. It is no accident that legal conformity is the final and probably least significant theory of jurist decision making. Like the proverbial iceberg, a judge's (not unlike a jury's) decision making is primarily "below the water"—mostly in the subconscious. The final decision on a ruling or a verdict is the justification of the law and evidence in the case, a rationalization for the accumulation of personal experiences, beliefs, values, emotions, preconceptions, and even misconceptions that lie below the surface.

One of the fundamental fallacies in the justice system is that justice is rational. The truth is that the decisions of juries and judges involve human judgment and thus are more than data-driven variables that are systematically entered into a great legal calculus.

THE MEDIA

June 26, 1919, saw the birth of a new kind of journalism in New York City in the form of the *Daily News*. Half the size of other newspapers at the time, it was designed to have a huge, eye-catching headline and a large picture on the front page. It featured short, sensationalized news stories with photos, illustrations, and human-interest stories about the trials and tribulations of both the famous and the obscure common man. The format and the editorial style were intended to titillate, frighten, and mislead the reader.

By 1924, the *Daily News* had the biggest circulation of any paper in the country.

Of course, this caught the attention of every publisher in the country, including William Randolph Hearst, and knockoff tabloids appeared in every major city. Because of this tremendous success, traditional newspapers started to copy the style, format, and even the tone of these papers. The seductive siren song of sensationalism with its promise of profit created a journalistic tension between education and stimulation that is still felt today.

While the public often feels that high-profile trials mirror the way all trials are conducted in this country, nothing could be further from the truth. Tabloid trials function in their own world and under their own rules. Whether it is the Scopes Monkey trial in 1925, where a teacher was tried for teaching evolution in Tennessee, or the espionage trial of Julius and Ethel Rosenberg in 1951, these trials rewrite history and define a cultural moment in time. In fact, the media actually changes the entire nature of how a case is brought and tried; their very presence makes them another party: part prosecutor, part investigator, always a judge, and occasionally a defender. Their omnipresence in these cases creates a combative collision between the First and the Sixth Amendments: the ultimate cage match of freedom of the press and the rights of a defendant to an impartial jury, free from bias.

These cases often salaciously succeed in a way dramatic movies and television cannot: they are real. Real bloodlust, real greed, and real consequences. They create both morality and cautionary tales for the viewing public. Through the jury, these trials fulfill the promise of a truly participatory democracy—a promise that has faded with our cynicism about the impact of our individual vote on our elected officials. That promise is fulfilled when we, at home, view the evidence, judge the credibility of the witnesses, and "vote" to convict or acquit. Through these trials, we see the actual mechanics of the Bill of Rights along with its clanging inconsistencies, inefficiencies, and crazy contrarian justice. It is the constitutional sausage factory.

High-profile trials are the perfect combination of Super Bowl, presidential election campaign, and prime-time police procedural. It is justice as a spectator sport, a civilized Coliseum, with both the public and the jury turning their collective thumbs-up or -down at the plight of the combatants. The prosecution and defense battle as gladiators, hoping to win the collective approval of twelve thumbs.

The camera and the Internet create a justice system on steroids. Facts fuel hyperbolic rage as the media channels the collective emotions of victims, the agenda of political interests, and the ambitions of everyone, vying for the brass ring that news coverage offers: more visibility, more business, more money, fame, and notoriety.

Television and the Internet make the world our community. The bombing of the Boston Marathon instantly becomes *our* bombing, as the coverage of the manhunt for the bombers seems to be happening in our neighborhood. That's why a televised trial puts everyone in the jury seat. Movies and plays are communal stories, shared experiences because we sit and experience the story together. Watching on television or the Internet is a private theater. We watch alone so the stories become our personal stories. They become the looking glass through which we see and judge ourselves. It is why there are at least thirteen judge shows on television at present count, and Judge Judy makes almost fifty million a year.

HLN #1 Among Ad-Supported Cable
as Arias Pleads for Her Life

HLN continues to be the ratings leader and complete source for coverage of the Jodi Arias Trial. **On Tuesday May 21, HLN ranked No.1 among ad-supported cable networks from 1:56p to 2:15p (ET) as Jodi Arias took the stand to plead for her life in front of the jury that found her guilty of Travis Alexander's murder.** *During that time period, HLN out-delivered the competition among both total viewers (2,540,000) and 25–54 demo viewers (691,000).*

—Actual press release from HLN on May 24, 2013
(emphasis added)

Steven Brill, who co-founded Court TV, once wrote, "We see so many 'trials of the century' and the next one could be tomorrow because you have this [mass media] machine that needs it." Media competition, content need, and ratings wars dictate that news organizations pick an angle, shape coverage to appeal to their audience, or regurgitate oft-cited misconceptions in order to feed their audience. The decline of the daytime soap opera is accompanied by the rise of the televised trial. In this amplified environment, the outrage is manufactured and pro-grammed into the shows. And part of it is there to kill time. Because televised trials, like sporting events, only fill a portion of the program time with actual testimony, hearings, and arguments, so the cable stations need commentary to fill the extra programming time.

Frank Magid made most of this possible. He was a social psychol-ogist that became the "news doctor" and transformed news broadcasts from the serious intonations of Edward R. Murrow and Walter Cronkite into the "Action News" format we see today. From his research, he told networks and local affiliates that their audiences wanted a formula of national and local news, liberally sprinkled with crime and human-interest stories. The phrase "If it bleeds, it leads" was generated from his research in the 1970s. Magid also helped to develop the *Good Morning America* news format interspersed with celebrity and lifestyle news.

Additionally, deregulation of television in the 1970s and 1980s also led to greater potential for advertising dollars as entertainment companies consolidated, while Nielsen told advertisers where to put their ad dollars by utilizing a system it developed in the 1950s to measure the "ratings" of viewers toward television programming. It took the O. J. Simpson case to realize the potential in a televised trial. For the networks, local stations, and cable outlets, it was a recipe for success in content-hungry media markets: a gripping drama played out every day for months. And the production costs were minimal, just the cost of the cameras, the cables, and the staff to carry the drama. No writers, no directors, no actors, and no unions.

Over the years, the networks and cable stations have refined their court coverage. Today, there is a cottage television industry in suspecting, condemning, and coveting young women. Prime time is populated with shows about manipulative, vulnerable, and tragic pretty girls. They are the subjects that a target demographic of channels such as Lifetime, the CW, and ABC Family want to see. Now, with media coverage of trials, cable and network news have tapped into the zeitgeist and contrast between innocence, sexuality, and murder. Casey Anthony, Amanda Knox, and Jodi Arias personify our prurient fascination and puritan condemnation of wanton sexuality and recklessness.

Tabloid trials become the looking glass into our own lives. Anthony activates our most primal fears about the worst thing that can happen to our children and our terrible ambivalence about our own families. Arias makes us look at the horrific rage that can lie underneath the love, sex, and dependency in a relationship. Sensationalism is rooted in sensation. And while it has a pejorative connotation by today's journalistic standards, sensationalism allows us to experience shocking, aberrant, and even horrifying conduct in a safe manner in order for our brains to try to make sense of that behavior. Sensational labels allow us to explain strange and unsettling human actions that would otherwise be unthinkable.

These scandalous cases become important because the press says they are important. Because the media places so much attention on a case, jurors pay more attention to these issues. And at that moment when the decision is made in an executive suite of a network or cable news station to cover a trial, the case becomes no longer about the evidence but about larger social issues. To make the coverage appeal to the widest possible audience, the producers, the editors, and the pundits discuss the wider issues of race, religion, or domestic violence, depending on the committed crime. We look to these commentators to give a voice to our sadness, our outrage, and our deepest beliefs about these issues. Haynes Johnson, in his book *The Best of Times*, states that television "democratizes experience" and televised trials democratize our justice system, giving every viewer a seat in the jury box.

However, the presence of the media changes the very nature of legal evidence. Daniel Boorstein speaks about pseudo-events in his book *The Image*. The book, published in 1962, describes how public life had become a series of staged events from political campaigns to quaint Hawaiian luau performances that "represent" Hawaiian culture. The courtroom is already composed of pseudo-events or staged re-creations of events. First, there is the actual crime, which is one version of reality. Then there is the police investigation, which produces another reality through police and expert reports as well as fallible eyewitness testimony with their erratic memory of events. Then there is the trial, which produces yet two more separate realities through the selection and presentation of evidence by the prosecution and defense. The media adds another reality with their interpretation of the evidence and the personalities of the players in the case.

What is sacrificed in this fast, sensationalized, and competitive media market is the measured, thorough, and sometimes slow evaluation of an actual trial. There is an innate pressure in television and Internet journalism to come to quick conclusions in an effort to accommodate the short-segment formats of programming and to scoop competing journalists. Also sacrificed is waiting and withholding judgment until the evidence is all in, replaced with instant opinion and rank speculation. Also sacrificed is individual thought, replaced with pressure to conform to the public opinion shaped by talking heads and water cooler consensus. And one of the worst results of the modern tabloid trial is the presumption of guilt that is carried by the defendant in the case.

Television favors the prosecution because television favors the familiar. We like to think we live in a just world where good things happen to good people and bad things happen to bad people. When bad things happen to good people, it must be because a bad person did it. We trust that prosecutors will always get the bad guy, so if a prosecutor has taken someone to trial, it must be because they know he's guilty. But acquittals are messy because they convey uncertainty. We don't like realizing that the prosecution might have, at best, made a mistake or, at worst, knowingly prosecuted an innocent man or woman. We like even less the idea that the defendant may be guilty but the prosecution just failed to prove it. The whole premise of a criminal defense is to get jurors to embrace the unknown and the uncertain. Prosecutors live in a certain world, and they want jurors to live there as well. They want there to be a reason for everything, a natural order. Most people don't invest weeks watching a trial in order to be left with doubt about the guilt of the defendant. Viewers, for the most part, watch with the expectation of conviction.

Additionally, jurors are also conditioned by broadcast, investigative, and Internet models of news information more than the judicial model of legal information. Here are a few statistics about our media consumption and digestion:

The average adult spends:

- 274 minutes a day watching TV
- 167 minutes a day on the Internet
- 94 minutes a day listening to the radio
- 65 minutes a day on a mobile device
- 26 minutes a day reading a newspaper
- 18 minutes a day reading a magazine
- 78.3 percent of Americans have Internet access
- 83 percent of Americans own some sort of cell phone
- 35 percent of Americans own a smartphone
- 84 percent of smartphone owners regularly use it to access the Internet
- 73 percent of Americans use text messaging
- 13 percent of Americans with Internet use Twitter
- 51 percent of Americans use Facebook
- 19 percent of American adults own a tablet
- 40 percent of people who own a tablet and/or smartphone use them while watching television
- 53 percent of Americans with Internet use Wikipedia
- 49 percent of all households have at least one video game console

According to Nielsen, the average American over the age of two watches thirty-four hours of television a week. If you multiply this by the population, America watches well over 530 billion hours of TV a year. TV-Free America, an admittedly partisan group, also has compiled statistics showing that 99 percent of all U.S. households have at least one television and two-thirds have three or more sets. Seventy percent of day-care centers use television during a given day. And while

American children spend an average of 900 hours per year in school, they spend 1,500 hours per year watching television.

Informing expectations of criminal cases, an average child sees 8,000 murders on TV by the time they finish elementary school and 200,000 killings by the time they turn eighteen. Over 50 percent of all news broadcasts are devoted to stories about crime, disaster, and war. And while almost 60 percent of Americans can name the Three Stooges, only 17 percent can name three justices on the Supreme Court.

Our vast amount of media consumption not only informs our perceptions and expectations about court cases, but also fundamentally shapes the way we process new information. Yet the courts routinely expect the average citizen to immediately switch to the legal model when they are sworn as jurors. Additionally, people who are watching or listening at home have a different role than those sitting in the jury box in the courtroom. At home we have the luxury of taking breaks and joining the trial when it suits our schedule or mood. We can skip boring parts and opt for the more exciting testimony that comes when a defendant or key witness testifies. Our viewing can become a social activity where we watch with others or share our observations with fellow employees at work the next day.

At home, we don't have any rules that govern the way we listen to a case. We can investigate, form immediate opinions, and discuss the case with whomever we wish. We listen to the experts speculate, give opinions, and add information about the parties that would certainly not be allowed in court. More importantly, certain legal coverage invites guests representing the prosecution and defense perspectives to debate the "merits of the evidence." This point/counterpoint discussion often prompts the audience to come to conclusions about the evidence prior to deliberations. Since the viewer at home is not charged as a juror in the case, they have no instruction on burden of proof, reasonable doubt, or circumstantial evidence. The media plays and replays selected footage of high-profile trials, whether it be the slow march of the defendant into the courtroom, pictures of the crime scene, or screen shots from the defendant's social media accounts. "Experts" opine in short sound bites on the guilt or innocence of the defendant. A key witness's testimony will be played over and over and over again. Additionally, much of the early news coverage of a case focuses on information that would be ruled inadmissible in a trial, such as character testimonials by a defendant's co-workers, friends, or ex-lovers. This media barrage creates an indelible impression on prospective jurors, and these impressions are carried into the courtroom.

Any good editor and producer knows that the viewer can click on another website or change the channel at any time. As soon as they get bored or hear something they don't like, they're gone. Therefore, news sites and stations use an "inverted pyramid" model when putting together their stories. In this news model, someone reading an article in a newspaper or on the Internet reads a headline that summarizes the event in a phrase. There is then an explanatory subhead, which discusses the event in a sentence. The first few paragraphs in the story synopsize the entire issue, focusing on what actually happened at the news event. Then the article goes back into greater detail on the background, history, or additional information, which gives the reader context and a more detailed picture of all of the players and acts that inform the story. Internet journalism also provides a lateral information flow, as readers are able to click on links of related stories or events to the news event being reported. Contrast these models with the repetitious, detailed, and contradictory testimony in a legal case, where jurors are given a vast amount of information, often without a headline or summary to give that evidence context.

In a news story, the reader, viewer, or listener sees the picture of the jigsaw puzzle before it gets put together piece by piece. In a trial, jurors do not know what the picture is supposed to look like—they just get a lot of pieces from both sides and have to put together a picture themselves.

Additionally, while TV is about watching, the Internet is about participating. While we shout with ineffectual rage at our televisions, we can be heard through the marvel of fiber, our comments posted for the world to see. Social media also affects how crimes are now investigated, with cell phone pictures, texts, and tweets of crime suspects circulated immediately after they are first identified. Over its twenty-five-year history, the show *America's Most Wanted* claims to have netted more than 1,200 suspected criminals. A willing crime-solving audience can participate in law enforcement investigations, all from the comfort of their living rooms. Jurors also carry an expectation of participation when they are seated for a case.

In order to describe the horror of some violent felonies, district attorneys and pundits use the adjective "evil" to characterize the defendant on trial. The term "evil" names and externalizes our fears and makes the unknown more understandable. It is the unknown that scares us in horror movies, but also touches a primal part of us. We blithely label Arizona convicted murderer Jodi Arias "evil" but at some level recognize the betrayal and the rage of rejection she may have experienced with her boyfriend Travis Alexander. We are fascinated and outraged at Casey Anthony because we feel inherently protective of our own children, have mixed feelings about the relationship between parents and children living at home, and look over our shoulder at the dark specter of abuse and incest. In identifying these ancient emotional themes in our televised trials, O. J. Simpson becomes a modern-day Othello for us, and Anthony becomes a Floridian Medea.

Russell Webster and Donald Saucier are two psychologists who have studied our beliefs in pure good and pure evil. In their research, those who had a belief in pure evil also voiced stronger support for the death penalty, preemptive military strikes, and support for torture as an interrogation tool. Those people also showed greater racial prejudice, opposed social and pro-racial programs such as affirmative action, and did not believe in criminal rehabilitation. Those with a strong belief in pure evil, not surprisingly, believe in a dangerous, hostile, and despicable world. Researchers Jessica M. Salerno and Liana C. Peter-Hagene have also published studies on a phenomenon that prosecutors are intuitively aware of in presenting their cases. These studies have shown that when the emotions of both anger and disgust are elicited in jurors, it increases their moral outrage, which in turn increases their confidence in a conviction verdict. For prosecutors, conviction confidence is the protective shield against a defense attorney's most utilized weapon: reasonable doubt.

These high-profile cases, with their narratives of good and evil set in dens and bedrooms just like ours, are carried to us by the flickering LCD of computer and television screens. They are a study in contrasts—these people look to be perfectly normal, living idyllic lives. But then someone dies and a darker David Lynch–like reality is exposed. These cases are deeply unsettling because they make us confront our deepest fears: that one day *our* idyllic lives can be similarly upended. If it could happen to them, it could happen to us.

THE AMERICAN JURY

I reject your reality and substitute my own.

—*Mythbusters*

Juries are the best judges in the system. They are not elected, they don't have the high-powered microscope of appellate review or the stern, disapproving-schoolmarm precedent looking over their shoulder, and they have no interest in the outcome of the case. Which is precisely the genius of our country's founders. They knew from their experiences with the monarchy that anyone deeply involved in a governing system was susceptible to influence.

Juries were created by those who believed in the wisdom of entrusting citizens with the power of judgment. It is a core value for both liberals and conservatives alike—a mutual distrust of unchecked, unfettered power. Juries are a key component of a representative government because they have direct involvement in the democratic process. They become both the voice of the community and the government, they endure gut-wrenching testimony and graphic pictures, they struggle to comprehend convoluted scientific and legal principles, and, for the princely sum of fifteen dollars a day, they fulfill the solemn duty of judging their fellow citizens.

Yet many mistrust juries and don't understand them. You often see this when a jury returns an unpopular verdict in an O. J. Simpson, a Casey Anthony, or a George Zimmerman case. Many attorneys and judges also dismiss juries as irrational and unpredictable. While most in the legal system pride themselves on the systematic way that they gather evidence and analyze the law in a case, they often think about juries in the most rudimentary and simplistic manner. This is how most judges and lawyers think of juries:

1. Jurors are obligated to be there, so they should be obedient to authority and do as they are told.
2. Jurors will willingly admit to their own biases, no matter how embarrassing.
3. If a juror says they can be fair, they can be fair. After all, they said it under oath.
4. Fairness and impartiality are the same thing.
5. Jurors can easily "set aside" and never use life-changing experiences and long-held beliefs when judging the evidence and the law in a case—kind of like wiping the hard drive on a computer.

6. Jurors can neatly load each side's case into separate folders on this new blank hard drive and consider each folder separately.

7. Jurors can sit and listen with rapt attention for days, weeks, or months, easily understanding even the most arcane concepts and complex subject matter.

8. Jurors are able to compartmentalize their emotions and disregard whatever the judge tells them to disregard.

9. Jurors want to be told how they should think and feel about a case.

10. Jurors can easily work with a group of strangers from diverse backgrounds.

Many of these attitudes toward jurors enable the courts to simplify a complex process of seating a jury and conducting a trial. However, common sense and a panoply of social psychology tell us that this is simply not how juries work. Here's what we know about how jurors go about accomplishing the complicated task of listening to a case, processing the information, deliberating with fellow jurors, and coming to a verdict.

Many cases involve two conflicting versions of facts and dense, complicated testimony about the evidence. Jurors face a heavy "cognitive load"—they hear incredible amounts of information on unfamiliar subjects and have very little time to process it. For example, in cases involving Wall Street brokers accused of securities fraud, we expect jurors to learn and understand in a few short weeks what it took an expert witness in that same trial four years in a PhD program at a business school to learn. Additionally, when jurors are confused, are confronted with gruesome images in a violent crime case, or experience conflict with other jurors, they often revert to what they know best: their years of personal habit and hard wiring. When jurors listen to the emotional testimony about the abuse of a child or the murder of a spouse, it is a faster neural path to their own memory bank than the winding intellectual road of evidence comparison.

Jurors use their own everyday experience and habits constantly as reference material during a trial. It forms the basis of their "common sense," which they are instructed by the court to use. It allows them to judge the validity and credibility of each side's case. These experiences help them to establish norms of how they expect the parties in the case to behave and to understand complex evidentiary and legal issues in a case. Rather than wade through the acronyms and formulas of a forensic accounting expert in a fraud case, it is easier for a juror to refer to what happened to "Uncle Dave when he was audited by the IRS."

When we do things or are told things over and over and over again, this behavioral repetition creates neural pathways in our brains. Hence the expression "creatures of habit." A single traumatic event like the untimely death of a family member can also hard-wire the brain, with the accompanying emotional intensity cementing this wiring. No amount of rational rigor or admonishment can entirely overcome years of habituated and deeply embedded wiring. This applies to jurors, attorneys, and judges. Supreme Court Justices Antonin Scalia and Ruth Bader Ginsburg are as much a product of their life experiences and resulting ideologies as a postal worker hearing a DUI case in downtown Detroit.

These habits of the mind and our explanations for the way the world works serve a neurological function—they create emotional equilibrium to reduce imbalance and uncertainty in our lives. Because of how we were raised and what we have experienced, we constantly seek to reconfirm this worldview. When something does not fit into our mold, we experience instability. This creates a physical sensation that causes an emotional reaction. In Star Wars terms, we experience "a disturbance in the force." Since we do not like disturbance and imbalance, we translate these sensations and emotions into linguistic labels we call *feelings*. And these feelings help us to create balance, because we can now explain these sensations we are experiencing. In fact, our experiences, our habits, and our emotions shape how we see, hear, think, and act. They define who we are in relation to the outside world. Without these explanations, we are wandering through the world without a map or a compass, in a foreign country where we don't know the roads, can't read the signs, and don't speak the language.

Jurors in criminal cases find themselves in bleak territory: drug deals gone bad, domestic violence, infanticide, and sexual assault. Real-life versions of *Breaking Bad*. In order to make sense of this disturbing foreign landscape, jurors' brains play a series of cognitive tricks to make the surroundings look familiar.

One of the most common and treacherous tricks is "confirmation bias." As we are creatures of habit, we look to confirm what we already believe. In a 2008 study, Yale political scientist John Bullock showed Yale University research subjects an ad published during Justice Roberts's confirmation hearing, which accused Roberts of "supporting violent fringe groups and a convicted clinic bomber." Among Democrats who saw the ad, the 56 percent who previously disliked Roberts climbed to 80 percent. However, when these same people heard that the ad's claims were false, Roberts's disapproval rating dropped to only 72 percent. This same study showed that refutation of false information sometimes even strengthened the misinformation. Only 34 percent of conservatives thought Iraq had hidden or destroyed its weapons before the U.S. invasion, but 64 percent who heard the Bush administration's claim and refutation thought that Iraq really did have the weapons. Confirmation bias demonstrates that we see what we *want* to see.

In order to make sense of their new and unfamiliar judicial role, jurors also look for familiar rules, standards, or "norms" for how police or suspects are supposed to act in order to judge whether their actions fall within these expected boundaries, even if these rules come from *Law & Order*, John Grisham, or Judge Judy.

Jurors also tend to think that the most important evidence in a case is what the prosecutors and defense attorneys spend the greatest amount of time disputing. In a trial, time + emphasis = importance. Since "availability bias" says we tend to give weight to that which we remember, the more time and emphasis that are placed on certain evidence in the trial tends to make the jury believe that it must be important. In the next chapter, I will discuss how the prosecutors in the O. J. Simpson trial actually created reasonable doubt in their own case by turning a two-week routine double-homicide case into a nine-month battle over evidence credibility.

Of course, jurors also apply twenty-twenty hindsight to what the defendant and law enforcement should or could have done differently. The George Zimmerman case involved a neighborhood watch captain who shot and killed a young man after a confrontation on a rainy night in a condo complex in Sanford, Florida. Jurors in that case were asked by both sides to use "hindsight bias" to guess what would have happened if Zimmerman had just remained in his car as instructed by the 911 operator or if Trayvon Martin had reacted differently when confronted by Zimmerman.

These are tricks of the mind that we all use as we live our everyday lives, whether we know it or not. These biases become more prominent in jurors as they try to navigate the complex and volatile waters of a criminal case. And this is the real art of jury selection—to engage jurors in an exploration of their life circumstances and attitudes in order to discover not if, but *how*, they will use their experiences and beliefs to interpret the evidence and law in the case. Understanding jurors is to step into their shoes and look at the world through their eyes. Overburdened attorneys with too many cases, too many motions, and looming opening statements find it easier to think of jurors as demographic categories: "Do I want men or women? Old or young? Educated or uneducated? Black or white?" But attorneys who are excellent at selecting juries have an inherent curiosity about what makes people tick. They engage jurors in a true conversation about who they are and how they see the world. This helps the attorney not only look at whether the juror is appropriate for the case, but how that attorney will speak to that juror, in opening statements, testimony, and closing arguments.

The difficulty in jury selection is that very few people will admit to being biased in a legal sense, unless they are actively trying to avoid serving on a jury. Similarly, asking a juror if they can "set aside their bias," as the court often asks, also achieves little. And the legal system actually has a poor definition of bias, thinking of it as a conscious process that renders a juror unable to be fair. In fact, bias tends to be more subconscious, and is simply a tendency or inclination to automatically make assumptions about people or issues based on preconditioned attitudes or experience. This can cause jurors to inherently lean a certain way or favor a certain side. Bias is not always negative or positive; it's simply a natural preference, regardless of strength, for one option over another.

No one wants to admit to having biases, especially in a room full of strangers, under oath, with a black-robed authority glaring disapprovingly at them. Even an outspoken racist will hide or shade his or her true opinions because of this social pressure to appear fair. But the reason impartiality is so important is that it is hard mental work for a juror to overcome their preconceived attitudes, making it more difficult for them to clearly listen to evidence. Moreover, instructions to suppress thoughts, for example, a judge's instructions to ignore prejudicial testimony or "put attitudes aside," can, ironically, make those thoughts hyperaccessible because of a rebound effect, increasing the application of jurors' stereotypes and prejudices.

While much of the social psychology literature on subconscious or implicit biases has focused on racial stereotyping, there is research suggesting that we hold all sorts of biases toward gender, sexual orientation, religion, age, disabilities, and body types, most of which we are not even aware exist. People can also be biased against professions (doctors, priests, lawyers), against industries (oil, banking, tobacco), and against entire communities (New Yorkers, Texans, Hollywood).

These biases can be triggered in a number of surprising ways, and we're usually not even aware we hold them. Studies have shown that a white male job applicant with a felony conviction is more likely to be brought back for a second job interview than a black male high school graduate. I have seen New York attorneys disparaged by Texas jurors and Mississippi attorneys ridiculed by Boston juries, based almost exclusively on their speech patterns. Implicit bias happens when you are introduced to a couple at a party, one of whom is named Dr. Hamilton, and you automatically go to shake the man's hand. We stereotype that which is not familiar in order to make it familiar. Most bias is not cruel, vindictive, or even intentional. It is just how we are raised. And it becomes our truth.

In fact, *our* truth and forensic truth always compete in a criminal case. What I think versus what I believe. What I believe versus what I *want* to believe. This is the conflict of conscience—the balance of biases and evidence that jurors, judges, and even zealous advocates struggle to reconcile.

THE POWER OF COMMUNITY

But just as individuals can hold biases against communities, communities themselves have their own biases, beliefs, collective values, and rules of social etiquette. Juries are composed of individuals that belong to the same community, so it is important to understand that community in order to understand how they will work together as a group.

I conducted jury research in New Orleans and Mississippi after Hurricane Katrina to study how people in those venues felt about insurance companies and claims by homeowners after the hurricane.

Our mock jurors discussed their mixed feelings about the aftermath of the storm that devastated that region. Many talked about their anger toward insurers and the federal government. Others spoke about their anger toward local officials in handling the disaster. Some spoke of losing friends, family, and neighborhoods with great sadness. Others spoke with scorn about watching their neighbors fraudulently causing damage to their own homes to get insurance payments. Our jurors were torn between the desire to help local homeowners, no matter the merits of the claims, and the fear that large verdicts would drive the already scarce insurers out of the area.

All of the cases I speak about in this book are also about the communities where these trials occur: Los Angeles, Houston, Orlando, and Little Rock.

A jury also becomes its own community in a trial, a group of individuals that develops its own persona and has its own decision-making dynamic. When I help to select a jury, I look to the group dynamic to project the deliberation process I most want to occur in the jury room. In looking at this dynamic, I consider the number of strongly opinionated jurors on the panel, the personality, temperament, or emotional state of the jurors in the group, and the combustibility factor: the likelihood of personality clashes between jurors. In a criminal case, this helps me to figure out whether I want a consensus jury, which is necessary for a prosecution's case or a defendant who is rolling the dice on an acquittal, or whether I am looking for a conflict jury, which is necessary for a criminal defendant who is dealing with difficult facts or a pervasively biased pool.

When Juror B37 in the George Zimmerman–Trayvon Martin case refers to the peaceful marches in Sanford, Florida, as "riots" in jury selection, this tells us she is already keyed into safety and protection issues that would make her side with Zimmerman. When another juror in that case says that she heard that the case was about "an altercation and then the gun went off," it tells you that she is already thinking that it was an accident instead of a murder. We see what we want to see. We see what we have experienced.

I try to listen to these hidden conversations that jurors have with themselves, conversations hidden even *from* themselves. This hushed dialogue occurs deep in the juror's brain where they utter their secret rules about the way the world works. If the juror has little awareness of their own biases and beliefs, they will always follow their own rules. If they have some awareness, they can reconcile the tension between their own hidden rules and the court's rules in deciding a case. Judges, attorneys, and witnesses also have their hidden rules. All of these rules are whispered in the back of their brains but revealed in a glance, a pause, a shift in posture, a grimace, a pupillary dilation, and a small held breath. The skill of a trial consultant is to understand and use all of these hidden rules to move the case toward the best verdict for the client.

TRIAL TRUTHS AND MYTHS

Under our Constitution, we are not guaranteed a fair trial or a fair jury. The Sixth Amendment says, "In all criminal prosecutions, the accused shall enjoy the right to a speedy and public trial, by an impartial jury of the State and district wherein the crime shall have been committed, which district shall have been previously ascertained by law, and to be informed of the nature and cause of the accusation; to be confronted with the witnesses against him; to have compulsory process for obtaining witnesses in his favor, and to have the Assistance of Counsel for his defence [sic]." That's it. You get a quick, public trial by an impartial jury. You get to see the witnesses against you, and you get to have witnesses for you. You get to have a lawyer. Nothing about fairness. There is plenty of legal commentary about how these due process provisions provide us with a fair trial. But we have no explicitly stated constitutional right to a fair trial. And we shouldn't. Because fairness is both relative and subjective. And what is fair for one party might be unfair for another.

I have been a trial consultant for almost thirty years. The reason I have been employed for so long is that the procedural strictures and aspirational concepts of our justice system clash mightily with what we know about the psychology of human decision making. In Jonathan Haidt's book *The Righteous Mind*, he describes the "rationalist's delusion": that we incorrectly believe objective analysis of facts is the motor for our judgment. This misguided hallucination that informed reason dictates our life decisions is prevalent in our society. We think that stock market fluctuations are guided by a careful analysis of the trends of company capitation, market values, and employment figures rather than fears of a Fed interest rate hike. We think we buy houses and cars based on careful comparisons of features and price instead of the way they look and feel. But nowhere is this rational delusion more codified than in the justice system.

The justice system plays a series of clever cognitive gambits with jurors to confound their work in trials. First, they are instructed that they should only decide the case based on the evidence and the law but are then told to use their common sense. They are not told what to do if their common sense collides with the law and evidence. For example, in working on the Spector case, when we conducted an analysis of the 192 questionnaires that we read in that case, we discovered that approximately 40 percent of our jurors believed that a criminal defendant is obligated to prove his or her own innocence. That was common sense for these jurors. Of course, the judge in that case instructed jurors that it was actually the state's burden to prove the guilt of the defendant. Jurors are not told *how* they should resolve this conflict between what they believe and what they are instructed to do, only that they should.

Jurors are also instructed that they should not be deciding a case based on passion or prejudice. However, in a death penalty case, jurors listen to victim impact statements, which discuss the wrenching effect that the victim's death has had on the surviving friends and family. Jurors also hear the presentation of evidence about the cruel and depraved manner in which the killings were carried out as an "aggravating factor" in the case. All of this testimony is truly geared to incite the emotions or passions of the jury, even if carries the label of statutory evidence.

In court, jurors are instructed that they may not speculate, but they do it all the time. Especially when there are critical holes in their narrative of the case where a judge has ruled that they can't hear evidence. In a situation like that, jurors feel they have to guess or the evidence won't make sense to them. A classic example of this is where jurors speculate about gang affiliation when they see tattoos on a defendant. To complicate matters, the courts actually invite speculation when they tell jurors to judge a witness's credibility based on their demeanor on the stand. Speculation is not an error; it is a natural consequence of missing information. When uncertainty exists, a juror's brain fills in the missing pieces until it makes sense to them.

When a witness says something that the judge rules is inadmissible, the jury is told to disregard these statements. Not surprisingly, they don't. Jurors are also told that they are only to use testimony from the witness stand. However, in their search to discover the true motivations of defendants, witnesses, and attorneys, jurors observe them in hallways, bathrooms, elevators, cafeterias, and parking garages to pick up on small nonverbal cues in order to match their character with the persona presented in court.

Even the concept of "reasonable doubt" is notably subjective. In our jury research and in post-trial interviews, we constantly hear jurors talk about "beyond a shadow of a doubt" or "90 percent certainty," which is a higher standard. We also hear jurors say that the prosecution's case was slightly more convincing than the defense's case, which is a lower evidentiary standard found in civil cases. To demonstrate juror confusion over legal standards, in one national poll we conducted involving almost three thousand respondents, we asked respondents to define the civil lawsuit standard of "preponderance of the evidence." More than half defined it as "beyond a reasonable doubt," the criminal standard, and only 28 percent defined it correctly.

Jurors don't measure evidence based on a doubt yardstick during the trial. Instead, a more natural gauge for them is what happened, what makes sense, and what they believe. Reasonable doubt becomes the final justification for all of these other instincts.

There is also a presumptive validity to eyewitness testimony, despite the fact that it has been shown in numerous studies over the years to be quite unreliable. Forensic evidence is also presumed to have a great deal of scientific strength, although the National Academy of Sciences in 2009 found glaring inadequacies in the way that this evidence is examined and evaluated by coroners' and medical examiners' offices across the country.

Fingerprints and DNA, hair and fiber, blood spatter, gunshot residue, emails, and rape kits all help the jury figure out who was where and what happened. All of it goes into the great circumstantial evidence gumbo pot, seasoned with judicial rulings, witness personalities, and attorney style. Keep it on a low simmer on the stove for days, weeks, and months and see how it turns out.

Although we think of evidence as the cataloged exhibits and transcripts of testimony, evidence really exists only in the minds of jurors. What matters in the final verdict is the *interpretation* of that evidence by a judge or jury and how that interpretation matches or fails to match their arguments about what happened in the case.

Aside from these contortions of comprehension, we also ask our juries to perform almost impossible tasks as if they were part of everyone's everyday practices.

1. Jurors must listen attentively to understand and critically evaluate *every* statement, question, answer, and argument in court.

2. Jurors must selectively compare the two separate realities being presented by the two sides in the case.
3. Jurors must understand complicated testimony presented out of order while being constantly interrupted by objections from the other side.
4. Jurors must wait until the end of the trial before making a decision.
5. Jurors must not ask questions or clarify confusion until deliberations, sometimes days and weeks down the road. (This is being changed in some courts.)
6. Jurors must listen to an entire trial and not know until the end of the case how they are supposed to apply the rule of law to the facts they have listened to for days or weeks.

In cases where people's lives hang in the balance, we assume jurors will be able to perform these complex tasks as if we were asking them to boil water for spaghetti or run a load of laundry.

CRIMINAL CASES

There is a curious momentum that is built into a criminal case. A crime is committed or thought to have been committed. There is pressure to solve that crime. A suspect is identified and an arrest is made. Because of the volume of other crimes that need to be investigated, and because a majority of arrests correctly identify the suspect, there is a strong incentive to make sure that the original arrest sticks. Therefore, evidence gathering revolves around proving a conclusion that has already been made. No doubt, suspects are freed when evidence does not pan out or leads move the investigation in a different direction. However, in multiple-defendant cases, the smart suspects are the ones that plead early in exchange for pointing the finger at a fellow defendant. Many times, the suspects that end up holding the short end of the stick in these situations are the ones with a lower mental capacity to understand that the system has rolled them. And even though they may be the least culpable of the crime, they are the ones that are charged with the most serious offenses.

This is the hard-knocks reality for defense attorneys in today's criminal justice system. Criminal defense lawyers deal with people's messy, complicated, and sometimes bloody lives. Accidents happen. People lose control. Bad things happen. In more than 90 percent of criminal cases, the defendant pleads out to something. Most of them are guilty and they know it. But many are innocent or provisionally innocent and just do not want to take the risk of going to trial. So they look to negotiate a plea deal.

But the deals have gotten worse over the years. Politicians have taken advantage of rampant voter fear and sensationalized cases in order to pass draconian legislation. Mandatory sentences have meant that judges have less leeway over sentencing a defendant if they are convicted. Three strikes laws have meant that convicted criminals can serve life prison terms for minor offenses. Human Rights Watch published a report in December of 2013 on how statutory sentencing increases in cases involving drugs, possession of a firearm, or a defendant's prior convictions allow federal prosecutors to threaten a defendant with sentences if convicted that are so severe, that in the words of one federal judge, "they could take your breath away." All of this has led to an increase in pleas and prison population. The United States currently incarcerates more than 2.4 million, which means one out of every one hundred adults is behind bars.

Our courts also persist in using nineteenth-century methods and definitions of psychology, qualifying sanity as "capable of distinguishing right from wrong" and competence as a defendant's ability to understand the proceedings and to rationally deal with his or her lawyer. If a defendant appears to be incompetent, he can be medicated to the point where he *appears* to understand the proceedings as if he were competent. If another defendant claims to be not guilty due to insanity, she may be forced to undergo psychological examination under the influence of truth serum, or using a polygraph, to recount the events of the crime. That defendant's statements under the influence of drugs, or her response to interrogation with a lie detector, can then be used against her to prove that she was *not* insane at the time of the crime. Crazy, right?

Additionally, forensic psychologists administer tests and come up with IQ or MMPI (Minnesota Multiphasic Personality Inventory) scores to artificially measure mental capacity, bipolar disorder, or scalable sociopathy. These scores are meant only to meet the court's narrow legal definitions of mental illness or incapacity, and in no way attempt to reflect the true state of mind of a defendant. It is another one of the legal system's rationalist delusions that they can quantify and categorize mental illness. No credible psychologist or psychiatrist would purport to diagnose or treat schizophrenia or bipolar disorder the way the courts demand they be defined. In fact, there is a great deal of debate in the psychological community about the scientific validity of measuring psychological disorders at all. Clinicians who treat patients routinely use the DSM-5, the Diagnostic and Statistical Manual of Mental Disorders, in order to categorize diagnoses for insurance purposes rather than to actually treat patients. Yet prosecutors and defense attorneys routinely rely on experts to chart out their statistical conclusions about the measurable mental defect, or lack thereof, in a criminal defendant.

The legal definitions of sanity and competence are defined situationally, a temporal contrivance of the criminal justice system that has no basis in scientific fact. A defendant can be labeled *temporarily* insane depending on the circumstances of the alleged crime, or *currently* incompetent depending on their mental state in court, as if their brain were on a timer. A defendant can have a diagnosis of schizophrenia, but that is not sufficient for a legal finding of insanity at the time of a crime. A defendant can have an IQ of 50 and be unable to read or write, but that is not sufficient for a legal finding of incompetency that would interfere with their right to counsel. And both of these defendants can be tried as if they had no mental issues whatsoever.

Additionally, while most people think that the death penalty is reserved for serial killers, particularly gruesome killings, or the murder of children, there are thirty-four special circumstances in California that can qualify a defendant for the death penalty. One of those special circumstances is "intentionally killed the victim while lying in wait." This is virtually indistinguishable from "premeditated murder," a noncapital offense. Another special circumstance is if a defendant kills someone *while* committing a robbery, burglary, or one of the many other crimes on a long list. The way these laws are written makes almost every first-degree murder case potentially eligible for the death penalty. Not that these are regularly charged, but it has the effect of allowing a prosecutor to leverage a plea deal in more cases when they can say, "I am willing to take the death penalty off the table if you accept a plea." Resigned acceptance and compromise are the currency of plea bargaining.

There is also a great deal of disparity in how a death penalty case is charged and conducted. The death penalty may be charged in a case in Ventura County, California, whereas the exact same crime may not be charged as a death penalty in adjoining Los Angeles County. Two offices can look at the exact same crime with the exact same circumstances and come up with two different charges. Additionally, there have been numerous studies that have shown a statistically disproportionate number of death penalty charges that are sought for minorities and people from lower socioeconomic strata. A death penalty case also entails a jury qualification process that has been shown to systematically load conviction-prone citizens onto juries. This means that most lawyers defending these cases are almost conceding the guilt of the defendant and are focused solely on the penalty phase from the beginning of the trial. In Alabama, a judge can overturn a jury's decision and impose the death penalty, which they have done almost ninety times since 1976. They can then campaign when they run for reelection on their support for the death penalty. One in five on death row in that state are there through judicial override.

A few years back, I was assisting with an Innocence Project case. The Innocence Project was founded by Barry Scheck and Peter Neufeld, whom I knew from the O. J. Simpson case. They had developed the Project as "a national litigation and public policy organization dedicated to exonerating wrongfully convicted people through DNA testing and reforming the criminal justice system to prevent future injustice." They had managed to uncover gross prosecutorial misconduct on the part of a district attorney in Tennessee that had led to the wrongful conviction of Paul Gregory House, where he had sat on death row for twenty-three years. Among other things, the prosecution was found to have ignored crucial witnesses, withheld evidence from the defense, and it even turned out that a crucial piece of evidence contained House's blood because a lab technician spilled a vial of it and never told anyone. The United States Supreme Court overturned the conviction and sent it back to Tennessee with a strongly worded opinion implying that the state of Tennessee had essentially framed an innocent man.

While most prosecutors would have dismissed the case, the current district attorney decided to re-try House, insisting he had to be guilty. Not only did he want to re-try House, he wanted to seek the death penalty again. I was asked to assist my friend Linda Kenney Baden, who was assisting the local public defender, with the retrial. We designed a questionnaire in which we asked the question, "Do you have any negative opinions about criminal defense attorneys or public defenders?" One of our jurors responded, "Just doing their job to defend the person whose [sic] being convicted." This juror's belief, like many others, is that guilt is a foregone conclusion and the system goes through the motions until that defendant is inevitably convicted.

And so the machinery of criminal justice slowly turns. District attorneys rely on conviction records in their election runs for higher offices or to get higher-paying jobs in the private sector. Judges rely on a tough-on-crime image in order to get reelected. Budgets are approved based on numbers of prosecutions. Private prisons charge hundreds of millions of dollars to the state to house prisoners and become powerful lobbies for crime legislation.

We live in a moral universe, and our judgments carry moral authority. Defense lawyers moralize about the injustices of the system, and the desperation, poverty, and hopelessness of their clients. Prosecutors moralize about evil, punishment, and loopholes. In fact, prosecutors and defense lawyers speak in two different narrative languages. Prosecutors speak in idioms of melodrama and certainty. Defense lawyers speak in a vernacular of realism and equivocation.

And while the courts think of criminal cases as the static weighing of evidence on the proverbial scales, the narrative structure of trials is emergent and dynamic. It becomes dynamic when both prosecutors and defense attorneys start telling stories to a jury to re-create the circumstances of the crime in question. When a woman kills her husband and claims self-defense after years of abuse, there is a tremendous emotional history in that relationship. And yet the criminal justice system demands that the relationship be judged on a fixed and limited set of facts and laws determined by the judge in the case. The dynamism of the system is the struggle between primal behavior and civilized rules, the rational and the emotional, the impulsive and the procedural. It has inherent tension and it is inherently dramatic. And that's why trials fascinate us.

> *This was a decision whether we're going to tell somebody they were going to be put to death or spend the rest of their life in prison. You've got Travis Alexander's family devastated, that he was killed, that he was brutally killed. You've got Jodi Arias's family sitting in there, both families sitting and seeing these humiliating images and listening to unbelievably lurid private*

details of their lives, and you've got a woman whose life is over, too. I mean, who's winning in this situation? And we were stuck in the middle.

—Bill Z., juror in Jodi Arias murder trial

TRIAL CONSULTING

In 1972, a group of sociologists and social psychologists assisted the defense in the Harrisburg Seven trial, in which a group of priests and nuns were charged with conspiracy to raid draft boards and other anti–Vietnam War activities. They are generally considered to be the first official "trial consultants." Similar individuals also were used in some of the early high-profile cases involving the Wounded Knee incident, in which two hundred Oglala Lakota Indians occupied the town of Wounded Knee in 1973, and a federal marshal as well as several American Indians were shot and killed. Beth Bonora, a noted trial consultant, worked the Attica prison riot cases, where one thousand prisoners in upstate New York took hostages and control of the prison in 1971, resulting in the death of at least thirty-nine people, including prisoners, correctional officers, and civilian employees. The McMartin preschool case, the Rodney King beating trial, William Kennedy Smith, the Night Stalker, the Menendez Brothers, Robert Blake, Dr. Jack Kevorkian, Scott Peterson, Martha Stewart, Michael Jackson, George Zimmerman, various Al Qaeda terrorist trials, and the case of Bernhard Goetz, the notorious subway vigilante, have all involved trial consultants, some on both sides of the case. None of us is trying to win any popularity contests. We work when the facts are tough or when the prejudice is high.

The American Society of Trial Consultants was formed in 1982. Today, it is a collection of clinical, social, and organizational psychologists; lawyers; crisis, media, and political consultants; speech and communication experts; linguists; and theater experts. Like most consultants, they are idiosyncratic. But they fulfill a critical function—they are the bridge between the vibrant and dynamic jury decision-making process and the legal profession's static, antique version of the jury. We see jurors as Instagram, constantly updating with fresh pictures and images, while many judges and lawyers see the jury in an old daguerreotype image, posed and serious.

Good consultants are clinicians and not just academics. They have good ears, good eyes, and good noses. They can hear a winning argument. They can see what the jury sees. They can hear the clear bell of truth in testimony. And they can smell the manure that is spread in a case to make something weak or artificial grow. Good consultants know the psychological literature. They know communication theory. And they understand patterns of the mind and patterns of behavior.

As consultants, we conduct pretrial research in the form of focus groups, mock trials, and community attitude surveys. We perform communication work in assisting witnesses to communicate *their* truth more clearly and effectively on the stand. We help attorneys define case themes, structure, and strategies. We help to write opening statements, closing arguments, and even witness examinations. We help to design litigation graphics to visually communicate the case more effectively and to design some of the overall production values of the case. That's right. Production values. We use techniques from the fields of communication, linguistics, educational psychology, public relations, journalism, historical research, documentary filmmaking, marketing, theater, and the visual arts to design the most evocative and compelling story of the case. The art of advocacy determines that every trial is a theatrical production where attorneys tell a story to an audience. However, in telling this story, I am always looking for the most authentic expression of the evidence, the thing that rings most true for the jurors. As the best advocate for your client, you need your jury to remember your story and use it in deliberations.

We also put together strategic plans to assist attorneys to best influence the decision makers in the case: the juries, the judges, opposing attorneys, the media, and the community. We assist attorneys to select juries by de-selecting jurors who are already predisposed against their clients or their cases. And we sometimes watch trials to help our clients understand how the jury and the judge may be seeing the case. Most importantly, we help to clarify confusing or prejudicial information in a trial.

We help our clients to be the best advocates for their clients by wearing three separate hats: with a jury hat, we tell attorneys how jurors will react to their case; with opposing counsel's hat, we tell them what the other side will do to win the case; and with an advocate's hat, we tell them what they need to do to win the case.

> *I think it's safe to say that few of us spend a lot of time considering the concept of justice. Being a juror forces you to do so, to think about what constitutes the evenhanded administration of the law. At several points during the trial, I was struck (in admittedly* Mr. Smith Goes to Washington*-esque fits of idealism) by the messy elegance of a system that requires twelve people to figure out, through conversation, false starts, and dead ends, where the truth of a matter lies. The truth, in administering justice, is emergent; cobbled together from the collective puzzle pieces in twelve minds, driven by emotion, confirmed by fact.*
>
> —Philip B., served for six months as a juror in the case of the People of the State of New York v. Anthony Marshall and Francis Morrissey

PERSUASION

Rhetoric, or the art and craft of persuasive language, used to be taught and was part of everyone's education until the late nineteenth century. Aristotle called rhetoric "the faculty of observing in any given case the available means of persuasion." Law schools usually give a cursory discussion about Aristotle's three rules of audience appeal: logos, pathos, and ethos. These were later organized in classical Rome into five canons: invention, arrangement, style, memory, and delivery. This was controversial even in ancient Greece, as Plato blamed the Sophists for using rhetoric as a means of manipulation and deception rather than a search for the truth. He also accused Sophists of using rhetoric to influence the ignorant masses. Sound familiar? Thus the semantic and philosophical battle over truth and illusion in public discourse is as old as civilized communication. But despite the debate over the use or misuse of these persuasive tools, the concept of rhetorical discourse was key to the Greeks' notion of participatory government.

Aristotle also defined three fields or types of rhetoric: deliberative, where a speaker tries to influence an audience toward a specific outcome; forensic, which is attributed to a presentation of evidence in a public forum such as in the courts; and epideictic, which is a formalized speech for ceremonies that incorporate more subjective "praise and blame" speech.

As civilization advanced, we developed the necessity to influence wider audiences in politics and society that preceded the revolution wrought by Johannes Gutenberg's printing press in 1450.

However, the art of rhetoric—the shaping of persuasive thought in order to affect an audience—is no longer taught in schools. Attorneys must develop it themselves or possess a natural gift. Part of the decline in advocacy training we owe to Harvard Law School dean Christopher Columbus Langdell. He developed the "case method" of law school training in 1890. Up to that point, lawyers had been trained in the law and had gone out into the field to get training from other lawyers. The old method blended a study of the law with an apprenticeship with a practicing attorney, a method that limited the number of lawyers. Langdell believed that law should be studied like a science, with appellate decisions of judges being the subjects of analysis. This also had inadvertent benefits for law schools. It allowed them to create a more systematic approach to legal training. According to the American Bar Association in their last survey in 2010, there were more than 145,000 students enrolled in law schools and over 1.2 million attorneys in the United States and territories.

The problem attorneys have is that law school is essentially a three-year foreign-language immersion program—it teaches them to speak legalese, a stultifying vernacular of acronyms, codes, statutes, and "expert" opinions. They stop thinking in plain English and start thinking in rules, laws, and procedures. While most law schools have trial advocacy courses, they rarely teach communication theory, storytelling, presentation skills, or how to both teach and engage the jury. In fact, the modern law school and court system seems to take a Platonic view of persuasion—defining it as deception or sleight of hand rather than the artful shaping of arguments to support positions. Today's lawyers get training in persuasion through forensic debate in high school and college, mock-trial experience in law school, or experience in a district attorney's or public defender's office. Some attorneys may have additional skills such as public speaking experience or performing arts training. For most attorneys, unless they participated in a moot court program in law school, their persuasion education begins the very first time they set foot in front of a jury.

Despite the mandated duty of an attorney to be an advocate for his or her client, we seem to have a more reticent Platonic view of persuasion in the courts: the quaint notion that "facts speak for themselves" and that persuasion is relegated to only an adjectival description of events in closing arguments. Instead of embracing the truth that *all* communication is persuasion, we would prefer to live in suspicion of those that would use "fancy words" to try to convince us.

Rhetoric, although used pejoratively these days, is neither Machiavellian in its strategic manipulations nor Rasputinish in its use of charismatic personality to convey a message. It is not all that mysterious. We just refuse to acknowledge the components of persuasion. As a result, we have lost our rhetorical swagger, flourish, and mojo. In 1928, Edward Bernays, an early public relations pioneer and nephew of Sigmund Freud, published the book *Propaganda*, which stated, "Conscious and intelligent manipulation of the organized habits and opinions of the masses is an important element in democratic society."

Interestingly, today's *political* environment is more rhetorically charged than ever. George Lakoff, a professor in cognitive linguistics at the University of California–Berkeley, and Drew Westen, a professor of psychology, psychiatry, and behavioral science at Emory University, have charted a neurological connection in modern political rhetoric.

We love facts because they seem concrete. We distrust rhetoric because it seems artificial. It's a quaint and clever skullduggery on the part of our brains to convince us that we are deciding cases based on "facts" when we are actually using these facts as a framework to justify our real decisions. However, these more subliminal influences— emotional arguments and community values—are equally concrete because they are both sensory and experiential. So, in a case where a coach or priest is accused of sexual molestation or a parent is accused of abusing a child, the visceral reaction to that kind of horror, the "What if that were my child?" question, easily drives a desire to convict. However, on the defense side, the rhetorical frame of "What if I were wrongfully accused of this crime?" can drive an acquittal. Neither of these frames have anything to do with evidence, yet they profoundly influence the outcome of the case.

The traditional model of human communication used in a courtroom is a static model. There is a sender of the message, the message itself, and the receiver of the message. It is a classic educational model—a teacher gives a lecture on a subject and the student takes notes on that subject. That's it. They do not take into account the passion of the teacher for the subject, their speaking skill, the learning style of the student, or their interpretation of the material. But what most classical education models fail to realize is that communication is not a linear, but a cyclical process of developing the message, testing that message against the audience's perception of that message, adjusting the message, delivering, and then even adapting the message to the reaction of the audience as you are giving it. This is the art of live communication. You are engaging the audience in you as well as your message. When you hear Martin Luther King Jr. deliver his famous "I Have a Dream" speech, it is artfully crafted, practiced, and passionately delivered. It is rhythmic, musical, filled with meaningful imagery and emotional language, building in both tempo and volume to a crescendo. As he is delivering it, you can also hear him responding to the crowd on the Washington mall, reacting to their reaction, their energy feeding his delivery, his eloquence.

A great speaker is constantly delivering and receiving communication. Real persuasion is in being persuaded as you are persuading. And great storytellers craft a meaningful story and simultaneously experience the audience's reaction, making minute changes that mean both storyteller and audience are telling the story together, creating meaning for both.

In 1925, Dr. Ossian Sweet, a Howard University–educated black doctor in Detroit, had the temerity to move into an all-white neighborhood. When an angry mob from the Waterworks Park Improvement Association ("improvement" meaning color consistency) tried to improve the neighborhood by raining rocks on Sweet's house, a shot rang out from inside his house and killed one of the white mob members. Sweet, his wife Gladys, and nine other men who were inside the house at the time were charged with murder. The celebrated attorney

Clarence Darrow was asked by the NAACP to assist, and he accomplished the heretofore unthinkable in most communities across the country—an acquittal of black defendants by an all-white jury. In his closing argument, he spoke to the jury.

"Who are we, anyway? A child is born into this world without any knowledge of any sort. He has a brain which is a piece of putty; he inherits nothing in the way of knowledge or of ideas.

"You need not tell me you are not prejudiced. I know better. We are not very much but a bundle of prejudices anyhow. We are prejudiced against other people's color. Prejudiced against other men's religion; prejudiced against other people's politics. Prejudiced against people's looks. Prejudiced about the way they dress. We are full of prejudices. You can teach a man anything beginning with the child; you can make anything out of him, and we are not responsible for it. Here and there some of us haven't any prejudices on some questions, but if you look deep enough you will find them; and we all know it. All I hope for, gentlemen of the jury, is this: that you are strong enough, and honest enough, and decent enough to lay it aside in this case and decide it as you ought to."

The rhetorical construct of this passage uses the theme of prejudice to condition the jury to its own inherent prejudice, forcing them to question whether they are convicting on evidence or bias.

Trial consultants are both translators and storytellers. They must speak the separate languages of the lawyer, the judge, and the jury to help shape the evidence and testimony so that the postal worker, the teacher, the linesman, and the account executive on the jury all hear, understand, and feel the import of the attorney's message.

As a trial consultant, the complexity of trial communication also demands that you have the eyes of the enemy. As you are listening to and crafting the best arguments for your side, you are constantly playing them against the other side's arguments and evidence. It is an exercise in self-induced schizophrenia, as you simultaneously hear voices of prosecutors, witnesses, defense lawyers, victims, and police officers, all try-ing to seamlessly blend those voices into a winning narrative.

In the arc of a case, "winning" is tenuous at best, lasting only as long as the last witness, the last question, the last ruling, and the last argument. Lawyers tend to think of verdicts as the cumulative weight of the evidence. But any issue is a potential doorway through which a jury can walk into what they think the evidence *should* be, or specu-latively *is* in their own narrative world. So you look to close every door, so that the jury only has one door to walk through, the door to your verdict. Some of the doors are evidence. Some are legal instruction. Some doors open into the jurors' personal experiences. Some doors are errant speculations, ghosts in the machine, random thoughts that occur to them as they try to put the pieces together and solve the mystery of your case. Some are what we call "just world" doors, the doors that jurors walk through to reinforce their reality that they live in a world that is fair according to the way they were raised. You try to know which doors jurors are likely to open and steer them through this hall of doors until they only have one door left: the door to your verdict.

But no matter your planning or your paranoia, trials have their own momentum, their own rhythm, their own direction. You look for these tempos and turning points to swing the jury to your case, to your reality. You then look for ways to keep that momentum building in your direction. But it's never guaranteed. The tides can turn in an instant. In most great court battles, you can look at who is defending to know who is currently winning. Toward the end of the O. J. Simp-son case, it was clear the prosecution was defending its case.

In the old power-persuasion model of advocacy, attorneys relied on their authority, their strength of personality, their vehemence, and a linguistic barrage to convince jurors of their cases. These days, this old model conveys arrogance because the message communicates, "Believe me because I am important." Arrogance is a case killer. Jurors will punish the arrogant attorney or witness more than any other quality.

Those powerful arguments a generation ago sound like arrogant sales pitches today because we no longer have the obeisance to authority we had a generation ago. There is a body of literature discussing "resistance persuasion," stating that any message these days is being filtered through skepticism and tested for veracity. There is no longer an open and receptive congregation, waiting with wide-eyed expectancy to hear the attorney's gospel.

What follows are my experiences from some highlights in almost thirty years of trials. In these chapters, I hope to pull back the curtain of the justice systems, to show you the machinery and the humanity that drives this perfectly designed and perfectly flawed human enterprise. To show you how lawyers, judges, defendants, politicians, witnesses, and jurors all struggle to find *a* truth to help them solve the mystery and restore order to their world.

> *We must not make a scarecrow of the law,*
> *Setting it up to fear the birds of prey,*
> *And let it keep one shape, till custom make it*
> *Their perch and not their terror.*
> — *Measure for Measure*, William Shakespeare

People of the State of California
v. Orenthal James Simpson

| | | | | | | | | | | | | | | | | | | **REALITY TRAGEDY** | | | | | | | | | | | | | | | | | | | | |

Whatever Fortune has raised on high, she lifts but to bring low.
—Agamemnon, Seneca the Younger

When O. J. Simpson flew to Chicago on the 11:00 p.m. flight out of
LAX on June 13, 1994, he looked down at the Tron-like grid of lights
and roads that is Los Angeles. As he made the slow arc over the Pacific
and headed out to the desert, he saw seventy straight miles of streets
and freeways crawling with red and white, the headlight and brake
light blood cells that make up the body of Los Angeles.

Los Angeles is movement. A restless, kinetic city of makeovers,
do-overs, and the shimmering mirage of the American dream. From
the early 1900s, people from the East Coast and the Midwest came
to Los Angeles to be free of the puritanical wince of repressed sexuality. African Americans came from the South to escape racism in
order to encounter a different kind of bias. And many came from
Mexico to escape poverty and pursue the immigrant's dream. Rich
people, poor people, bored people, and the oppressed all came to the
Golden State to remake their lives, remake themselves.

And they all got in their cars and drove.

From the early twentieth century, Los Angeles has always been synonymous with cars because it allowed these new dream seekers to move. Automobile manufacturers tested all of their cars in Los Angeles to find out what these new freedom riders needed, to find out what these consumers wanted to buy to reinvent themselves. Because the main industry in Los Angeles is reinvention. Hollywood is called "The Dream Factory," but it is a moniker that is attached to all of Los Angeles.

So it is apt that American justice reinvented itself in a Ford Bronco on a stretch of freeway from Orange County to Brentwood, California, on June 17, 1994.

The news reinvented itself that day too. Both the way news agencies covered events and the way they profited from them. Never before had one hundred million people continuously watched a single event for five hours. Pandora's box was opened that day and can never be closed again.

By 1921, Paramount Pictures had paid Fatty Arbuckle three million dollars to star in eighteen silent films. He had just signed another million-dollar contract when he was arrested for the murder of a thirty-year-old aspiring actress named Virginia Rappe during an alleged sexual assault. With Arbuckle sitting in cell number 12 in the San Francisco Hall of Justice, various newspaper headlines screamed, "Evidence Shows Conclusively He Was Directly Responsible for Death," "Three Striking Poses of Virginia Rappe, Victim in Arbuckle Orgy," and "Plan to Send Arbuckle to Death on Gallows." He had two hung juries before he was acquitted of all charges. But his career was over and he died of a heart attack in a hotel room at age forty-six.

Bruno Richard Hauptmann was tried for the kidnapping and murder of the infant son of Charles Lindbergh, the famous aviator. He was tried in a one-hundred-year-old courthouse in Flemington, New Jersey. Tens of thousands clamored for tickets to the courtroom, distributed by the sheriff's office, and approximately two hundred journalists covered the trial, touting it as "The Trial of the Century."

The jury was sequestered in the same hotel as the journalists and could hear their radio broadcasts at night from neighboring rooms. The jurors also had to wade through crowds shouting for the execution of Hauptmann, while vendors sold miniature "Lindbergh ladders," replicas of what had been used to kidnap the boy. Five newsreel companies covered the trial, and a hidden microphone was installed over the jury box to capture the proceedings.

When the jury retired to discuss its verdict, ten thousand people waited in the streets below, chanting "Kill Hauptmann! Kill Hauptmann!" When the jury returned a death sentence, the crowd roared its approval. In their living room, the Lindberghs listened to both the verdict and the crowd's approval. Reportedly, Charles Lindbergh turned off the radio and with disdain said, "That was a lynching mob."

The Lindberghs knew that the public verdict was not for them or the death of their son. They knew that justice by popular condemnation serves a different purpose than justice sought for personal loss or a state's regulation of criminal conduct.

Dr. Sam Sheppard lived with his pregnant wife in Bay Village, Ohio. On July 4, 1954, while fireworks flecked the night sky over this bucolic Lake Erie town, Sheppard's wife was found slain and he was arrested. He was charged with second-degree murder.

Immediately, the newspapers dogged the story, not only reporting on every detail, but also writing editorials sharply criticizing the police and Sheppard. First, they scolded Sheppard for refusing to make statements to the police without his lawyer present and refusing to take a lie detector test. He finally relented and was interviewed for several hours by the police without counsel. At the request of the coroner, Sheppard reenacted his version of the events on the day of his wife's death. The coroner invited newsmen to attend, and this version was widely reported the next day.

The newspapers also questioned why the coroner had not held an inquest. Lo and behold, an inquest was held the next day in a school auditorium, where Sheppard was searched in front of hundreds of spectators who cheered, booed, and blew kisses to the coroner, the proceedings broadcast live on radio. The day after two rebuking newspaper editorials questioned why he had not been detained, Sheppard was finally arrested and charged with murder. He was brought in to the Bay Village City Hall in front of hundreds of people, newscasters, photographers, and reporters, who were awaiting his arrival.

When his trial finally started, the first rows of the audience gallery were given to the media, with Sheppard's family and the public given the back rows of the courtroom. The judge was interviewed on the front steps of the courthouse and all the lawyers, witnesses, and jurors ran a gauntlet of photographers when they walked down the halls to the courtroom.

Most of the jurors subscribed to the newspapers that ran daily stories of the trial. They were photographed by hundreds of reporters and a helicopter captured footage of their site visit to the Sheppard home. The jurors sat for posed pictures the day before the verdict, and over forty stories about the jury appeared in the newspapers. The jurors admitted during the trial that they had seen the numerous damning articles that appeared almost daily in the newspapers, implicating Sheppard in the murder.

When the jury finally convicted him, the Ohio appeals court ruled, "Murder and mystery, society, sex and suspense were combined in this case in such a manner as to intrigue and captivate the public fancy to a degree perhaps unparalleled in recent annals. Throughout the pre-indictment investigation, the subsequent legal skirmishes and the nine-week trial, circulation-conscious editors catered to the insatiable interest of the American public in the bizarre. . . . In this atmosphere of a 'Roman holiday' for the news media, Sam Sheppard stood trial for his life."

This judgment went all the way up to the Supreme Court, and they overturned the verdict, ruling that in this "carnival atmosphere . . . the massive, pervasive, and prejudicial publicity prevented him from obtaining a fair trial . . ." and, "The trial court failed to invoke procedures which would have guaranteed petitioner a fair trial, such as adopting stricter rules for use of the courtroom by newsmen as petitioner's counsel requested, limiting their number, and more closely supervising their courtroom conduct. The court should also have insulated the witnesses; controlled the release of leads, information, and gossip to the press by police officers, witnesses, and counsel; proscribed extrajudicial statements by any lawyer, witness, party, or court official divulging prejudicial matters; and requested the appropriate city and county officials to regulate release of information by their employees."

Twelve years later, a young F. Lee Bailey re-tried the case and won an acquittal for Sheppard. But the words of the Supreme Court have gone unheeded for more than fifty years.

On the early morning of June 13, 1994, a confused and crazed akita was heard barking in a Brentwood neighborhood. Sukru Boztepe was walking along Bundy Drive shortly after midnight when he was pulled to a bloody scene by the dog. When he looked down a path to a condominium in the upscale neighborhood, he saw a blond woman lying in a pool of blood.

When the police were called, they discovered the bodies of Nicole Brown Simpson and Ron Goldman. Nicole was the ex-wife of football star and movie actor O. J. Simpson, and Goldman was a young waiter who worked at the nearby Mezzaluna restaurant.

When the detectives on the scene discovered that one of the victims was the ex-wife of Simpson, they went to his house, two and a half miles away. The house sat behind a fence and private gate, and seeing some blood on a door of a car parked next to the house, one of the detectives,

Mark Fuhrman, climbed over the fence and recorded in his police report that he found a bloody glove behind the house. While at the house, the detectives found out that Nicole Brown Simpson's ex-husband flew to Chicago the night before. He was contacted at a hotel near the O'Hare airport and immediately got on a plane back to Los Angeles.

W hen Simpson flew back from Chicago on June 13, 1994, he passed over the homes of Armanda C., Carrie B., and Marsha R. J. They lived less than a dozen miles but a world away from Brentwood. They and nine other jurors would be inextricably tied together with Simpson in a trial that would last over eight months and capture the attention of our entire country.

I grew up two miles from the Bundy condo where Nicole Brown Simpson and Ron Goldman were murdered. For those of us who grew up in Santa Monica, our experience of police was at the Fourth of July parade, or if your party got too loud and the neighbors complained, or, God forbid, you got pulled over for going 40 in a 30 mph zone. But if you were Armanda C. or Carrie B. or Marsha R. J., you had a different experience of police altogether.

I watched much of the Bronco chase from a CNN studio where Larry King was interviewing trial consultant Jo-Ellan Dimitrius. Jo-Ellan and I had been colleagues and friends for years. She had handled a few high-profile cases before, most notably that of the police officers who were acquitted in the Rodney King beating case in 1992. She had called me on April 29 of that year, and we had a long talk. As the riots raged in many parts of the city, she felt terrible that the result of the trial had caused such pain and destruction. We discussed the nature of working on high-profile trials and the difficulty of representing unpopular clients or unpopular decisions under the disapproving glare of parents where your kids went to school and the censorious glances of friends and even family.

When the terrible events happened at the Bundy condo in early June of 1994 and the media firestorm started, Jo-Ellan asked me to come with her to the Larry King interview as part of our ongoing discussion of the media in these cases. And there we were in the studio, watching as that white truck rolled up the I-405 freeway, making O. J. Simpson's pain transparent to one hundred million people. On that day, he became their O. J. They became his prosecutors, his defenders, and his jury. He was no longer a running back or an actor. His iconography transformed that afternoon from sports star and actor to accused murderer.

The Bronco chase, like many other pivotal points in the case, divided the strategies of the prosecution and the defense. For the prosecution, any suspect who runs shows "consciousness of guilt." However, this was no ordinary runner. This was O. J. Simpson, arguably the greatest running back of all time. Simpson, who in 1973 became the first man in NFL history to rush for two thousand yards, who led the league in carries, yards, and touchdowns, was on the run. For the defense, the Bronco chase was the act of a desperate, suicidal man.

The police, along with the district attorney's office, are charged with following the evidence wherever it leads and in preserving the rights of the defendant as well as the state's interests. But that all goes to hell in a handbasket in a high-profile case. Political pressures make these cases win-at-all-costs scenarios because they go on the reelection résumé for the office.

Almost immediately, the district attorney's office released Nicole and O. J. Simpson's previous domestic abuse 911 calls to the press. There was only one intention behind this release: to poison the public against O. J. prior to the trial. Prosecutors have long relied on the "perp walk," mug shots, and press releases to sway jurors in high-profile cases. Once the public sees an accused in handcuffs or glaring mug shots with a bleary-looking defendant holding numbers across their chest, the jury thinks they *look* guilty. And while the district attorney's office often protests when the defense in a high-profile case makes statements to the media, prosecutors themselves are able to make their case to the jury pool ahead of the trial by leaking evidence to the press. From the beginning, we knew that the prosecution planned to try this case in the press before they got to court.

We also knew that Jo-Ellan's work on the Rodney King case made her a leading candidate for the trial consulting job on Simpson's case. But Jo-Ellan was ambivalent at first. She had been asked by a couple of networks to work as a paid consultant and on-air commentator and was seriously considering it. She asked me what I thought. I told her that we were *trial* consultants, and while she could get a lot of exposure and contribute to the public's understanding of the jury system, this would be a historic trial with a lot of important jury issues. She thought about it and agreed that the trial was where we could make the biggest contribution.

Sure enough, we were asked by attorney Robert Shapiro to come in to discuss jury selection. Jo-Ellan had spoken to another longtime colleague, Dr. Paul Strand from San Diego State University, about conducting a survey of Los Angeles jury-qualified residents to see how they initially saw Simpson's guilt, given all of the pretrial publicity and the release of the 911 tapes. We wanted to go into the meeting demonstrating we had done our homework and already had some information about how a jury looked at the case. Strand conducted the survey out of his lab in San Diego, and the results proved to be both revealing and counterintuitive. As a result, we were hired.

PRETRIAL WORK

One of the biggest concerns the defense team had was that the unprecedented pretrial publicity, along with the release of the 911 calls, would prejudice the public into prejudging Simpson. Indeed, numerous public opinion polls conducted by news organizations already indicated a majority of Americans were predisposed toward Simpson's guilt. We thought that the more potential jurors were exposed to the mostly pro-prosecution stories in the media, the more they would be preconditioned to Simpson's guilt, making it exceedingly difficult to seat a fair and especially impartial jury. However, when Strand's polling came back on a couple of refined questions, we found an interesting result. The more people had heard about the case, the more they were inclined to think Simpson was *not* guilty. Even more important was that half of those polled didn't *want* to believe that he was guilty.

We were learning, as became more apparent in later "celebrity" trials, the great barometric test in the changing weather of public opinion is how much the public *wants* an O. J. Simpson, Michael Jackson, or Martha Stewart to be guilty or innocent of the alleged crime. And early on in the Simpson case, the images of the crime so contrasted with the public's image of the man that most did not want to believe that the USC and Buffalo Bill running back they had rooted for, or Officer Nordberg in the Naked Gun movies that they had laughed at, could have done such a horrible thing.

Experienced trial consultants spend a great deal of time in trial listening to juries in voir dire and talking to them, if possible, after a verdict. However experienced, smart, or intuitive we think we are, the real staple of consulting is research. Because research in the form of surveys, mock trials, and focus groups lets you look at a jury's decision-making patterns. Good jury research digs below the surface of a jury's reaction to the case and looks at the blueprint of the decision-making machinery of *how* they arrive at a verdict. The *how* allows the consultant and the trial team to present the evidence in trial so that the jury you have will more easily understand and be influenced by your case. Lawyers and judges talk about juries being unpredictable, but they are actually unpredictable in very predictable ways. Juries have patterns in their decision making, and if you ask the right questions and listen carefully enough, they will tell you exactly what they need in order to come to the verdict you want.

We decided to have two tracks of research, public opinion polling and our own research. I asked Dr. Sharon Gross, a brilliant social psychologist and one of my mentors, to track the public opinion polling. Predictably, it was overwhelmingly negative toward Simpson. Armchair jurors around the country were seeing news reports about the 911 calls, hearing leaks about the blood evidence, and listening to District Attorney Gil Garcetti's proclamations about Simpson's guilt.

However, as we have seen from the public's outrage to other high-profile cases, the public mind and the private juror mind often differ. In addition to Strand's survey, we also wanted to understand how our jury pool thought about what they had heard in the news. We had to carefully plan the research as we knew the media was hungry for stories, and would love to hear about how the trial consultants would "spin" the case. So we carefully screened our focus group "jurors" to make sure that there were no leaks. Ironically, DecisionQuest, a national trial consulting firm who was hired by the district attorney's office, decided to conduct their focus group research in Phoenix to avoid being discovered by the press. This was an odd choice, as Maricopa County jurors are nothing like Los Angeles residents, so any feedback they got would have been a false read for the Los Angeles jury pool. The media managed to discover their focus group location and hounded the DA team all the way back to Los Angeles. We managed to conduct our focus group research undetected.

When we looked at our survey data and our focus group results, some interesting patterns emerged. While only a little more than a third of our respondents thought Simpson was actually innocent, two-thirds thought that Simpson did not have enough time to commit the murders, giving the defense team an insight to an important theme in the case. When looking at our research, two other key findings emerged: almost half of those expected to show up in the jury pool had been treated poorly by police at least once, and almost a third believed that blacks were rarely treated well in the justice system.

CBS's hit show *CSI* did not premiere until 2000, so DNA evidence was a relatively new concept for the general public. In our research, the prosecution's evidence of a DNA match to Simpson did not get a strong reaction except for one particular demographic: young people. Almost two-thirds of the under-thirty-five set leaned toward acquittal but also believed in the strength of DNA evidence. We knew we would have to keep an eye out for this group, as these jurors could swing toward either acquittal or conviction.

And in another counterintuitive twist, almost half of the divorced or widowed women we spoke to leaned toward acquittal. Surprisingly, Nicole Brown Simpson's history of 911 calls and domestic abuse did not impress them as a motive for murder. We knew from the release of the 911 calls that the prosecution would be trying an escalated spousal abuse case. We believed that the prosecution's primary motive evidence would be:

1. O. J. was possessive of Nicole and extremely jealous, even after they were divorced.
2. In uncontrolled rages, he would lose control and beat Nicole.
3. He would obsess about Nicole and spy on her.
4. He felt excluded and dismissed at his daughter Sydney's dance recital on the day of the murder, which made him furious.
5. He killed Nicole and Goldman in a jealous rage.

Although the prosecution does not have to prove motive, jurors always consider it when they are trying to solve a crime, especially a gruesome murder. It did not take an expert to figure out that the district attorney would want women on the jury who could relate to Nicole's circumstances and condemn O. J. as an abuser. And it was here where our research provided some insight into our jury-selection profile. I asked some of the women in our focus group why they were reluctant to convict Simpson. Some who had been in troubled relationships shared that they themselves had contributed to the volatility with their partners. And the stronger women I spoke to were proud to claim they gave as much as they got. They said that although they did not stay in relationships with their abusive husbands and boyfriends, it was too big a leap to say that the fights and physical abuse alone provided motive for murder.

The prosecution, in pursuing this "abuse equals murder" angle, also left narrative inconsistencies in their motive story. The physical evidence pointed to a rage or impulse killing, while the prosecution's timeline suggested a carefully premeditated murder to fit into a prearranged alibi for Simpson. The premeditation scenario did not fit our jurors' perception of domestic abuse being a "heat of passion" reaction and the gruesomeness of the attack. And the jealous rage scenario did not make sense with the prosecution's theory of how Simpson had carefully planned the killings to be able to make his flight, as well as the coincidence that he just happened to be carrying a knife. These may seem like small inconsistencies, but for a jury considering a first-degree murder conviction, these can be the seeds of doubt. In our focus groups, a number of jurors spoke about how these stories did not seem to "fit."

So we learned from the research that we did not have to be overly concerned with strong women who had been in physically combative relationships with boyfriends and husbands. And this provided a big strategic advantage by allowing us to keep jurors that the prosecution would also want, gambling that our research was better than their intuition.

Finally, the jury research told us that the pretrial publicity had a counterintuitive effect. The media's furious competition for the "exclusive story" made rampant rumors and speculation fair game. And because most traditional journalists had no-pay policies, the *National Enquirer* became one of the most trusted sources for breaking news on the case, specifically because they could pay and pay well. So everything Simpson was a story. Everything was for sale. The trial became a commodity, fueled by the public's insatiable desire to hear anything and everything related to not only O. J. and Nicole, but the police, the lawyers, and anyone who knew a family, friend, or foe associated even remotely with the trial or that terrible night in Brentwood.

The more that prospective jurors heard about the case, the more they could not distinguish real facts from the hype and sensationalized coverage. Thus, evidence got buried in the slag heap of hearsay and rank speculation that ran amok in the scramble for scoops. Jurors were already suspicious and had more than a modicum of doubt about everything that they had heard, even the prosecution's hardest of hard evidence.

This unprecedented media feast also desensitized jurors to the evidence they were going to hear in the actual trial. The 911 calls and pictures of the Bundy crime scene had lost the visceral punch of the first time seeing those bloody images and hearing the fear and anguish in Nicole's voice.

All of the defense lawyers were savvy enough to understand that the trial had started long before jury selection. The police and the prosecutors were conducting their investigation. The defense also set up a tip line and fielded hundreds of calls and letters. And the media was conducting their own investigation, fueled by advertising dollars and Nielsen ratings. Tracie Savage of KNBC News in Los Angeles had to testify in a court hearing after she reported on a DNA match of Nicole that was found on one of O. J.'s socks, even before the defense had heard of the lab results. Credible witnesses became discredited overnight when it was found out that they had sold their stories to the tabloids.

Between evidence leaks from the prosecutor's office, the separate investigations conducted by hundreds of journalists, and the interviews given by the Goldman and Brown families on one side and O. J.'s friends and family on the other, the pretrial PR wars were at a fever pitch. Hundreds of letters flooded the jail in support of O. J.

And in this both heady and noxious air of public scrutiny, everyone became an instant celebrity. Robert Kardashian, whose young children Kim, Khloe, Kourtney, and Rob would later become famous for being famous, would get better tables at his favorite restaurant in Beverly Hills. Jo-Ellan went to the White House Christmas party with Larry King and met Bill Clinton. *Vanity Fair* wanted to do a glamour photo spread of the defense team.

At the office, we received dozens of calls every day from media outlets in Japan, Sweden, and Australia asking us about this strange phenomenon called the jury trial. And everyone wanted in on the action. Graphologists, phrenologists, and psychics all called to help us "read" the jurors and to be a part of the Big Show.

Larry King famously quipped, "If we had God scheduled and O. J. wanted to be interviewed, we would have to move God." Ultimately both prosecution and defense teams paid way too much attention to the media in the case. It was all new, the spotlight was seductive, and no one really knew how important it would be for the case or their careers.

In this environment, the mantle of impartiality, including Lady Justice's blindfold, is ripped away, revealing the naked body of justice with all of its scars and flab. Presumption of innocence and burden of proof take on new meaning. The prosecution's challenge was to present a case that had already been presented, to meet the expectations of those who had already heard the evidence and arguments.

Our job was to maintain the balance of power prior to jury selection. In the iconography of this trial, we wanted to make sure that the defendant Orenthal James Simpson remained a human being and not the crazed, manipulative monster in the evidence leaks and news stories. In humanizing the defendant, we wanted our jury, at the beginning of the trial, to presume him innocent of the crimes for which he was charged. More importantly, we wanted them to still *want* to believe he was innocent.

JURY SELECTION

In 1968, Martin Luther King Jr. was assassinated, and a week later, an Iowa schoolteacher named Jane Elliott tried an experiment. She told her class of seven-year-olds that the blue-eyed kids were superior to the brown-eyed kids. Within minutes, these superior children were denigrating and dismissing their brown-eyed counterparts. She then reversed her instruction, telling the brown-eyed children that they were better. They in turn also treated their blue-eyed classmates—their friends—with scorn.

This in-group/out-group phenomenon is one of the best-tested and recognized phenomena in the social sciences. We like people who are like us. Look like us. Talk like us. Behave like us. We mistrust all others. Until we decide they actually are kind of like us. Then they're okay.

This is a very old biological and neurological mechanism, older than language. Yet, when we speak about race, with good intention, we often reinforce the very stereotypes and clichés that we seek to dispel. Every poll that describes how African American, Latino, or Asian populations differ from Caucasian folks reinforces the concept that somehow, skin pigment determines belief systems.

And this is natural. Because our ancient predator-prey instincts demand that we create labels for every out-group difference as a matter of survival. It is also easier to label differences as "black," "white," "men," or "women" than to delve into the subtle complexities of culture, geography, linguistics, and psychology.

But it is actually not that complicated. We all have biases, whether they be race, gender, religion, sexual orientation, politics, music, or food choice. These biases are bred and fed from the time we are born, and nurtured by the personal experiences in our lives.

But we will never admit we have biases. Which is a bias itself, for us to think we are bias free. Biases are as natural as breathing. And the more we deny that we have them, the firmer they become cemented in our psyche. We just find more and more elaborate explanations for why we feel we don't have them. Racism is a slow-growing weed, fertilized with subtle biases over the years and denied the light and air of tolerance.

In 2011, 120,000 African American and Latino kids got stopped and frisked by the police. It is so commonplace that for most minorities, it is not a matter of whether they will be stopped, but how many times. The more times they are stopped, the more likely they will be arrested. The more times they are arrested, the more times they are likely to be charged. The more times they are charged, the more times they are likely to be convicted. It is basic math.

In communities like Inglewood, Compton, and East Los Angeles, the kids grow up being schooled in these basic equations. And transplants to Los Angeles from East St. Louis, Philadelphia, and Biloxi are also familiar with these formulas. For those jurors who lived in these areas, the claims of police profiling and evidence planting and tampering, were not the desperate attempts of a defendant trying to escape conviction—they were a reality of living with the Los Angeles Police Department. And because poorer minority communities cannot afford the lawyers or the legislators to challenge this pattern, this became the norm. So they were not shocked when they saw a video of police officers raining almost sixty blows on Rodney King in eighty seconds. They were not shocked when they heard that five young black men in New York's Central Park "wilding" case were coerced into confessing and were prosecuted, convicted, and served years in prison for crimes they did not do.

A cooperative democracy has always been counterintuitive given our antediluvian tribal beginnings. Over the course of history, we have spent much more evolutionary time building our neurological instincts for survival than our social instincts for tolerance and cooperation.

Thomas Jefferson wrote "all men are created equal" in the Declaration of Independence while owning slaves. Abraham Lincoln issued the Emancipation Proclamation in 1863, yet thirty-three years later the Supreme Court, without a shred of irony, decided on the "separate but equal" doctrine in Plessy v. Ferguson that legitimized racial discrimination through Jim Crow laws until the Brown v. Board of Education Supreme Court ruling in 1954. Our nation still struggles with the issue of race in the form of affirmative action rulings by the Supreme Court, immigration reform in Congress, and the daily confrontations of George Zimmermans and Trayvon Martins across this country. Our struggle will continue until we confront our biases and accept our differences.

On July 19, before the trial, there was a meeting between District Attorney Garcetti, John Mack of the Urban League, the NAACP, and the Southern Christian Leadership Conference. Garcetti wanted to assure the African American leadership in Los Angeles that a jury would be selected that was fair, representative, and racially diverse. This promise became one of the anchors for jury selection, one that we would remind the district attorneys of again and again.

Since the trial's conclusion in 1995, a myth has been perpetuated that if only the prosecution had filed their case and tried it in Santa Monica, it would have had a different outcome. It wouldn't have. Both Marcia Clark and Chris Darden had tried lots of African American defendants in front of African American juries and won convictions. The district attorney also had plenty of sound logistical reasons for trying this case in downtown Los Angeles, including proximity to their main office just above the courtroom; Parker Center, where the evidence was stored; and the central jail where Simpson was housed. Downtown was also their home turf. The place where they won convictions in 90 percent of their cases. But most importantly, juries are selected randomly from a twenty-mile radius of each courthouse. Predominantly the same jury pool would have been called to Santa Monica, because jurors from lower socioeconomic areas like South Central were all within twenty miles. We had also prepared and filed a motion with the jury commissioner to make sure that, when jury notices were sent out, these lower socioeconomic geographic areas were fairly represented. And finally, Garcetti had made political promises to the African American community about the racial diversity of the jury.

Think about the racial implications of the concept: "If only it had been tried in Santa Monica, it would have had a different outcome." In other words, "Rich white people would have gotten it right." This is the type of thinking that has been alienating both minority and lower socioeconomic jurors across this country for decades.

Nationally, juries convict defendants in criminal trials around 90 percent of the time. When polled, judges approve of jury verdicts almost all of the time. Yet a few high-profile cases that have ended in acquittals have translated into a public distrust of the jury system. Cries of abolishing citizen juries and empaneling expert juries resound, and legislation is introduced to try to reform a jury system that, by all measures, works. It works so well, in fact, that other countries around the world, including Japan, South Korea, and Mexico, have started implementing jury systems.

Yet even lawyers fear juries as "unpredictable," constantly advising clients to plead out criminal cases or settle civil cases because "You never know what a jury will do." Most of the public's distrust of juries comes from a lack of civics education in schools and a misunderstanding of a jury trial's true function. Most attorney distrust of juries comes from a misunderstanding of their own role in relation to a jury. Lawyers think that it's the jurors' job to listen with rapt attention to every word of their case, when it is in fact the attorney's job to communicate their case so that the jury fully understands it. It is a subtle, yet important distinction that profoundly affects the ability of attorneys to accurately represent their clients and for jurors to make their best decisions in trials. When lawyers in expensive suits speak ten-dollar words with the arrogant expectancy that jurors who struggle to pay their rent, work long hours, and worry about their kids' health and safety should pay attention to them, a significant communication gap occurs. As I said, two countries, two languages.

One of my privileges is to be a translator. To not only understand the idiosyncratic language of any given jury panel but their culture, customs, habits, and beliefs. One of the ways you do this is by carefully designing a jury questionnaire to try to understand as much as possible about the jurors you will be interviewing.

We submitted a fifty-page questionnaire to Judge Ito and Decision-Quest, the prosecution's consultants, proposed a one-hundred-and-twenty-page behemoth. Even a fifty-page questionnaire was larger than I liked, but given the nature of the case we had to cover a number of areas: personal background history of all of the jurors, the pretrial publicity they had seen and how it had affected them, experience with the police and domestic violence, knowledge of O. J. Simpson, attitudes toward the criminal justice system, interracial marriage, and DNA evidence.

There was also a one-page hardship questionnaire in which jurors discussed their potential difficulties in serving as a juror on the case. And it was here where the prosecution ran into a real problem. According to them, they had a "mountain of evidence" that they were eager to bury Simpson with. But it takes a long time to build a mountain. And most employers simply could not afford to pay their employees to be gone for the estimated six months that the trial would take. So a large portion of the jury-qualified citizens were eliminated because of financial hardship, medical reasons, preplanned trips, and caretaking requirements of children or elderly parents.

After the hardship phase, the overall jury pool for the defense improved immensely. Many higher-income, conservative jurors who were more reliant on law enforcement and less willing to believe in police tampering or misconduct did not want to serve on this long a trial.

The pool that was left was populated with citizens whose employers would pay for unlimited jury service: postal workers, teachers, utility employees, personnel of large companies with generous jury service policies, as well as the retired, unemployed, and people who were on disability leave. The people who worked in government or large organizations had seen firsthand the frequent backstabbing, political infighting, and cover-your-ass behavior, thus were more receptive to the defense themes of police error and misconduct.

We also had to consider how sequestering the jury would affect the outcome of the case. There was, and still is, very little research on the effects of sequestration on jury decision making and verdict preference in a criminal case. We wondered if such a long period of time spent apart from a juror's family, friends, and home environment would result in the jurors identifying and building relationships with law enforcement, the sheriff's office in this case, who was charged with protecting them and guarding them during the trial, resulting in jurors giving more credence to police testimony.

On the other hand, we also wanted to protect jurors from the daily media rumor mill that kept churning out negative stories against Simpson. When I consulted with Dr. Gross, who had been tracking the public opinion polling, it was apparent that the public's attitude was deteriorating toward Simpson and the defense team as a whole. As a result, we decided that sequestering would probably be a better course.

This also factored into a personality profile that we considered for jury selection. In a normal criminal case, defense lawyers know the deck is typically stacked against them with both evidence and juror attitudes. As a result, they sometimes look for just one or two contrarian or loner jurors to push for an acquittal or to hang the verdict. However, in this case, it was clear that we wanted an acquittal jury. For this, we needed jurors who would be able to manage the pressures of a long trial, work together, and reach an acquittal consensus.

Dr. Paul Strand, who had done our survey polling, had also developed a unique statistical model especially for the trial. This model used our prior survey data to create a jury profile. Strand then input the information from each of the juror's questionnaires into the model to come up with a positive, neutral, or negative ranking for each juror. This was especially useful when we had a juror with both positive and very negative questionnaire responses. Based on their cumulative responses to our key questions, the statistical model could tell us whether that juror was ultimately favorable or unfavorable for us. Strand would meet with Johnnie Cochran during the selection process to go over these rank orderings so that when we reached the final strike phase, Johnnie would know how to make strategic calls in the chesslike, peremptory challenge phase.

Just as we were about to start the individual questioning of jurors, Dove Books published Faye Resnick's autobiography. She was a friend of Nicole's and had damning things to say about O. J., which of course the tabloids splashed all over the headlines right before jury selection. The team was thrown into a quandary about whether to delay the trial. But we did not want to give the prosecution more investigation time, so we decided to forge ahead. This latest sensationalism also reinforced our desire to have the jurors sequestered.

We spent several weeks questioning jurors individually about the pretrial publicity (including anything they had heard about Resnick's book) as well as numerous other specifics contained in the jurors' seventy-nine-page questionnaire. Both Cochran and Shapiro did an excellent job of weeding the jury pool, identifying jurors who had a hidden agenda, had already formed an opinion about Simpson's guilt, or who were already leaning toward the prosecution. Cochran also spoke candidly to the jurors about race, to find out if some jurors would already lean toward guilt because they disapproved of O. J. and Nicole's interracial marriage.

When we finally got to the strike phase, the prosecution used a number of challenges on African American jurors. We issued a Wheeler motion (California's version of a Batson motion) to make them explain the nondiscriminatory reasons they had for kicking off those jurors. As the prosecution decided to make more and more strikes on black jurors, they were also reminded of the promises they had made to the African American community about the representativeness of the jury. They finally had to stop and we had our jury. Twelve jurors and twelve alternates. Although much has been made of the racial composition of the original jury, for us it was much more important to understand the life experiences of those jurors, as those experiences profoundly affected how they saw the world, and thus the case. The final jury included:

1. A twenty-eight-year-old married woman who worked for the post office and said that as a young child, she watched her father beat her mother. She stated that, "As an adult I don't go for any man being abusive to me." She was "shocked" to hear that Simpson was a suspect in the murders.

2. A twenty-four-year-old single woman who worked at a Los Angeles hospital.

3. A fifty-year-old divorced woman who worked as a county collections vendor and who said she "respects [Simpson] as an individual based on his past accomplishments."

4. A thirty-two-year-old single man who delivered Pepsi and said Simpson was "a great football player."

5. A thirty-seven-year-old married woman who worked in the post office and said she didn't think Simpson "acts too well" in movies. She described the freeway pursuit that ended in Simpson's arrest as "stupid."

6. A thirty-eight-year-old single woman who was an environmental health specialist and whose father was a police officer. She said the 911 tapes of Nicole calling for police help "sound frightening."

7. A fifty-two-year-old divorced woman who was a postal worker and described O. J. as "only human."

8. A twenty-two-year-old single woman who handled insurance claims and said she was shocked when she heard Simpson was a suspect.

9. A forty-three-year-old married man who worked as a phone company salesman and said he thought O. J. was a good football player.

10. A sixty-year-old divorced woman who was a retired gas company employee. She was the lone holdout in another murder case and managed to get other jurors to change their minds.

11. A forty-four-year-old single woman who fixed computers and printers for the county superior court. She said Nicole "wasn't a saint."

12. A seventy-one-year-old married woman who was a retired cleaning worker and said, "I don't know nothing about no O. J. Simpson."

Juror Marsha R. J. was raised in Oakland, California, in a neighborhood where hers was one of the few black families. Her sister was a Black Panther.

Juror Armanda C. grew up in a small town ten miles from Gary, Indiana, twenty-five miles from Chicago. She recalled, "There were certain cities in Indiana we [black people] could not live in, such as Griffith and Highland, during that period of time. Where I grew up we were not even allowed to go to certain stores. When I went to certain stores, the salespeople would look at me like they knew I was stealing something, and while they're looking at me thinking I'm stealing something, the white kid's got it and gone." She also remembered living across the tracks in a predominantly black neighborhood where some white kids went to her school. She said, "The white kids let you know that being white carried some kind of superiority."

Juror C. was an alternate juror who was raised in the South. He felt that "the white man will hold you back if you let him." It became clear to many jurors that he held a deep-seated hatred for white people. He never made it on the jury.

Most significantly, three-quarters of our jurors had negative experiences with law enforcement. Either they themselves, family, or friends had been pulled over for a DWB—"Driving While Black" as it's known in Los Angeles—or been arrested and harassed for insignificant infractions, or had drugs planted on them by the police.

Recently, President Obama spoke candidly and personally after the Zimmerman verdict in Sanford, Florida, in July of 2013, "I think it's important to recognize that the African American community is looking at this issue through a set of experiences and a history that doesn't go away. There are very few African American men in this country who haven't had the experience of being followed when they were shopping in a department store. That includes me. There are probably very few African American men who haven't had the experience of walking across the street and hearing the locks click on the doors of cars. There are very few African Americans who haven't had the experience of getting on an elevator and a woman clutching her purse nervously and holding her breath until she had a chance to get off. That happens often. And, you know, I—I don't want to exaggerate this, but those sets of experiences inform how the African American community interprets what happened one night in Florida."

Writing about Simpson's eventual acquittal, Michael Wilbon, an African American columnist for the *Washington Post*, wrote, "You see evidence. I see a plant. I see a racist cop. You see a defense attorney's diversionary tactics. The lines aren't always that clear, but they are in this instance."

The challenge for any trial attorney, especially when they know they have a tough audience, is adjusting their presentation for the jury they have, not the jury they wish they had or the jury they think they should have. The prosecution failed to learn this lesson.

THE TRIAL

Suit the action to the word, the word to the action, with this special observance: that you o'erstep not the modesty of nature; for any thing so overdone is from the purpose of playing, whose end, both at the first and now, was and is, to hold, as 'twere, the mirror up to nature; to show virtue her own feature, scorn her own image, and the very age and body of the time his form and pressure. Now this overdone, or come tardy off, though it make the unskillful laugh, cannot but make the judicious grieve, the censure of the which one must in your allowance o'erweigh a whole theatre of others.

—*Hamlet*, William Shakespeare

Whether some saw this case as Shakespeare's *Othello*, a Jacobean tragedy, or political retribution for the acquittals in the Rodney King case, the Simpson trial marked a new era in modern media trial coverage. This was the mother of all reality shows: a football star turned actor, a beautiful estranged wife, her young boyfriend, a horribly violent death, a slow freeway chase, a yearlong daily soap opera, all played out on television in front of millions.

According to some reports, approximately two thousand reporters covered the trial from the initial discovery of the bodies to the aftermath of the verdicts. There were more than 121 video feeds with eighty miles of cable from the Criminal Courts Building, an electric jungle of black snakes carrying footage of witness testimony, reports, and pundit opinion to the world. The *Los Angeles Times* published over one thousand articles on the case, while television ratings soared for everything O. J.

It became the first reality TV presentation, a version of *The Truman Show*, the 1998 Peter Weir–Jim Carrey movie, where 24/7 coverage focused on the personalities of players as much as the trial. Marcia

Clark's makeover and Kato Kaelin's hairstyle, the disputes among the Simpson defense team, and the Hollywood parties all seamlessly blended into coverage from CNN to *Entertainment Tonight*.

There was dinner at Drai's and Halloween parties at Spago with Robert Shapiro dressed as a boxer. A screening party at movie producer Robert Evans's house. A Christmas party at Robert Kardashian's house, meeting the future stars of *Keeping Up with the Kardashians*. The press wore Shapiro masks on Halloween, and the USC marching band played the USC fight song in front of the courthouse one day.

It was a bizarre and seductive carnival for all of us involved, distracting at times from the job at hand—defending a man against allegations that he brutally murdered his ex-wife and her companion.

The most memorable times for me were sitting in a conference room in Century City and looking around the room. There was Johnnie Cochran, Robert Shapiro, F. Lee Bailey, Alan Dershowitz, and Barry Scheck. There was Shawn Chapman, Carl Douglas, Sara Caplan, Peter Neufeld, and Bob Blasier. There was Dr. Michael Baden and Dr. Henry Lee. All extraordinary lawyers and experts. All with résumés that had touched history before this trial—the assassinations of the Kennedys, Dr. Martin Luther King Jr., the Serbian genocide, and the civil rights movement. And while much has been made over the divisions in the team, there we all were, looking at the evidence and trying to come up with a unifying strategy.

Simpson had been hit hard on the field for most of his career and knew the value of a front line. So when he hired Shapiro, then Cochran, and then the rest of the attorneys and experts, he wanted the best defense and the best offense he could have. He also wanted to challenge the traditional league rules.

Trials are not only about which evidence you can get the jury to focus on, but what you can get your opponent to focus on. The side that wins is the one that is able to control the focus of the trial. This is a concept called "framing." It occurs in both political elections and product advertising. And, make no mistake, high-profile cases are political campaigns.

Frames are different than themes. Themes are related to the narrative structure of the evidence while frames are about focus—where you spend your time in trial and how you define the roles of the participants—the judge, jury, witnesses, and your opponent. You can have a great theme, but if the other side has a great theme as well, the jury gets to choose which one they prefer. And in a criminal case, it is always easier for the jury to choose the prosecution's theme. But if you control the frame—the essential focus of the trial and what jurors should be deciding—it is easier for them to adopt your themes and even to incorporate your opponent's themes into *your* frame of the case.

Rather than just defend against the murder charges, Cochran took the position from the very beginning that the trial itself was an "outrageous travesty of justice." The extremity of his position demanded a response, demanded that the prosecution defend itself against this allegation. Strategically, it called into question every action by the police and the prosecution, as well as every piece of evidence or testimony. This "rush to judgment" phrase became a significant frame for the case. It made us into prosecutors and eventually pushed the prosecution into trying the case we wanted them to try.

Prosecutors usually control the pace of a case. They make allegations and the defense responds. But they were put on the defensive immediately by the defense's frame of rushing the investigation to find a convenient suspect. They responded by talking about the "mountain of evidence" against Simpson, and this eventually became a problem for them. First, it made them seem arrogant. How could they lose with such an abundance of evidence? Second, it forced them to justify their evidence collection, a defensive posture. Third, this overwhelming evidence demanded scrutiny and time, by themselves two variables that can create reasonable doubt for a jury. The closer and longer that jurors look at evidence, the more they can skeptically pick it apart, questioning its credibility and those that are presenting it.

We often speak about case evidence when we really should be discussing the jury narrative. There are at least eight narrative cases a jury uses to piece together their own story of the case. First, before they hear evidence, it is what each individual juror's experience and common sense tells them is going on. Then there are the two opening statements, which are the stories the prosecution and defense want to tell. Then there is the prosecution's case, and the defense's case, which are similar to but different stories than opening statements. There are then two closing arguments, with each side trying to tell the jury what it all means. Finally, there is the collective story that the jury as a whole negotiates and puts together using their individual interpretations of the seven narrative strings. Eight different stories.

Prosecutors usually think they need to pick a single case theory and stick to it. This fixed approach does not take into account the emergent way that jurors decide cases. With these numerous narratives, jurors are figuratively putting together a composite jigsaw puzzle from two different boxes of puzzle pieces. The fallacy in conceiving of trial strategy as a single set of facts is that jurors accept multiple explanations of factual scenarios all the time. Jurors will also add pieces of the puzzle from their own box of experiences and beliefs. Thus, it is difficult with all of these puzzle pieces to show resolutely that all of these pieces reveal *only* one picture.

Part of our job in this case was to defuse, diffuse, and confuse the prosecution's approaches in order to create reasonable doubt. To make every witness *our* witness to support our frame of the case. To create a clearer and more realistic picture out of the puzzle pieces. To point out where the prosecution bent or cut the pieces to force them to fit.

THE INVESTIGATION

Our two interconnected themes for the police investigation were: 1) Mistrust the Collection, Mistrust the Results; and 2) Mistrust the

Messenger, Mistrust the Message. As we knew that Clark and Darden would have to lay a foundation for their evidence by introducing it through all of the police witnesses, these key themes were geared toward trying our case in the prosecution's case.

Given our jurors' experience with the police, we knew we had a receptive audience for these themes. The prosecution presented evidence of how detectives Philip Vannatter, Tom Lange, Mark Fuhrman, and Ron Phillips had originally only gone over to notify Simpson about his wife's death. Then, noticing a small amount of blood on the door handle of the Bronco, Fuhrman had leapt the fence fearing for the safety of those inside the house. This already struck a false chord with the jury.

Said one of the jurors after the verdict, "It seemed the police spent all of this time trying to cover up the fact that Mr. Simpson was not a suspect and how they originally went over there because they had just been to a double homicide and they just wanted to make sure nothing was going on at Rockingham. . . . No one ever goes upstairs. No one ever searches the house. You've got no protection. Your guns aren't drawn . . . Remember, too, that time in the '89 incident when [Nicole] ran out of the house and she had mentioned to the police that he [Simpson] had guns in the house." It was obvious to jurors that Simpson was an immediate suspect and that the officers concocted "exigent circumstances" to avoid obtaining a warrant to enter the house. This lost them serious credibility points and tainted how jurors saw the collection of *all* the evidence.

The jurors also did not like Vannatter and commented that he never looked at the jury when he was testifying. So when Vannatter took a vial of blood collected at Bundy over to Rockingham instead of booking it into evidence at Parker Center, the jurors thought he was counting on what police have been counting on for decades: that they could take a case that looked pretty good and make it look even better. And for jurors, it was no coincidence that the officers had not seen the blood drops in the driveway when they first got to Rockingham, but after they had been there a while, lo and behold, there was the damning evidence.

In a high-profile case, jurors believe that the police will take extra precautions and have higher standards in conducting their investigation. The sheer number of officers and medical examiners at Bundy communicated the importance of this case. Realistically, the more personnel involved, the more chance for mistakes. However, for jurors who had created this higher investigative standard, these errors and inconsistencies started looking like more than simple mistakes. They looked suspicious.

Jurors heard that some of the blood evidence from Bundy was stored in a hot van all day instead of taking it directly to Parker Center to book into evidence. They heard of O. J.'s blood being found on a gate two weeks after the original investigation. They also heard that EDTA, a blood vial preservative, was found on some of O. J.'s blood evidence collected at the Bundy crime scene, including the gate. There was testimony from one officer and investigative reports that did not see or catalog O. J.'s socks (that supposedly contained Nicole's DNA) in his bedroom, but later the socks appeared right at the foot of the bed. Finally, there was testimony that .08 milliliters of O. J.'s collected blood was unaccounted for, making jurors suspicious that some of O. J.'s collected blood had been planted at the Bundy crime scene.

At the very least, jurors thought that blood, clothing, and other evidence had been mishandled. This provided an easy explanation of how police negligence allowed some of O. J.'s blood to be found at Bundy and how some of Nicole's blood was found at Rockingham. In forensic circles, this is called cross-contamination. Said one juror, "First the socks [in the bedroom at Rockingham] weren't there, then they were there. Contaminated. Degraded. Then two weeks later you come back and look, and if there is still blood there [on the gate at Bundy] and you can see it with the naked eye, why wasn't it seen in the beginning?" In questioning the glove evidence, another juror stated, "I have a problem with understanding why there was so much blood on that glove [Rockingham] versus the other glove [Bundy]."

When you spend a great deal of time on certain areas in trial, you invite greater scrutiny and skepticism from jurors. So when LAPD criminalist Dennis Fung testified for nine days about the collection and testing of the blood, jurors raised their own reasonable doubts just to alleviate the boredom. They also started to interpose their own investigative techniques as pseudo-detectives. One juror said after the verdict, "Had [O. J.'s] cut been as bad as they say it should have been, some of his blood should have been on the Rockingham glove somewhere, but none of his blood was on it." Trial attorneys are always wise to look at these "shoulds"—these are the personal rules that jurors impose on both evidence and attorneys.

Another common myth in the Simpson case is that the defense, through Simpson's wealth, was somehow able to outresource the district attorney's office. This is sheer nonsense. Although Clark and Darden were making all the calls in the courtroom, the Los Angeles District Attorney's office had dozens of lawyers and investigators, as well as other law enforcement resources like the FBI's Counterterrorism and Forensic Science Research Unit lab in Quantico, Virginia. Certainly the Simpson case commanded many more resources than a normal criminal trial, but the district attorney spent many more millions on this case than the defendant. This myth also tells us where the balance of power lies when it comes to advocacy in the criminal justice system. We commonly believe that the government and the defendant start out on an equal footing at the beginning of a trial. But nothing could be further from the truth.

This was one of those rare instances where the defense could even start to approach the resources of prosecutors. Investigators Pat McKenna, Bill Pavelic, as well as attorneys Scheck, Neufeld, Blasier, Douglas, and Chapman collectively spent hundreds of hours, all combing through the dozens of boxes of documents looking for inconsistencies in the evidence collection and witness statements. At times, we would get boxes of documents from the district attorney where the files would be randomly shuffled so that we would have to spend hours putting them in order.

And then there was Detective Fuhrman. The furor around Fuhrman was clearly one of the turning points in the trial. But not for the reasons that most people think. In the public's mind, the controversy around his recorded boasts to a screenwriter about planting evidence, physical intimidation of suspects, and the use of the n-word was a shocking revelation for the public who rely on the integrity of the police. But for our jurors, living where they lived, seeing what they had seen, Fuhrman lost credibility the moment he denied ever using that word. One of our jurors said, ". . . but I disbelieved Fuhrman when he actually said he didn't use the word *nigger*. I believed that he was lying then. I hadn't heard the tapes then. As soon as he said no, I thought, 'Oh come on. Sure you have.' He should have come right out and said, 'Of course, I've used the n-word. Tell me who doesn't use the n-word out there dealing with these people?' For him to sit up here and pretend that he never used it, it made me feel like just jumping up and slapping him right down right then and there."

As we have seen time and time again with both political and corporate scandals, the denial is often more costly than the misconduct. Jurors and the public just crave some humility and humanity from our political, corporate, and government leaders. They hunger for an authentic moment when these esteemed leaders accept responsibility for their actions. I say *authentic* because we have become used to the canned, scripted apology that sounds more like an excuse than real accountability. When I have worked in high-stakes civil litigation with corporate clients faced with a scandal or crisis, I always look for ways for them to create understanding for their actions instead of excuses and to sincerely accept responsibility for their own conduct and those they are accountable for. Had Fuhrman gotten up on the stand initially and confessed that he *had* used the n-word, his willingness to be honest about something so publicly shameful would have given jurors more confidence in his testimony about the evidence.

But because of Fuhrman's main role in the investigation, his absolute denial and Fifth Amendment assertion once the tapes became known called into question most of the prosecution's key evidence in the trial. Jurors are constantly evaluating witnesses on both a verbal and nonverbal level. In fact, they are instructed by the judge in any trial to pay attention to the demeanor of the witness to evaluate his or her credibility. While lawyers tend to like their witnesses to look polished in their testimony, jurors are looking for small, authentic cues to let them know the witness is being real. One of the jurors said about Fuhrman, "I just sort of knew that he was a snake. Fuhrman seemed too clean-cut and too calm, too cool. . . . But when the defense started to interview him, his whole demeanor changed. His breathing patterns shifted and, from where I was sitting, you could see him squirming."

Although the defense's leverage started increasing at the beginning of the trial, the power shift at this point in the trial was both significant and unexpected for the prosecution. In the jurors' eyes, Fuhrman, Vannatter, and the LAPD were actually on trial. And these two detectives were viewed as the source of the most damning evidence against Simpson. For assistant district attorneys who are constantly dealing with public defenders, it is rare for defense attorneys to so aggressively attack police and prosecutors. Especially when defense lawyers depend greatly on prosecutors' cooperation to cut plea deals. Although the prosecution surely understood the setback with Fuhrman's testimony, they had no choice but to plow ahead with their badly damaged case.

The glove incident in court, where Simpson tried in vain to put on the gloves found at Bundy and Rockingham, became an indelible image for the journalists and public who viewed the trial from their couches and dining room tables. However, the jurors were decidedly mixed about it. One juror said, "I was sick when I saw they didn't fit because I just thought for sure that they were going to fit." This suggested that she had become convinced by some of the other evidence and actually wanted to confirm that Simpson's gloves were involved in the murders. Another juror was clearly convinced that they were Simpson's gloves: "Those gloves fit. He wasn't putting them on right. Sure, you know, they fit."

When you lose credibility in a trial, jurors become suspicious of all of your evidence. For jurors in this frame of mind, even Simpson's "opportunity" to commit the murders became questionable. While the prosecution was confident they would show that Simpson *could* have committed the crime within the allotted one-hour time frame between his attempted cell phone call to his girlfriend at 10:02 p.m. and limo driver Allan Park seeing him at Rockingham at 10:55 p.m., the timing was extremely tight. When all of the conflicting testimony and timeframes from witnesses at Bundy were added in, it created doubt for jurors about the ability of Simpson to commit these murders in the allotted time. For an already doubting jury, it appeared to be more a series of tragic Shakespearean coincidences than a premeditated act on the part of a jealous ex-husband.

In most murder trials, motive is pretty clear-cut. A drug deal gone bad, an escalated argument, a grudge by an employee or a neighbor. But in a long, drawn-out, high-profile trial, the psychology of motive disfavors the prosecution. Prosecutors don't traffic in the *why*, often arguing that physical evidence obviates the necessity for motive. "We have a glove. We have his blood. It doesn't matter why he did it. But (sigh) if you must know, O. J. was jealous and possessive. Here, we'll play you the 911 tapes again." And that's usually where they stop.

But jurors, in their own lives, have a much more nuanced and complex understanding of the nature of jealousy or possessiveness in a relationship. So the *why* becomes a prosecution weakness because it leaves a series of questions. Simpson looks happy at the recital, so what makes him snap? What makes him decide to kill her now? If he is possessive and jealous, wouldn't this be more of an impulse killing if seeing her with Goldman sets him off? If it's an impulse killing, why is he carrying a knife around? These questions beget more questions all in search of the *why*. This search for motive is more important when it is a public figure accused of the crime, as jurors try to reconcile his or her positive public image with the crime he or she is accused of committing.

As one juror said, "But I could not consider it as a heavy motive in terms of him building up some type of rage because of the time period we heard testimony about. They were always drinking. Here they are, drinking, tempers are flaring, and I think Nicole was a little scrapper herself, not so quick to sit down. My husband is 6'1" and weighs 210. I had jumped on him one evening. He did something I didn't like . . . But I say women are women and abuse is abuse. I divorced my husband after three years because he came home and jumped on me and I left."

In these comments, jurors use their own life experiences to make sense of what they are hearing. This again validated our research prior to trial. Women who were divorced and had been in volatile relationships believed that *both* people in the relationship contribute to its volatility. Although it is unfair that Nicole could not speak for herself, jurors do not necessarily ascribe purely angelic qualities to murder victims. This jury was sequestered for 265 days and they had had almost nine months to ponder O. J. and Nicole's relationship.

THE ATTORNEYS

Great attention was paid to the personalities of the lawyers in the Simpson case mainly because they were on television. But the public's perception of the lawyers' performances often differs widely from jurors' expectations of the role of advocates. Different jury panels are responsive to different personality types. When Scott Peterson was tried in San Mateo, California, for the murder of his wife and his unborn child, the press criticized the dull and plodding presentation style of the prosecutors while praising Mark Geragos's more dynamic rhetoric.

However, the jury in that case appreciated the clear and methodical way that those prosecutors presented evidence. Scott Peterson was convicted and sentenced to death.

Jurors mainly look to the attorneys for clarity. The attorneys they understand have a better chance of persuading them than an attorney with dramatic flair. When they are bored and confused, they look to attorneys for emotional cues as to how they should feel about the evidence. One Simpson juror said, "Although we all thought Marcia Clark did an excellent job, a few of us had problems with her attitude." And this tells us about some of the subtle ways that jurors pick up on attitude in the courtroom. The attitudes of the attorneys and the witnesses communicate more loudly than their words. Clark did not trust the jury. And they knew it. At one of the many jury misconduct hearings during the trial when the jury was supposedly exposed to some publicity or errant comment, Marcia asked Judge Ito to dismiss the entire panel. When he refused, she requested they be given lie detector tests. It's hard to trust someone who doesn't trust you.

Jurors would also keep paralinguistic score during the trial by looking at the body language of the two camps. One juror commented, "On the prosecution side, Marcia would just get too frustrated. I'm sitting right in front of her and I'm watching all her sighs and that to me was a sign of weakness. You're here to do a job and if something is bothering you, don't let them see you sweat. And Darden, too."

To show how sensitive our jurors were to the issue of race, one of the jurors commented, "When the district attorney's office first sent Chris Darden down, I remember thinking he was there as a token because the jury was predominantly black. I felt the prosecution needed this particular balance. To me, this was the first 'race card,' as it has come to be called, and it was played by the prosecution."

The jurors responded better to the demeanor of the defense than the prosecution. Jurors thought Clark did a good job but could not relate to her, thus were not as receptive to her themes and arguments.

Jurors understood the cadence and linguistic patterns of Cochran, and not just because of his skin color. One of Cochran's many skills was that he understood more what the jury needed than what the case needed. Like a great director, he knew not only the story that he wanted to tell, but knew how the audience would react to that story and how to develop that story to create the greatest impact on that audience.

The jurors also responded well to the feistiness of New York attorneys Scheck and Neufeld. The combativeness of these attorneys appealed to the personality of this jury and helped to keep them awake during the long and complex testimony about the scientific evidence.

Three blocks away from the Criminal Courts Building, the jurors were sequestered at the InterContinental Hotel and were dealing with their own group dynamic. Juror sequestration in the Simpson case was like taking a nine-month road trip with friends. Rooms were nice, food was good. But after a while, the excitement wore off. The jurors missed their home life, their family, their routines. Small things became big things. They were in the nicest jail in Los Angeles, constantly monitored, guarded, and shepherded from courtroom to hotel cell. They had curfews, conjugal visits, and limited videos they could watch.

As a result, the jurors formed their own ingroups, and feudal rivalries broke out. Jurors were dismissed for misconduct. Deputies were dismissed because of accusations, and jurors staged a protest about their dismissal, first refusing to come to court, and then wearing black armbands in protest.

In all of this, Simpson, like all high-profile defendants, tried to maintain control of the trial, giving stage directions to various attorneys in the case. For public figures, there are two separate trials: one in the criminal court and the other in the court of public opinion. Many celebrities have been in the spotlight for so long they've become dependent on the constant feedback of the populace. Naturally, they feel an attack on their public image is an attack on them personally. They have become so identified with this image that maintaining a positive public presence in the midst of the trial becomes almost more important than their ultimate exoneration.

Most criminal defendants relinquish their control to Lady Justice, throwing themselves on her mercy, whim, and convenience. But Simpson had a personal mission of redemption. He was a public figure. He resolved to redeem himself and build his personal salvation from the wreckage of the disastrous pretrial publicity and the damage to his brand. He wanted to testify, to exert his charisma once again. And everyone wanted to hear him. But no one would listen to him. So he couldn't testify. No matter what he said, his image, his brand, was transformed forever on June 14, 1994.

As we approached the end of the trial, we wanted to refine our final approaches to closing arguments. We conducted another set of focus groups with mock jurors who had similar backgrounds to the actual jury. Since most had followed the trial, we asked them what they most wanted to hear in closing arguments. Blasier presented a prosecution closing, and Chapman the defense. Most importantly, there was a dispute among the defense team as to whether—in closing arguments—we should talk about a wider conspiracy within the LAPD to frame Simpson. Our mock jurors said they did not believe that. From what many of them had seen in the trial, they thought that there was some valid evidence against Simpson, but Fuhrman, Vannatter, and Lange were so eager to nail him that they had tampered with the evidence and directed the investigation to point only toward Simpson. The mock jurors concluded that the rest of the police department chose to turn a blind eye to the detectives' malfeasance.

The closing arguments in the actual trial were more for the media than the jury. The jury had heard enough over the nine long months of trial. Gerald Uelmen's "If it doesn't fit, you must acquit" became a perfect theme. Although jury foreperson Armanda C. dismissed this phrase as not having the great impact that all the pundits claimed it did, it helped to summarize, explain, and justify all of our evidence and arguments in the case. We wanted the jury to remember and use the phrase "it doesn't fit" in deliberations, remembering the image of the glove. We hoped the combination of this simple, evocative phrase and image would help our opinion leaders in deliberations to convince opposing jurors and uncertain fence-sitters.

But the jurors did not need the drama that both sides provided in their closing arguments. One of the jurors commented that she thought Marcia presented the case well but disliked the emotion revealed by Clark's expressions, and felt she was speaking down to the jury. "I thought, 'Jesus Christ. Please. Somebody help me. Get these people to understand that I am not totally illiterate here.'"

Jurors didn't care for some of the theatrics, the celebrity glamour, and the joking during the trial. One juror said, "After we got out, I was surprised to learn that everybody thought we bought the show-boating from Johnnie Cochran . . . after nine months, honey, I don't need that. When Johnnie Cochran put that hat on his head, everybody wanted to die. You could see stomachs literally moving, trying to contain the laughter. I hated it because at that point you're supposed to be tying in all evidence and tying in everything."

THE VERDICT

Jurors are not instructed by a judge *how* they should deliberate in a given case. We have found that there are two typical types of jury deliberation processes: evidence driven and verdict driven. In an evidence-driven verdict, jurors typically organize and pore over the documents, exhibits, and transcripts in the case, reviewing and debating the testimony and issues in the case. In a verdict-driven deliberation, jurors take a vote and then organize their discussions around that vote. If the jury is mostly in agreement, the majority may spend some time convincing the few jurors who are not convinced or discuss which evidence they are in disagreement about. Not surprisingly, verdict-driven deliberations are much quicker than evidence-driven deliberations.

When the Simpson jury took its first vote, it was 10–2 for acquittal. In a jury of twelve, deliberation takes longer, and there is a greater likelihood of a hung jury if you have three jurors or more in disagreement with the majority. But one or two jurors have a harder time holding out against the consensus. Henry Fonda in *12 Angry Men* is a very rare phenomenon.

The jurors in Simpson's case took about four hours to discuss the case in a verdict-driven deliberation before acquitting Simpson on the charges of first- and second-degree murder.

One hundred and forty-two million people were estimated to have watched the verdict and listened to it on radio, with 91 percent of all viewers changing their channels to watch the outcome.

With 150 witnesses, 857 exhibits, 433 motions, and fifty thousand pages of transcripts over nine months at the cost of an estimated twenty million dollars, it was the longest and most expensive trial in California history. Reportedly when Russian president Boris Yeltsin stepped off his plane to meet with President Clinton, his first question was, "Do you think O. J. did it?"

The jurors had been sequestered for 265 days, sheltered from the media firestorm that had erupted at the verdict. When they made their way through the back corridors of the Criminal Courts Building, they could feel the palpable anger from the sheriff's deputies. They were loaded into a county jail bus in an underground garage that was set as camouflage to take them to their hotel to gather their things and then to an undisclosed location where they could meet with their families. They were told to keep their heads down. And sitting on a bus where prisoners sat every day, they were not prepared for what they saw when they emerged from that garage. They had not been watching television. "It was shocking," said juror Carrie B. "When we came out from the underground, there were policemen as far as you could see. Cops on horseback, cops in riot gear." Armanda C. said, "We're sitting in that hotel room feeling that O. J. is free. He's home with his family. He's laughing. He's having a good time and enjoying the moment, whatever it was, of freedom and here we are fugitives from justice . . . We're running trying to hide from the media . . . The way I see it, I'm the one on trial now."

I was working on another case in Phoenix on the day of the verdict and flew back that evening. I joined the defense team for dinner at Georgia's, a southern restaurant on Melrose Avenue. It was not a celebration. There is always a mixture of emotions at an acquittal verdict in one of these cases. Satisfaction at the job you have done for your client. Defensiveness because of the anger you will inevitably encounter from people who wanted another verdict. Sadness at the loss of life.

I drove over to Rockingham in Brentwood to speak to Simpson. There were crowds jeering and roaming the streets outside his home, some outraged at the verdict, rich Hollywood kids partying, tourists trying to get a picture of the now-infamous house, trying to sneak a glance at macabre celebrity. Yet another tent in the carnival that had set up its big top in downtown Los Angeles.

I was let in by security at the gate. I stood briefly to look at the place in the driveway where Simpson had been chipping golf balls the day of the murder, where the blood drops had been wiped away, and where the Bronco chase had ended a year and a half earlier. Simpson's son Jason let me in the door. Simpson was back at home, sitting on his sofa, his Heisman in the case. He was tired and we only spoke briefly. There was no trademark Simpson charm. Just a melancholy and an air of uncertainty, as if to say, "What now?"

On February 4, 1997, in Santa Monica, an all-white jury found Simpson civilly liable for the crimes he was acquitted of a year and a half earlier. President Clinton was scheduled to give his State of the

Union address that night, and many networks and cable stations split their screens to cover both the president and the verdict. There was popular celebration and approval of the civil verdict.

There is an expression used by those who teach law and those who work in the criminal justice system, "Better to let ten guilty men walk free than to convict one innocent man." But we don't really believe that. We would rather convict ten innocent men. And we have. I always ask those who are still angered by the verdict in O. J. Simpson's case whether they are similarly upset by the verdicts against Cameron Todd Willingham, Troy Davis, Larry Griffin, and David Wayne Spence. Of course they say no, because they have never heard of these men. Because these men were never on television. All of these men were convicted, sentenced to death, and executed despite tremendous doubt of their actual guilt or abundant evidence of their actual innocence.

Armchair justice is not new. Celebrity justice is not new. But on a stretch of the I-405 freeway on a sunny June afternoon in 1994, Pandora's box was opened, and the chaotic clash of news media, journalism and advertising dollars, public craving, criminal investigations and prosecutions, celebrity culture, and constitutional protections was unleashed on our unwitting justice system. And we are still trying to close the box.

People of the State of California v. Heidi Fleiss

| | | | | | | | | | | | | | | FARCE OF FELONIES | | | | | | | | | | | | | | | | | |

I remember the first time I had sex—I kept the receipt.
—Groucho Marx

Once upon a time, in a faraway land called Hollywood, there lived a young princess named Heidi Fleiss. She and a number of other princesses went to visit kings and princes in their castles. For their charm and skillful dancing, they were showered with riches, adoration, and travel to exotic, faraway lands.

Until they were arrested.

Fleiss made her court appearance almost exactly one year before O. J. Simpson and foreshadowed the coming media spectacle. Flanked by her renowned Los Angeles attorneys Tony Brooklier and Don Marks, she dodged a fusillade of camera flashes on her way to court hearings. Sunglasses donned for her moment of celebrity, she would smile broadly and toss her hair as she entered the courthouse for hearings. She was arraigned on five counts of attempted pandering and one count of possession of a controlled substance: cocaine.

But the princess grew tired of the questions and court proceedings. She became surly and would snarl at reporters. It wasn't fun anymore. After all, she catered to sheiks and A-list actors. And while she waited those endless months before trial, she would periodically test positive for drugs. Normally, this would have landed her squarely in jail. But such was the skill of her attorneys, they managed to land her in a Pasadena rehab center instead.

This was a far fall for Fleiss, who had purchased a million-dollar home in Bel Air only a couple of years after hanging out her own shingle, subsequent to leaving the employment of another procurer of sexual dalliance, Madam Alex.

Fleiss's success came at a particularly lascivious time in Hollywood history. (Not that there is any other time in Hollywood.) This was pre-Internet and DVD, so box office grosses went through the multiplex roof as Tom Cruise defined American machismo with *Top Gun* and *Days of Thunder*, while Richard Gere and Julia Roberts glamorized prostitution in *Pretty Woman*. Studios and stars were shoveling money and cocaine, just looking for a testosterone sandbox.

Fleiss saw the business opportunity and took it. She catered not only to the movie establishment, but also to their coterie of financial backers. Los Angeles has always been a playground for inherited and international wealth. The moneyed trust funders, kings of Wall Street, European royalty, and Asian businessmen all sought their name on a blockbuster. They wanted their legacy to be popular entertainment instead of junk bonds, family money, or leather upholstery. And when the money came to play in movies, it also came to play in the boudoir.

For centuries, geishas, call girls, and escort services have all recognized that the companionship sought by paying customers is not strictly relegated to sex and kink. Some sell a deeper emotional connection by training their charges in the art of conversation, the nuances of a look and touch to tell the customer they care. Some sell an iconic image of a tall blonde or a sophisticated brunette to hang on an arm at an event. Some just want the forbidden fruit of what they can't get at home: fetish, bondage, and youth.

Historians have records of prostitution all the way back to Mesopotamia in 1800 BC, and the Bible implies the frequency of prostitution in ancient Israel, even though it's forbidden by Jewish law.

The Greeks and Romans were much more open about their prostitution. Hiring a male or female prostitute was legal, common, and didn't incur moral judgment or legal consequence for the purveyor of such services. However, prostitutes in both Greece and Rome risked losing the legal protections of citizenship if they fell into this profession.

Japan had widespread male and female prostitution all throughout the Edo period, from the 1600s to the mid-1800s. The precursors to the geisha were the *oiran*, who were high-ranking courtesans only available to very wealthy or noble Japanese men. Like the geisha, they were well trained in many art forms while also offering sexual services. Around the beginning of the 1800s, the *oiran* were starting to be seen as excessive and gaudy, and were eventually replaced by the geisha. While some geisha chose to have sex with clients, many acted strictly as entertainers. Prostitution was legal in Japan until the early 1900s.

Europe in the Middle Ages also had widespread prostitution, creating a heady mixture of religion, sex, shame, and stimulation. While the Catholic Church considered prostitution sinful, they never made a strong effort to eliminate it because they thought it a "lesser sin" than rape, sodomy, and masturbation. This mixed message manifested in both a geographic and psychological split personality. Many cities and hamlets in the Middle Ages forbade prostitution within the city walls, but participated actively outside their civic boundaries. Other cities set up specific streets or areas that were essentially red-light districts where prostitution was legal. Those who indulged in prostitution could purge their sin later with religious penance, allowing for both indulgence and consequence, creating the tremendous ambivalence about sex that is still prevalent in the church. European attitudes became more condemnatory toward the devil's temptations after outbreaks of syphilis and gonorrhea started sweeping regions, with many towns shutting down their brothels as houses of Satan.

For the European nobility, courtesans were common. This profession was similar to the geishas in that they were often well educated, wealthy, and usually upper-class women who provided a variety of services and entertainment. Most courtesans viewed it as a political position, so to speak, and used their status and skills to try to rise in social standing.

Much like Japan, prostitution slowed down in most countries around World War II. The United States actually banned it around 1910, as the National Woman's Christian Temperance Union advanced a number of morality laws. Prostitution remained illegal in the United States after that, tolerated as black-market sex in some communities depending on their political and religious temperament. In the 1980s, because of the AIDS scare, there was a renewed focus on harshening prostitution laws.

Generally, prostitution has been accepted through most of our civilized and uncivilized history and it was common for married people to openly sleep with prostitutes. Although historically condemned by religious leaders, prostitution only became morally unacceptable starting around 1900, particularly as modern Christianity started gaining a foothold.

With the illegality of the profession, men were rarely prosecuted for sleeping with prostitutes—even when arrested for it, a lot of times the police didn't bother showing up in court. Most of this is because of significant gender disparity in the criminal justice system, but law enforcement also found it easier to drive down the street and round up a bunch of sexual street vendors than to set up an elaborate female cop "sting" to catch johns.

While geishas and courtesans provided entertainment and eroticism, and other prostitutes served fetishism and taboo, Fleiss sold a party to her customers. And she sold parties with Playboy Playmates and Penthouse Pets. The daughter of a prominent Westside pediatrician in Los Angeles, she grew up in the pot-fueled, baby-oiled perpetual parties that accompanied beach life in the 1970s. She met girls that were climbing the Hollywood ladder—sleeping with producers, directors, and actors to get that one chance at their dream of fame. She met others that were just living the beautiful life and having fun. Why not get paid?

And she had buyers: financiers, businessmen, producers, owners of sports franchises, and foreign dignitaries. She became a Westside courtesan service for those who sought the suntanned surf-and-star promise of "California girls."

The problem with Fleiss was not that she was Hollywood's madam. It was that she flagrantly flaunted it. Discreet illegality is tolerated in small doses, but advertised transgressions create the kind of embarrassment that brings retribution.

The problem for the Los Angeles District Attorney's office was how to prosecute Fleiss without her clients—her very powerful and established clients who often made campaign contributions. Fleiss held this leverage in the long-rumored "little black book" with the names of customers: sheiks, studio heads, politicians, and a proud Charlie Sheen. So Fleiss was charged alone—no clients were named in the indictment.

I met her for the first time after a pretrial hearing and was immediately struck by her arrogance, aloofness, and adolescent attitude. She was depressed and used anger to relieve her sadness and confusion. She was not what you would call a cooperative defendant. She would roll her eyes in court, was constantly in violation of her bail terms by testing positive for drugs, and was so outraged at the conditions of her rehab assignment that she threatened to go back to jail rather than continue her rehabilitation. With all of her savvy, cynicism, and worldliness, she was just a lost little girl in the criminal justice system.

When my mother graduated from law school in 1955 and applied for jobs at various law firms, all she was asked in her interviews was, "How many words can you type a minute?" Having worked during the day for the better part of four years to put herself through law school at night, the thought of using her law degree as a secretary did not appeal to her. So she started her own practice, representing underrepresented women in family law matters such as divorces and child custody hearings. She was keenly aware of the gender bias during her career as a lawyer and a judge. Growing up, I heard many stories about the "good ol' boys" club my mother constantly faced in the ranks of lawyers and the judiciary. When she was appointed to the bench by first-term California governor Jerry Brown in 1977, the conservative faction in the state called her one of the governor's "Three B appointees: the blacks, the browns, and the broads."

So when Marks and Brooklier told me that Fleiss's girls had been threatened with serious jail time unless they testified against her, and that none of Fleiss's male clients would be prosecuted for partaking in these same consensual but illegal services, the stench of hypocrisy bothered me. I agreed to work on the case.

Fleiss's trial was scheduled to start in the midst of the Simpson jury selection. Although I was spending time on the Simpson case, I checked with that defense team, and since my colleague Dimitrius was in court every day for Simpson's jury selection, I was able to bounce back and forth between the two courtrooms, which happened to be almost next to each other on the ninth floor of the downtown Criminal Courts Building.

The first order of business was to help prepare Fleiss as a witness.

Even though Marks and Brooklier never anticipated that she would testify in trial, defendants are always witnesses in the case, and their conduct at counsel table is as clear as if they had taken the stand.

Jurors always look at a defendant's demeanor as a measure of their attitude. And the attitude they see in court is how they see the character of the defendant. It is simply easier to believe that they could have committed a violent crime if they *look* hostile and aggressive. In a trial, the jury is hearing about the alleged conduct and motive of the defendant from the witness stand. They then look at the defendant (especially in unguarded moments on breaks) to nonverbally confirm or contradict what they have been hearing. In the back of their minds, they constantly ask themselves, "Do they look like the kind of person that would do these things?" They subliminally measure how well they can relate to the life and choices of the defendant. Although jurors are judging the overall impression of the defendant, that impression is composed of a number of minute paralinguistic cues such as body type, clothing fit and fabric, eye contact, posture, grooming, tattoos and piercings, body angle, movement, breathing, weight, height, features, and gestures.

Demeanor is one of what I call the "hidden drivers" of jury decisions: factors outside evidence and testimony that drive a juror toward a guilty or not guilty verdict in a criminal case, and liability and damages in a civil case. Although many judges and attorneys may dismiss this kind of character evaluation as irrelevant, it stems from a juror's simple human desire to understand the defendant's motivation. In fact, jurors are also instructed by the judge that they *should* pay attention to the witness's demeanor to judge his or her credibility.

So I visited Fleiss at rehab on a shady, eucalyptus-lined street in Pasadena. This was before Dr. Drew and *Celebrity Rehab*. I looked around as I was led into her room. The carpet was worn, the furniture was old, and you could see the sheets of plywood under the thin mattresses on the bunk beds. I waited a few minutes and Fleiss shuffled into the room, wearing green scrubs. She had on no makeup and her hair was unruly. She was a long way from her million-dollar Bel Air abode. But here we were. Just this slender, disheveled twenty-eight-year-old woman and me, talking.

I preferred it this way. Because there are no masks, no pretense. And it is much easier to talk to clients when they are vulnerable, because they listen.

She complained bitterly about her treatment at the center. How she had to share rooms and shower in front of other women. How the women at the center were abusive to her. And how she was punished by being made to carry jars of urine or mud around the yard. She said she was about to ditch the center. I explained she would be arrested and put back in jail if she left court-ordered rehab. She said she would prefer that to her current conditions.

I listened sympathetically and told her I understood how hard it must be for her. But I emphasized that she had to stay at the center. I told her that it makes a world of difference to a jury whether they see a defendant arrive in a car, ride in the elevator, and eat in the cafeteria rather than emerge from a jail holding area. Judges are careful not to let jurors see a handcuffed or orange-jump-suited defendant. But the jurors give a greater presumption of innocence to defendants who are walking among them than those who wear chrome bracelets and disappear into the condemning catacombs of a holding cell.

Most defendants want to defend. They want to be heard. Fleiss was no exception. She had a big personality and a lot of scorn. I had seen her in action in court, slumping back in her chair, rolling her eyes, and scoffing at the prosecutor's claims. But the bigger the defendant's personality, the bigger a target they are for the jury. I spoke to Fleiss about how to make herself small. I told her that I wanted her to disappear from the courtroom. This surprised her. I explained that jurors hunt the biggest prey in the courtroom, and when she flopped about in exasperation, shook her head, and sighed, she became the largest beast on the savannah. I explained that she should remain solemn and still in court, paying careful attention while leaning forward at counsel table. She could take notes and confer quietly with her attorneys, but she must imagine she was moving through molasses. This was meant to slow her general energy and to communicate the image of what jurors expected her to be: a contrite and flawed victim of police over-zealousness. Jurors expected a defendant in her position to be humble. If she didn't look humble, it would be easy for them to believe she was flouting the law. And they would punish her.

If this sounds like manipulation, it is. In an advocacy forum—really in any communication situation—we are all constantly manipulating our image through appearance, words, and deeds. It is called "impression management," and in a courtroom, it can be the difference between a guilty verdict and an acquittal.

Don't get me wrong. Just throwing a sweater or eyeglasses on a contract killer will not automatically make them warm and fuzzy. Jurors have pretty good mendacity meters, and they know when they are being sold. But bringing out the positive side of a defendant's or a witness's personality is important, to keep the jury from being drawn into the prosecutor's negative characterization.

As the trial approached, I spoke to Marks and Brooklier about the case. Both had an extraordinary amount of trial experience and had been through the media firestorm before. They had represented a num-ber of notorious figures including organized crime figures, "Super Freak" singer Rick James, and accused Beverly Hills madam and Fleiss mentor, Elizabeth Adams, also known as Madam Alex. Marks was a native of New York before moving to California, serving briefly as a deputy attorney general for the state before starting his own criminal defense firm. He brought a gravitas and measured credibility to the courtroom. Juries just believed him when he spoke. Brooklier was crafty, had a big personality, a big smile, and jurors just liked him. You could easily mistake him for a Brooklyn mook but he was actually born in Lynwood, on the outskirts of Compton and Watts, and was raised in Anaheim near the "happiest place on earth." But Marks and Brooklier both had the best attribute of any criminal defense lawyer, the respect of the district attorney's office.

While most think that zealous eloquence in trial is the best quality in a criminal defense lawyer, the truth is that most cases never see a jury; they strike a plea deal. Ninety-five percent of actual criminal defense work and skill is looking at the file and sitting at the negotiating table with the assistant district attorney. So a good working relationship is critical to obtaining the best possible outcome for your client. Jury verdicts are the most visible part of the criminal justice system, but deal making is the real engine.

I spoke to Marks and Brooklier about Fleiss's case and what they thought were our evidence strengths and weaknesses as well as what jurors would find compelling and concerning. I then put together a profile of jurors who would be most receptive to the prosecution's story and to ours.

I wanted to make sure that we stayed away from socially conservative jurors who had puritanical views about sex. Those with rigid moral righteousness would obviously be more likely to convict. I also wanted to avoid some strongly liberal jurors who would think that Fleiss was exploiting her "working girls." Those who were strongly reliant on police, and women who had been cheated on, were also candidates for my strike list. I also wanted to avoid jurors who would be put off by Fleiss's overall attitude or threatened by some of the beautiful call girls who would be testifying. And obviously, we wanted to avoid anyone who had followed the case and had already formed a negative opinion of Fleiss and her courtroom antics.

On the positive side, I wanted jurors who thought that prostitution was a victimless crime and had a negative experience with the police. I wanted socially liberal jurors who were comfortable with themselves and their relationships and would not feel threatened by the existence of Fleiss's services or her escorts. I wanted women who would see the unfairness of the law that prosecuted a woman for having sex (even though Fleiss was not the prostitute) but let walk free the man who paid to have sex with her. But most importantly, I wanted jurors with a sense of humor.

Under the law, the police cannot induce a suspect into committing a crime they would not already have committed. That is called entrapment. The problem for us was the LAPD had Fleiss on tape boasting about the size and quality of her escort service. But it was the lengths to which the police would go to catch Fleiss that were both laughable and the basis of our entrapment defense.

We finished picking the jury, and I was generally pleased with the composition: a mixed panel with slightly more women than men and with different sensibilities and outlooks. There was one woman, Sheila M., a Pac Bell line tech, who had copious laugh lines and a "no crap" attitude, who I thought could be very good for us.

Deputy District Attorney Alan Carter, a cooperative and corpulent man who was affable with Marks and Brooklier, started laying out a perfunctory and somewhat lackluster case against Fleiss. Maybe it was because the district attorney's office felt they had such a strong case because they had all of the "transactions" on tape. But I also wondered whether they were on strict orders not to pursue the case too aggressively for fear of uncovering a powerful political figure in Fleiss's client list.

The prosecution presented their case through the LAPD investigation. The LAPD decided to set up an undercover investigation into Fleiss's services. They had a task force of twenty officers assigned to the investigation. That's right. Twenty officers to set up a sting for a woman who was pretty out in the open about her business. Their "cover" was to play Asian businessmen who wanted to purchase call girl services while they were in town on business. They secretly taped a meeting where Fleiss is sitting in a restaurant in the Beverly Hills Hotel with LAPD detective Sammy Lee, discussing in an oblique manner the various services her girls provided. Of course Fleiss was too studied to discuss the specifics of what the women would do, but boastful enough to claim that she was the best madam in Los Angeles. This obviously was very bad evidence for the defense.

But Marks and Brooklier were very careful in their cross-examinations to point out how the undercover officers were always the ones leading the conversation and asking for the services. In fact, after this initial meeting, Fleiss never followed up with the detective. Lee was so eager to make this operation work that he kept calling Fleiss until she finally agreed to send one of her girls to meet him. This was important: to establish that the LAPD had induced Fleiss to offer the girls in this situation, even though she had bragged generally about her extraordinary skill as the purveyor of feminine flesh. It was a narrow distinction, but sometimes it's all you have when your facts are thin.

Fleiss agreed that one of her girls would be provided to an "Asian businessman" in a suite at the Beverly Hills Hotel. A hidden camera was set up in the room in order to record the transaction, while other officers would watch in a room next door via a live feed. A tall, beautiful brunette arrived and was let into the room.

In order to establish the crime of prostitution, you have to engage in three actions: 1) you have to talk about sex for money; 2) you have to exchange money; and 3) you have to engage in what is called "furtherance," which is legalese for the woman's stripping or the unzipping of a fly.

A carefully orchestrated signal was arranged for the undercover officer in the room with the girl. Once she started taking her clothes off and had completed the three requisite steps, he would get an "emergency business phone call" and would dismiss the girl so he wouldn't have to actually go through with the act.

It was all going according to the LAPD plan. On tape, you could see the "Asian businessman" and the call girl talking about sex for money. Then the undercover officer carefully and slowly counted out fifteen one-hundred-dollar bills for the camera. Then this lovely woman started to take off her clothes. But, before the cue could be given for the officers next door to ring their partner, a smoke alarm sounded shrilly on the recording.

In trial, you could see the jurors try to stifle their laughter. But suddenly, they could not contain it. They laughed out loud at the absurdity. While not a word was spoken in evidence to explain the smoke alarm incident, Brooklier asked the officer who was testifying how many officers were assigned to this undercover operation. It was clear that most of the task force was there, crowded into a Beverly Hills hotel room, smoking, and watching Fleiss's girl strip. They had set off the smoke alarm.

This was the exact effect I had hoped for. In a single moment in the courtroom, jurors captured an image quite outside the evidence that characterized the preposterousness of the trial: a cadre of officers watching a striptease for their own enjoyment while gathering evidence to prosecute the unwitting women of this folly.

This was just the first setup, however. They wanted more counts against Fleiss in order to increase their leverage. So they set up an even more elaborate guise.

Fleiss was again approached. Under the auspices of a party at the Beverly Hills Hotel, Fleiss would provide three women for the Asian businessmen's "entertainment."

On the designated day, a hidden camera was again put into the hotel suite to capture the evidence. The three lovely ladies arrived, charming the eagerly assembled men in a practiced manner. In the room, the businessmen spoke among each other in Japanese, with one minor inconsistency. None of the undercover officers actually spoke Japanese. So they sat there speaking pseudo–samurai movie Japanese gibberish while Fleiss's girls stood by with looks of puzzled bemusement, none the wiser.

One of the undercover officers and Fleiss's designated money-collection girl retired to an adjoining room in the suite to discuss payment and services, again captured by a recording device. Since this cop was playing the role of an ESL-challenged Asian man, he would ask in halting English whether the girls would use, for the agreed amount of money, "mouth," "front," and "buttfucku." On this last phrase, the woman looked puzzled and asked "Joey Buttafuoco?" referring to another infamous case, where Buttafuoco, an auto body shop owner in New York, had an affair with a sixteen-year-old girl who later shot Buttafuoco's wife in the face. When Fleiss's girl finally understood that the Asian businessman was referring to a type of sex, she smiled and responded that each of the girls has their own preference but as long as it wasn't too weird or aggressive, it would probably be fine. And again, the officer counted out the hundred dollar bills slowly for the camera. The jurors tried to contain their smiles and take it seriously.

When the agreement was reached they went back into the next room so that the third vital step, the "furtherance" festivities, could begin. One of the cops asked the girls, in halting English, whether they could do a striptease. Politely, they responded that they usually did their striptease to music. This was not something the police had thought of. So all of the businessmen started awkwardly humming the classic brassy strip song, "The Stripper."

The girls shrugged and started taking off their clothes, trying to get into the spirit while the men built their song to a robust crescendo. The jurors at this point could not restrain themselves and the whole courtroom burst out in laughter at the strangeness of the scenario: cops posed as fake Asian businessmen singing strip ballads while beautiful women, about to be arrested, gyrated in this off-key, off-kilter comedy as the first bra dropped.

Of course, this was the cue. Numerous police burst into the room at that point, shouting and waving badges. The girls, scared out of their minds, tried to cover themselves, not quite sure what was happening. And as soon as the courtroom was laughing at this antic caper, all of a sudden it was serious and a little sad.

This mood shift underscored for me the mismatch between the silliness of the situation and the severity of the penalty that Fleiss faced. Because unknown to the jury was the fact that any conviction on a pandering charge carried years of mandatory prison time.

The prosecution finally finished its case, and the defense put on a short case, having established most of its entrapment defenses in the prosecution's case. One of the most important arguments that Brooklier was able to make in order to get the judge to allow an instruction to the jury on entrapment was the unfair disparity in the charging of men and women in the prostitution statutes. Under the law, both providing sex for money and paying for sex were felonies. Yet, in the state of California, no man had ever been prosecuted for paying for sex, while women were prosecuted all the time. In his closing argument, Brooklier was able to mention this disparity and discuss how law enforcement set up these operations only with the intention of inducing the women to violate the law, while turning a blind eye to their male customers.

Jurors were finally given the case to decide on November 29, 1994. It was not a long case, and we did not expect a long deliberation. I was back to spending time on the O. J. case down the hall. On breaks or at the end of the day, I would look for clues as to how Fleiss's jurors felt as they marched down the hallways.

Deliberation dragged on for four days. There was obvious contention among the jurors. On one of the days, Sheila M. was selected as foreperson and brought a coach's whistle to deliberations. Its shrill shriek could be heard in the courthouse hallways as Sheila tried to keep the jurors under control.

I had to fly to New Mexico later that week, so was looking for any sign of a verdict. At the end of the fourth day, my favorite juror, Sheila M., gave me a slight wink and subtle thumbs-up as she passed me in the hallway. I took this as a good sign. But still no verdict that day.

The following day, I boarded a plane to Santa Fe to conduct a training session for, ironically, the New Mexico District Attorney's Association. Just as we were about to leave the gate, I got a frantic call from Marks and Brooklier's office. The verdict was back. Guilty on three counts of pandering and not guilty on one count of pandering and the drug charge. Marks and Brooklier asked me if I could contact the jurors to conduct post-trial interviews.

The jurors had given a press conference after the verdict and had looked both stunned and upset when they had found out that the pandering charges were more serious, carrying mandatory jail time, while Fleiss would have easily gotten probation for the cocaine possession. The following day, when Deputy District Attorney Alan Carter was giving a press conference about his confidence in how jurors could make the right decision in a high-profile case in Los Angeles, jurors Sheila M. and Zina A. appeared on Geraldo Rivera's show, discussing how they had made a terrible mistake with their verdict.

Approximately 6 percent of trials nationally end in hung juries. In some urban areas like Washington, DC, or the Bronx, that can double. While it is certainly the desire of the justice system to arrive at a unanimous verdict in a case, there are cases where juries simply cannot agree. A hung jury, where a number of jurors cannot agree on a verdict, can tell prosecutors that the jury has problems with the evidence or the charged crimes. Hung juries can also reflect personality differences on the panel, or jurors with different agendas. Sometimes they see the evidence differently, sometimes they do not get along with other jurors, and sometimes they are an annulment juror.

Jury annulment occurs when a juror or jury refuses to convict a defendant, despite the evidence, on what they consider to be an unjust law. It is civil disobedience and has its roots in the birth of our nation. In colonial days, juries were often encouraged to defy the unfair laws of King James. The most famous of these rebellions was the Tea Party in Boston Harbor in 1773, which spurred the "no taxation without representation" movement. British Parliament responded by passing the Intolerable Acts, which ended self-rule in Massachusetts. Jurors in court responded by refusing to convict defendants charged with punitive British laws. In fact, these acts led to the convening of the First Continental Congress and, ultimately, the Revolutionary War two years later. Since our country was founded in revolution, this defiance of the law is part of our American psyche.

Psychologically, jury annulment has a much more practical application. As jurors are instructed to use their common sense in evaluating a case, it stands to reason that they will pay attention and give more weight to issues that make sense and are more familiar to them, even if they are not in sync with the evidence or the law in the case. Even more importantly, jurors will create an internal narrative of what they think happened in the case, even if that narrative has only a fleeting or tangential relationship to evidence or law. So if a prosecution of a particular defendant just seems unfair to a juror, they will look for reasons to dismiss or disregard evidence, or to minimize or interpret legal instructions in order to support what they feel would be a fair outcome in the case.

Finally, even though jurors are instructed to not consider how a defendant will be punished when the jury is deciding on a verdict, they do. They know that their verdict will have a direct consequence on the life of the defendant and are mindful to reach a verdict where the punishment not only fits the crime, but the character of the accused.

When there is a criminal conviction, juror misconduct is often alleged in an attempt to overturn the verdict. But the appellate courts are very strict about what they consider to be actual misconduct. The basic test is whether the courts believe that the misconduct outweighs all of the evidence against a criminal defendant. In other words, without the misconduct, the jurors would never have convicted. Appellate judges don't care about the thought process of jurors, because they recognize that the thoughts and impressions of a juror are changeable. If every juror who had misgivings about a verdict came forward to talk about their misunderstanding of the law and evidence, there would be scores of verdicts overturned every year. The appellate courts need demonstrable proof that jurors engaged in an activity that was in violation of the judge's instructions. And that this violation in some way directly affected the outcome of the case. So it can't be a small misconduct. It's got to be big.

I came back the following night from New Mexico and started going through questionnaires to see if I could find contact information on the Fleiss jurors. Because of their press conference and their media interviews, I managed to learn a little bit more about their backgrounds and their attitudes about the case. I finally reached Sheila M. the following week and she agreed to talk.

I met her at a smoke-filled City of Commerce casino. When I am interviewing jurors, I just let them tell me the story of the trial. They have invested so much time, concentration, and emotional commitment that they often just need someone to listen to them talk through their feelings. I try to ask as many open-ended questions as possible and avoid putting forth a prescribed list of topics. That tends to smack of an agenda, which can make a juror defensive and less candid.

Right away, Sheila told me how bad she felt about the verdict. She thought the police investigation was unfair and that Fleiss had gotten a raw deal. She said she was stunned to find out about the potential prison time that Fleiss faced. Jurors are specifically instructed that they should not consider punishment in their verdict, but, in judging a defendant on a crime, they naturally calculate what they feel would be a fair sentence.

I asked Sheila to describe the deliberation process for me. She said that one of the jurors had slammed the table at the beginning of deliberations and stated that he thought she was guilty from the beginning. She said he was the most stubborn of the pro-prosecution jurors, but said that the jury was evenly divided, six for guilt and six for acquittal. And no one would budge after four days. This would have been a great victory for us, as the district attorney would have to think hard before trying Fleiss again with a jury so deeply divided.

Jurors know that the world is watching in big cases. They don't like to come back with a hung jury after all the time, resources, and press coverage that have been invested in the case. So Sheila described how she and her other acquittal jurors made a deal with the guilt jurors. They were convinced that the drug charge was serious and would carry a hefty sentence but felt the pandering charges would result in minimal prison time. So they agreed to a conviction on three of the pandering counts in exchange for the acquittal on the drug count and one other pandering charge.

This type of horse-trading votes, by itself, is not misconduct. Jurors do it all the time. The courts have said that as long as it is not random or by chance, like flipping a coin, swapping votes is not misconduct. I was starting to feel hopeless about finding something to help Fleiss. But then Sheila said that she and her fellow "not guilty" jurors had a private meeting after court to see if they could strike this bargain.

This *was* jury misconduct. The judge is clear that the only discussions about the case are to happen in the jury room. This meeting outside to discuss vote swapping directly violated the court's instructions. I was excited that I might have stumbled across some direct proof that would help Fleiss avoid up to eight years in prison. But it is one thing for a juror to tell me this story in a seedy casino within wheezing distance of the I-5 freeway in East Los Angeles. It is another thing for that juror to admit to a judge that she had violated the jury instructions.

So I asked if she knew how I could get in touch with any of the other jurors in her well-intentioned negotiating team. She gave me what contact information she had on them. I thanked her and asked if she would be willing to meet with the lawyers in the case to discuss it with them. She eagerly agreed.

I contacted four of the other jurors and they all confirmed Sheila's story about the vote swapping. I asked if they would be willing to meet with the attorneys, and they all agreed. We met at Marks and Brooklier's office in Century City, and they all told the attorneys the same story about how they had met outside of deliberations to strike the verdict bargain. We explained that this was a violation of the judge's instructions and asked if they would be willing to state in an affidavit that this was, in fact, what they had done. We told them they were under no obligation to do so but it would obviously go a long way toward an appeal.

They all looked a little concerned and asked if they could be prosecuted for not following the judge's instructions. We looked it up and could not find an instance where a juror had actually been prosecuted for such an infraction. They hesitantly agreed. Now that they knew the consequence of their actions, they genuinely wished they had stuck with their true feelings about the evidence and had continued to insist on acquittal, even if it meant a hung jury.

We submitted five juror affidavits, all stating that they had met outside the presence of other jurors and had discussed the case. Juror Zina A. said in her statement, "The only reason I voted guilty was because I discussed the penalty and potential punishment of Ms. Fleiss with other jurors, and I believed that by so voting I could obtain a not guilty verdict on the narcotics offense. . . . I agreed to and did trade my guilty vote on the pandering counts in exchange for a not guilty vote on the narcotics offense." Juror Joseph L. also said in his affidavit that he did not think Fleiss had received a fair trial, because two jurors "presumed her guilty before the foreperson was even selected."

These were brave and extremely rare admissions. Most jurors are never willing to concede that they have done anything wrong to exact a verdict. And while there are some jurors who may try to manipulate the system for a preconceived verdict, most engage in misconduct out of an earnest effort to do the best job possible. They bring in a dictionary definition to help clarify an instruction. They talk about their uncle Henry's treatment by police in order to help them discuss the propriety of an investigation. But most go silently back to their lives.

Deputy District Attorney Carter was furious when he received the motion for a new trial based on jury misconduct. In the media, he threatened them with prosecution, and the jurors called me, their worst fears starting to be realized. I felt horrible and tried to reassure them. Marks and Brooklier went on the offensive, calling the DA's threats an intimidation tactic to try to dissuade the jurors from testifying. The judge set a hearing for this motion, but the jurors said they would not testify if they could be held in contempt by the judge. Marks and Brooklier finally brokered a deal where three jurors would testify about their misconduct without the threat of a contempt citation. Two of them that had originally submitted affidavits were scared off and said they would not testify.

Three brave souls admitted in court that they had made a mistake and disobeyed the judge's instructions. They were forthright, even though Carter cross-examined them and the judge angrily admonished them.

Even with this clear evidence, the judge refused to grant a new trial. Fleiss was able to stay out of jail on bail while her appeal was being heard. Less than two years later, when the appeals court finally read the motion for a new trial, they issued their ruling and granted a new trial in a week, unprecedented for the appellate court. In a rebuke to the judge, they stated how obvious it was that this misconduct was prejudicial to Fleiss's guarantee of a fair trial and how the jurors' misconduct was far worse than Fleiss's original crimes. With Fleiss's federal case looming and the prosecutors smarting from the appellate court decision, the district attorney decided not to re-try Fleiss. She had avoided at least eight years in prison.

But the princess did not live happily ever after. She served prison time for federal tax fraud charges and was re-arrested for DUI charges. She opened a clothing store, then a brothel and a Laundromat in Nevada, then went on reality shows and raised parrots.

United States v. Jim Guy Tucker

| | | | | | | | | **BANK FRAUD AND BLUE DRESSES** | | | | | | | | | |

The jury, passing on the prisoner's life,
May in the sworn twelve have a thief or two
Guiltier than him they try: What's open made to justice,
That justice seizes: What know the laws
That thieves do pass on thieves?

——*Measure for Measure*, William Shakespeare

ARKANSAS

In June of 1978, Susan McDougal named a 230-acre parcel of land "Whitewater" after she bought it with her husband, Jim McDougal; then attorney general of Arkansas Bill Clinton; and Hillary Clinton. They had visions of developing the land into vacation homes for those wanting a peaceful place on the river to sit and fish.

And there is good fishing on the White River in Arkansas. Trout anglers occupy cabins along the smoky Ozark mountain banks and exchange advice on flies and strategies. The brown trout found in deep pools are suspicious, diving and hiding when they see a fisherman's shadows. To catch them, you need overhanging cover and great patience. Cutthroat trout are ambush predators and strike most often with the coming of a storm. Fishermen look for boulders, logjams, eddies, and transitions between fast and slow water to lie in wait for them. Rainbows like the fast water, leaping and tail-walking to dance and taunt a fisherman. They are caught more easily with light spinning tackle, but good anglers use a fly rod.

In November of 1978, Bill Clinton was elected governor of Arkansas in a landslide vote. In Arkansas at that time, gubernatorial elections were held biennially. Two years later, in 1980, Clinton was narrowly defeated by Republican Frank D. White and lost his seat. He ran again in 1982, where he first beat Jim Guy Tucker in the Democratic primary and then reclaimed his seat from White by beating him in the general election. These two-year election cycles put fund-raising and reelection plans on the fast track as soon as a new governor took his hand off the Bible. It also bounced a politician from public to private sector if they were defeated, handing them a bill for election debt they incurred from the campaign and causing them to look for private sector solutions for that debt.

In 1984, Arkansas finally passed an amendment that changed term limits to four years. Clinton clobbered White again in the next election in the new term limit cycle in 1986 and won again in 1990 against Sheffield Nelson, building a groundswell of popular support in Arkansas. He vowed not to run for president, even as he started garnering national attention from kingmakers in the Democratic Party.

Jim Guy Tucker was born in Oklahoma City but moved to Arkansas as a child, where he attended public schools in Little Rock. After receiving a degree in government from Harvard University in 1964, he joined the Marine Corps Officer Training program, but was disqualified due to chronic ulcers. He worked as a freelance civilian reporter in two tours of Vietnam in 1965 and 1967. After his tour ended, he attended the University of Arkansas Law School at Fayetteville, where he graduated in 1968 and was admitted to practice law the same year.

From early on, Tucker effortlessly intertwined his law, business, and political careers, which began with his being hired by the prestigious Rose Law Firm in Little Rock in 1968. In what would later be seen as strangely ironic, he was first elected prosecuting attorney for the Sixth Judicial District of Arkansas in 1970 and then as the state's chief prosecutor, the Arkansas attorney general, where he served from 1973 to 1977. Following that, he was elected as a Democratic congressman before giving up his seat in 1978 to wage an unsuccessful campaign for the United States Senate, which was fruitlessly followed by his failed attempt against Clinton in 1982 to become governor.

As one of the oldest law firms in Arkansas, the Rose Law Firm traced its roots back to 1820, when one if its founders, Robert Crittenden, served as territorial governor and negotiated Arkansas's successful application to become the twenty-fifth state. Uriah Milton Rose co-founded the American Bar Association and later became instrumental in drafting the articles for the Second Hague Convention in 1907. Hillary Rodham Clinton became the first female associate and partner at the firm. She was later joined by Vince Foster and Webster Hubbell, both of whom would end up in President Clinton's administration.

Jim McDougal had one foot in the political world and one foot in the business world. He worked on the staff of Senator J. William Fulbright in 1967 and continued to work for him in both Washington and later back in Little Rock. Wanting to feel the power of elected office himself, he tried to claim a seat in the House of Representatives, but lost a heated electoral battle to unseat Republican John Paul Hammerschmidt in 1982.

McDougal and Tucker, both smarting from election defeats, turned their attention to the business of making money. Tucker was hurting the most from the lost election, saddled with more than $250,000 of election debt.

Tucker and McDougal looked to real estate development to rescue them from the penury of campaign obligations. In 1979, they bought a condominium project in Little Rock. McDougal, who had served as Clinton's economic development director when Clinton was governor, bought the Bank of Kingston and renamed it Madison Bank and Trust. Tucker obtained a small amount of ownership shares in the bank. McDougal also bought a savings and loan in Georgia and moved it back to Little Rock, renaming it Madison Guaranty Savings and Loan.

Small banks, especially savings and loans, are tempting acquisitions for businessmen. They have a constant source of investment funds in the form of depositor accounts, and they are federally insured in case something goes horribly wrong. However, they also face the scrutiny of federal regulators with sharp eyes, sharp noses, and even sharper pencils, who can pore over the bank's books at a moment's notice to make sure that the bank is fiscally sound. And then there is the matter of the paperwork. Bad record keeping or fudged documents can make those in business civilly liable, but when a bank is insured by the federal government, that same poor documentation can be a criminal offense.

After McDougal bought Madison Guaranty in 1982, his hunger for land increased with the new cash liquidity he had in the form of depositor funds. He, as Madison Guaranty, bought a 3,460-acre mobile home park, a 3,900-acre development parcel, and a 1,300-acre farm parcel that was set aside for residential development in Pulaski County, the seat of Little Rock. He was quoted as saying proudly, "I became known as the junk dealer. If it didn't have a road to it, if it had a problem that would depress the price, they'd come to me." Keeping their circle of friends and rivals tight, McDougal and Tucker formed a partnership with one of Clinton's aides, Stephen Smith, to also develop real estate projects in the Ozarks.

At the same time that McDougal was intent on becoming a land baron, Jim Guy Tucker set his sights on a different investment: cable television. A handshake deal with Billy Cost, a Louisiana businessman, created a business where Cost would obtain the cable rights and Tucker would handle the financing. They would split the profits fifty-fifty. One of Tucker's first cable businesses, County Cable, took out a $50,000 loan from Capital Management Services, an investment bank started by former Pulaski County municipal judge David Hale, who would later become a key figure in the Whitewater investigation.

Hale was born into a family that was heavily involved in state politics, and he was a member of the business community almost immediately after graduating from the University of Arkansas. He was involved in many local business and service organizations, and when he was elected as a judge in 1981, Hale continued to run Capital Management Services while remaining on the bench, unusual for a sitting judge. While there is nothing preventing judges from earning independent income while they are on the bench, it is rare for a judge to run an independent business, because judges have such a high ethical duty that they must avoid even the appearance of impropriety.

Capital Management was backed by the Small Business Administration (SBA), a U.S. government agency, and was originally created in 1953 to provide funds for "socially or economically disadvantaged" individuals. Hale's bank, however, soon became known for frequently making loans to powerful and influential politicians in Arkansas's government. Between McDougal's source of unlimited depositor funds and Hale's SBA-backed loans, the money flowed.

These were not your standard home and auto loans. If you had a connection, you had a loan. A phone call was made and you got money—no written applications, no down payments, no feasibility studies, and no collateral. Tucker borrowed over $725,000 from David Hale's company and $500,000 from McDougal's Madison Guaranty and never went through an approval process. As one of McDougal's associates put it, "If your story sounded good or if you were an insider, it was a done deal."

Between his salary and bonuses, Jim McDougal took home more

than $350,000 a year from Madison. Susan McDougal had a marketing firm, Madison Marketing, which was set up to promote Madison's real estate ventures. She was paid more than $1.5 million in a four-year period. She starred in television commercials for the real estate ventures, one where she sat astride a white horse wearing hot pants. The McDougals also set up Madison Financial Corporation, which bought a fleet of vehicles: Mercedes, Jaguars, a Bentley, and a twin-engine Piper aircraft. And the money kept flowing.

Jim McDougal and Tucker struck another deal in February of 1986: McDougal would lend him some more money if Tucker agreed to buy some land in the Castle Grande development, a thousand acres of a previously failed industrial development. McDougal's plan was to simply turn it into a trailer park—half-acre lots where you could park your "grand castle," a double-wide trailer home. He would also have some of the area zoned off for commercial usage so there could be a shopping center. Tucker's cable company had been expanding, and this would be a natural extension for his lines, so he agreed.

However, state law says that a bank cannot loan more than 6 percent of its total assets to a single borrower. McDougal needed a way around that to give Tucker the amount of money he needed, so he just brought in a second borrower. His friend Seth Ward was given a $1.15 million loan from Madison that would simply go toward the Castle Grande deal. Even worse, this loan was a "nonrecourse" loan, which meant there were no consequences if Ward personally did not repay the loan—the money would simply vanish. This was illegal and McDougal knew it. But like most people who end up reading their name in a criminal indictment for a white-collar crime, they start by edging right up to the line of illegality. When they don't get caught, they step over the line. When they still don't get caught, they keep walking until they don't even know where the line is anymore.

Also at some point in 1985, according to Jim McDougal, then-governor Bill Clinton jogged by his office one day, stopped in, and strongly suggested that his wife Hillary at the Rose Law Firm should handle some of McDougal's Madison Guaranty work.

Remember the federal regulators? The ones who specialize in scrutinizing banks and asking questions? They looked at Madison Guaranty, and they had a whole lot of questions. Questions like, "Why would a federally insured institution in Little Rock, Arkansas, have invested so heavily in real estate and not kept a fiscally sound, balanced portfolio to ensure the safety of depositor money?"

McDougal knew he was in trouble with federal regulators when they came to audit Madison's books about its top-heavy real estate portfolio. But, by that point, he felt he was in too deep. There is a tragic turning point in every crime, a moment of realization and desperation when a person realizes they have gone a little too far. It might have been a mistake, they may have not been paying attention, they act impulsively, or they simply have gotten a little too greedy. And instead of stopping, they decide to keep going, justifying and rationalizing their actions. Criminals follow Newton's first law of motion: objects in a state of motion tend to remain in motion, unless an external force is applied. In this case, bank auditors were the external force.

Before the federal regulators visited, McDougal and Tucker decided to drive Hale up to the Castle Grande. McDougal was in trouble and asked Hale for help. The feds were about to audit his bank, and he needed to move some bad loans off his books before they noticed them. McDougal and Tucker needed Hale to bail them out.

To correct Madison's questionable loan portfolio, Tucker and McDougal devised a plan to have Dean Paul, a local lumber company operator they knew, buy a piece of property from Hale for an extremely inflated price. Hale was able to extract money from the SBA to add to profits of the sale, which he then spun back to entities owned by Tucker and McDougal. They were essentially buying and selling their own assets in order to write Seth Ward's illegal nonrecourse loans off the books. A few adjustments here, a loan shift there, and, lo and behold, everything was in order right before the federal auditors arrived. Everyone breathed a sigh of relief. They had cleared all the loans and moved the properties so everything looked legitimate. They felt they were in the clear.

On April 3, 1986, Hale made another loan to Susan McDougal's new company, Master Marketing, for $300,000. It was backed by an SBA loan for the "socially disadvantaged," which she qualified for as a female business owner. The $300,000 loan was deposited in the McDougals' personal account at Madison and partially used to pay off some personal loans and Whitewater-related investments.

And of course, to make sure everyone had legal protections for these deals, Tucker's law firm had done work for Hale's company and state regulatory work for Jim McDougal's Madison Guaranty.

But they weren't in the clear. Even though the bank auditors did not pick up on the illegal nonrecourse loan, the McDougals could not hide all of the questionable and risky real estate investments and their own involvement. In July of 1986, Jim and Susan McDougal were replaced as officers of Madison Guaranty by the Federal Reserve Board for irresponsible lending practices.

It took a few years, but in 1989, Madison Guaranty finally collapsed under the weight of its debt, bad loans, and speculative land investments as well as changes in government accounting procedures. The federal government spent sixty million dollars bailing it out. As a result of the detailed financial scrutiny that ensued from this collapse, McDougal was indicted on fraud charges for his management of the Madison Guaranty real estate subsidiary. McDougal was also indicted for bank fraud for his illegal use of Madison Guaranty's funds. He was tried in 1990 but was acquitted of the charges.

While McDougal was fighting fraud charges, Tucker was preparing another run for governor against Bill Clinton in 1990. But despite Clinton's assurances that he would not run for president, Tucker saw the writing on the wall. He knew the political animal that was William

Jefferson Clinton, and he knew Clinton would eventually be president. So, rather than face him in yet another losing gubernatorial election, Tucker decided to run as a candidate for lieutenant governor instead. If Clinton were elected president, Tucker would automatically become the governor without having to face Clinton head-to-head in a primary again.

Clinton was, unsurprisingly, handily elected governor in 1990 over the Republican challenger Nelson, and Tucker won his much-easier campaign to become lieutenant governor. Clinton, who was clearly preparing for a presidential run, had no real interest in being governor after he was elected. He turned his attention to the national stage and left the day-to-day running of the state to Tucker. However, Clinton seemed unwilling to give his former rival Tucker the necessary information to actually run the state, and Tucker was often left scrambling. Later, Tucker would be further infuriated when Clinton, after being elected president, left Arkansas in a financial mess for Tucker to dutifully clean up.

Clinton decided to house his national presidential campaign headquarters in Little Rock, a first time in the national spotlight for Arkansas. Scores of reporters covering the campaign flooded the town, curious about the "Comeback Kid" phenomenon. They were fascinated with the narrative about the boy-who-would-be-president raised by a single mother in poverty from the little town called Hope.

Although Clinton was born in Hope, Arkansas, he moved to Hot Springs when he was eight and lived there through high school. Hot Springs was known for being an illegal gambling hub of the American South from early in the twentieth century. Much of the activity occurred out in the open with the mayor and law enforcement doing little to stop it.

Owen Madden owned the famous Cotton Club in Harlem in the 1920s and 1930s. After serving time in prison in New York, in the '30s, he decided to leave town and ended up in Hot Springs, Arkansas.

When Madden arrived, he fell in love with the local postmaster's daughter and married her, and soon after became a controlling partner in the biggest gambling ring in town, the Southern Club. As word got out that Madden owned this new haven, a lot of his mafia friends started coming down to visit, mostly well-known mobsters from the East Coast and Chicago.

Because of Madden's connections, Hot Springs became a place that a lot of gangsters would flee to if they found themselves in trouble in their home cities. Al Capone owned a year-round suite in one of the nicest hotels in Hot Springs, in case he ever needed to unexpectedly hole up there.

Years later, Clinton was an excellent student and a member of the jazz band at Hot Springs High School. When he was seventeen, he was elected Arkansas representative to the American Legion Boys Nation, when he was able to travel to the White House to meet President John F. Kennedy and future investor in the McDougals' and Tucker's land deals, Senator J. William Fulbright.

Clinton attended Georgetown University on a scholarship, and won a prestigious Rhodes Scholarship to study at Oxford. He then went to Yale Law School, where he met Hillary Rodham, and after graduating, married the bright young woman and moved back to Arkansas.

But, even though Clinton had lived in Hot Springs, Washington, DC, Oxford, and New Haven, the press narrative was always the boy from Hope who overcame an abusive stepfather and protected his single mother on his way to the White House. The press loved the story, but the more they heard, the more they wanted additional details about Clinton's life.

That curiosity also brought scrutiny to Madison Guaranty and the Rose Law Firm. After all, Little Rock is a small city, and secrets are hard to hide. A *New York Times* reporter wrote an article on March 8, 1992, that exposed how the Clintons lost money in the Whitewater Development and a partnership with the now-disgraced McDougals.

After seeing this article, a senior criminal investigator hired by Resolution Trust Corporation to investigate the failure of Madison Guaranty Savings and Loan looked into ties between Clinton and the McDougals. She finally sent a criminal referral to the U.S. Attorneys Office, stating that the Clintons may have been beneficiaries of the McDougals' illegal scheme. The FBI and the U.S. Attorney's Office decided the claim had no merit but she continued to investigate and insist on the connection. She ended up proffering ten criminal referrals to the Department of Justice.

Despite these questions and the growing suspicions of untoward influence on the part of the then-governor or his wife, Clinton was elected president in 1992. His surge during the campaign overcame George H. W. Bush's popularity as a result of the Desert Storm invasion of Iraq, the emerging scandals about Clinton's past affairs, and accusations about his avoidance of military service. This reaffirmed the narrative that the reporters themselves had started to believe—that a boy raised in adversity could overcome all odds. Tucker, the newly appointed governor of Arkansas, came to Washington for Clinton's inauguration, leaving a Little Rock dentist as the Arkansas Senate pro tem in charge of the state.

In January of 1993, William Jefferson Clinton looked out on a sea of hopeful faces as he was sworn into office on the Capitol steps and later danced to Fleetwood Mac's "Don't Stop." In order to protect the president from further inquiries, Jim McDougal offered to buy out the Clintons' interest in Whitewater for one thousand dollars.

In June of that year, Vince Foster, now a deputy White House counsel, filed three years of late Whitewater tax returns for the failed venture. Foster was also a native of Hope, Arkansas, as well as friend and law firm partner of Hillary Clinton at the Rose Law Firm before coming to Washington. Unexpectedly, less than a month later, he committed suicide in Fort Marcy Park in Virginia, less than seven miles up the Potomac River from the White House. Files found in his office prompted more questions about Whitewater, and conspiracy theories abounded about whether he was killed because of his proximity to the blossoming Whitewater investigation.

In 1993, Hale was indicted for fraud related to the SBA loans he doled out to the McDougals and others. He cooperated with the prosecutor in exchange for a plea agreement and said that he was pressured into giving Susan McDougal the $300,000 loan by both Jim McDougal and Clinton.

By reason of the title and authority of those involved—a state governor and a sitting president of the United States—what started out as an inquiry into questionable loans escalated into a full-blown investigation. Because these new allegations directly related to the commander in chief and her boss, Attorney General Janet Reno appointed former U.S. attorney Robert Fiske as independent counsel to investigate these allegations.

THE SATURDAY NIGHT MASSACRE

The appointment of a special independent counsel to investigate sitting presidents wasn't a new thing. Twenty years earlier, in 1973, another scandal was unfolding—Watergate. As the House and Senate demanded answers to the "White House Plumbers" and other direct connections to the Oval Office, President Richard Nixon did his best to cover up his involvement.

To look into the Watergate allegations, Elliot Richardson, the attorney general at that time, appointed an independent special prosecutor named Archibald Cox, who began looking into the Watergate break-in. As a special prosecutor, Cox was working under the attorney general and could not be fired or removed by any politician unless he had explicitly done something wrong or illegal.

Cox immediately butted heads with Nixon, as Nixon tried to completely stonewall the investigation into the Watergate plumbers' ties to the White House. He refused to turn over documents and recordings to Cox's office, offering strange compromises like having a hard-of-hearing senator of his choosing review the recordings and give Cox a summary of the White House tapes. Cox, however, wouldn't stand for any of this, and refused all of Nixon's offers.

Enraged, Nixon tried to get rid of Cox, but it took him three tries. First, he demanded that Elliot Richardson remove Cox from his position—something not allowed by the rules governing an independent special prosecutor. Richardson refused to fire Cox, and resigned in protest. William Ruckelshaus, Richardson's deputy who became attorney general after Richardson quit, was ordered to fire Cox as well, but he also refused and resigned. As both had been a party to the investigation by Cox, they felt they could not ethically or legally fire Cox, despite a conflicting ethical obligation to obey an order from their commander in chief. After these two back-to-back resignations, the next person in line for the attorney general position was Robert Bork, who at the time was the solicitor general and was not a party to the investigation.

When Nixon asked Bork to fire Cox, Bork acquiesced to the man who had just made him attorney general. Unlike his predecessors, Bork believed that the president had the legal right to fire the special prosecutor. Under Nixon's orders, Bork had Cox removed on Saturday, October 20, 1973, becoming known as the "Saturday Night Massacre." It was later revealed that Bork had considered resigning as well, but ended up firing Cox after Nixon promised him a seat on the Supreme Court. Despite Nixon's attempts to shut down the Watergate investigation, it snowballed, engulfing his entire administration. Facing almost certain impeachment, Nixon resigned on August 8, 1974.

A few years after Nixon's resignation, Congress wanted to make sure the Saturday Night Massacre couldn't happen again and passed the Ethics in Government Act in 1978. To prevent a president from wielding too much influence over a supposedly "independent" auditor, the law stated that future independent counsel would be supervised by a special panel of three federal judges, supposedly immune from the reach of the president. The attorney general would make a request to this judicial board, and they would approve or deny it—completely outside the purview of the president. This law briefly expired in 1992, when Congress did not renew it but it returned as the Independent Counsel Reauthorization Act of 1994.

The Whitewater scandal created another situation where a sitting president needed to be investigated. However, because Congress had not yet reapproved the statute, Attorney General Janet Reno did not have the Ethics in Government Act or its procedures involving the three-judge panel. Like Richardson with Watergate, she appointed a new special prosecutor to look into President Clinton's involvement with Tucker and McDougal. In January of 1994, she selected Robert Fiske, a moderate Republican who was a former U.S. attorney, to conduct a preliminary investigation into the initial Whitewater allegations. Congress, knowing that they no longer had an independent formalized procedure to investigate a sitting president and could end up with another Saturday Night Massacre, worked on legislation in 1993 to reauthorize the independent counsel procedure.

At the end of Fiske's six-month investigation in June of 1994, he wrote an interim report stating that there was no evidence that Clinton or anyone from the White House had tampered with or interfered with the current investigation into Madison Guaranty. Ironically, the day Fiske released his report was the same day Clinton formally signed the Independent Counsel Reauthorization Act of 1994.

The sudden reauthorization of this law meant that Fiske's position was no longer valid, as it had not gone through the approval of a three-judge panel. Janet Reno approached the newly formed panel, asking that Fiske be reinstated. But the panel wanted someone new who had not been assigned by a Clinton appointment. Led by Judge David Sentelle, the judicial panel appointed Kenneth Starr to replace Fiske as independent counsel and authorized him to continue Fiske's investigation. They conferred upon Starr "jurisdiction and authority to investigate other allegations or evidence of violation of any federal criminal law . . . by any person or entity developed during the Independent Counsel investigation referred to above and connected with or arising out of that investigation."

Sentelle was appointed in 1985 by President Ronald Reagan to the U.S. district court for the Western District of North Carolina. He served there until 1987, when Reagan then nominated him to the court of appeals in Washington, DC, as a replacement for Antonin Scalia, who had just become a Supreme Court justice. As a judge, Sentelle was known as a strong Republican, issuing many rulings and decisions in line with conservative positions and the goals of the Republican Party.

Starr attended Sam Houston High School in San Antonio, where he was a popular straight-A student. He went on to attend Harding University, a Churches of Christ–affiliated school in Arkansas, where he was an active supporter of Vietnam protesters and a member of the Young Democrats club. In fact, the young Starr was a Democrat while attending a string of reputable schools, earning degrees from George Washington University, Brown University, and Duke University. At some point, Starr found his conservative roots.

He clerked for Chief Justice Warren Berger and was a counselor to Attorney General William French Smith in the Reagan administration, where, in an interesting twist, he drafted Reagan's opposition to the renewal of the Independent Counsel Act, the administration still stinging from the Iran-Contra investigation by aggressive Independent Counsel Lawrence Walsh.

At age thirty-seven, he was appointed by Reagan to the appellate court, and two years after that he became solicitor general to President George H. W. Bush. Soon after, Starr founded the James Madison Club, a nonprofit organization that did a great deal of fund-raising for the Federalist Society. The Federalist Society is a group of judges, lawyers, law professors, and law students that are committed to judicial restraint and "originalist" or textual readings of the Constitution, eschewing judicial activism. Three of the society's founding members include Edwin Meese, former attorney general for Reagan before he resigned while being investigated by independent counsel; Theodore Olson, counselor to Reagan during the Iran-Contra investigation and solicitor general for George W. Bush, arguing for the president in front of the Supreme Court in the Bush v. Gore election controversy; and Robert Bork, Nixon's solicitor general who fired Cox on that fateful Saturday night.

When Fiske was dismissed, and the three-judge panel appointed Starr as independent counsel in 1994, the political finger-pointing began in earnest. While Starr was roundly criticized for his Republican connections, he was also scolded by the staunch right for not more zealously pursuing the Clintons in his investigation. In fact, Starr kept up with his law practice at Kirkland & Ellis while he was still performing independent counsel duties. Despite the political backbiting, a high school friend discussing Starr's motivations said simply, "He has firm beliefs about what's honorable, what's right, and he's presenting those. He has a goal, his mind is set, and he's going with that."

On June 7, 1995, as a result of his investigation into the Whitewater scandal, Starr indicted Tucker on three counts of conspiracy to commit tax and bankruptcy fraud related to his cable company venture. The indictment stated that Tucker created a shell corporation in order to hide profit from a Florida cable venture that netted him nearly three million dollars.

Starr was not the only one conducting a Whitewater investigation. The Senate Whitewater Committee began an eleven-month investigation in July of 1995. Republican Alfonse D'Amato, who was the chair of Bob Dole's presidential campaign, chaired this committee. At the same time, the House Banking Committee, also chaired by a Republican, was just finishing its investigation into the McDougals' Madison Guaranty implosion by concluding that no illegalities had occurred.

These investigations were chum in the water for a ravenous Republican Senate. Whitewater had all of the earmarks of a classic political scandal: financial fraud, backroom deals, and a suicide. The conspiracy theorists fed hungrily on the promise of a tainted presidency so early in its infancy. Twenty-nine of Clinton's administration officials were subpoenaed, or testified at congressional hearings. None were implicated in any wrongdoing.

Stemming from the independent counsel's investigation, in August of 1995 the McDougals and Tucker were charged with multiple counts of bank fraud. But the presence of the Clintons still cast a shadow over the continuing Whitewater investigation.

Early in 1996, Hillary Clinton became the first First Lady to ever testify before a grand jury, speaking about her role as an attorney and whether billing records from the Rose Law Firm were ever intentionally withheld from Starr's or the Senate investigation.

Later, Clinton's friend and campaign advisor Dick Morris would allege that Tucker, furious at being criminally charged, would issue a not-so-veiled threat to Clinton that should Tucker be prosecuted, he would let the investigators know about Hillary's role in the failed Castle Grande land development project. Morris claims that Clinton called up U.S. district court judge Henry Woods, who was friendly to the Clintons and later told Morris that he "handled that thing today." Three weeks later, Woods threw out the charges against Tucker, saying that Starr had exceeded his authority, although the charges were later reinstated and Woods was recused from the case. In October of 1995, the Senate Whitewater Committee, reacting to the Department of Justice's criminal indictments, issued forty-nine subpoenas related to the Madison Guaranty fiasco.

And it is at this unique three-way intersection where the judicial, legislative, and executive branches arrive at exactly the same time, all carrying different passengers headed in different directions. They all demand the right-of-way, trying hard not to end up in a head-on collision. The legal becomes political, the political becomes personal, and it all becomes public. All of these forces—legal, political, personal, and public—each exert its own influence on the process, both pulling and repelling each other.

In April of 1996, the McDougals and Tucker stood trial on the bank fraud charges. One female juror wore a Star Trek costume to court every day until she was dismissed for giving a television interview. Hale testified that then-governor Bill Clinton intervened to put pressure on Hale about the $300,000 loan he was asked to give to Jim McDougal. In another jurisprudence first, a sitting president, Clinton, testified via videotape that he had no knowledge whatsoever about Hale's loan.

The McDougals, Tucker, and Hale were all convicted on May 26, 1998, and the pundits and partisans saw it as a rousing rejection of the Clintons' credibility and a clear indication of their wider participation in the scandal. They called for even more congressional hearings.

Finally, in June of 1996, the Senate Whitewater Committee issued a finalized report, divided along party lines, about whether the Clintons committed any ethical breaches.

Tucker, convicted of felonies, resigned on July 15. He then immediately withdrew his resignation, saying that he would not resign until his appeal was heard in the case. The public outcry was tremendous, and Mike Huckabee, who was attorney general, threatened to start impeachment proceedings. Tucker finally conceded and formally resigned as governor of Arkansas. He was given a four-year suspended sentence because he was suffering from a liver disease, which would have likely been fatal to him in prison. McDougal, who was cooperating with federal investigators, was given a reduced sentence of three years but ended up dying in prison one month before his release. Susan McDougal was given two years in prison but would not cooperate with a grand jury. She was cited for contempt of court and sent to jail, where she would stay for seven months. The convictions convinced multiple committees that there was more investigation to conduct, more wrongdoing to uncover, and more political gain to be made.

At the sentencing of Jim McDougal, Starr addressed the Little Rock court by saying, "Truth is a bedrock concept in morality and law."

Both political machines were in high gear now. Clinton was facing reelection in mere months, and this potential scandal was looming over the upcoming vote. Clinton's election guru, James Carville, ramped up the rhetoric against Starr, calling him a right-wing hatchet man for the Republican Party.

The Whitewater grand jury's term was extended. The White House attempted to refuse to turn over notes requested by Starr and made an appeal to the Supreme Court. The Court ruled against them, and forced them to turn over all of their documents. Starr's investigators began questioning Arkansas state troopers about President Clinton's personal life and extramarital affairs. As his investigation stretched further and further, Starr looked down the long road at the White House.

There is a subset of crime that is perpetrated by denial and fear of consequence. When any defendant is being investigated, they have a tendency to deny, to shade, or to cover up behavior that may not actually be illegal, but the suspect believes will be used to shame, humiliate, gain political advantage, or prosecute them in court. And that reaction, that overreaction, ends up propelling the investigation much further than it would have gone in the first place. It also creates a crime that actually may not even have been there in the first place. While seven of the Watergate burglars were convicted of participation in the break-in at the Democratic National Committee, twelve in the Nixon administration were convicted of crimes related to the cover-up.

And it is here, in the boulders, logjams, and the transition between the slow and fast water that the patient federal fisherman waits for "perjury" and "obstruction of justice." The reaction becomes the crime, and the reaction becomes the story.

OFFICE OF THE INDEPENDENT COUNSEL

Tom Dawson was born in Texas and raised in Mississippi. He originally got a degree in chemistry but got tired of smelling of acetone and wearing a lab coat, so he took the LSATs. He went to law school at "Ole Miss," the University of Mississippi.

Dawson had been in private practice a short time before he was recruited by the Department of Justice and moved to Washington. He ultimately moved back to Mississippi where he worked in Oxford as an assistant U.S. attorney, prosecuting significant drug, white-collar, and public corruption cases.

Hickman Ewing, a prominent DOJ attorney whom he had known for years, called Dawson one day. Ewing was Starr's deputy at the time, and Ewing asked Dawson to come to Memphis to meet with him and Starr. Because Tucker's original trial on tax fraud had been delayed by Woods's rulings, the original prosecutors who were handling the case had returned to their home offices. Since all of the local Arkansas U.S. attorneys had been recused from working on these cases, Starr and Ewing were looking at two separate qualities in a deputy U.S. attorney to work with their office: they wanted someone who knew right from wrong and someone who could "speak Southern" to try cases in front of a Little Rock jury.

D awson and Ewing met Starr at the Memphis airport. They boarded a private plane, and Starr came in disguised in a baseball cap through a rear entrance of the plane, accompanied by a U.S. marshal. For an hour, they discussed Tucker's case and the political environment of the investigation.

Afterward, Ewing and Dawson spent another two hours discussing the matter at Mrs. Winners, a chicken and biscuit place in Memphis. It was a complicated case, involving bank loans and numerous shell corporations. Ewing used Styrofoam cups on the table to try to describe the various entities Tucker had set up to avoid paying taxes on approximately three million dollars in profit from the sale of one of his companies. As Ewing described the case against Tucker that they wanted Dawson to take over, Dawson calmly asked Ewing, "Wait, you are asking me to prosecute a case where I did not do the investigation and I did not convene the grand jury or issue the indictment. It's in a district and a circuit where I do not practice, and it's against a sitting governor of the state?" Ewing said that that about summed it up. Dawson paused, and then said, "Well, all right."

The U.S. Attorneys Office can make its own calls on the direction they take on any given case and dictate the timing of subpoenas, grand jury testimony, indictments, or even when to end an investigation. In other words, they call all the shots. The Office of the Independent Counsel takes direction from a panel of judges who have some say over the scope and direction of the investigation.

But Whitewater was different. It took on a life of its own because of news stories, a Resolution Trust Corporation investigation, White House staffing misconduct, a civil lawsuit, and a suicide. There were multiple investigations going in different directions: one with the

McDougals, one with Tucker, one with Hale, one with the White House travel office, and one with the Clintons. They intersected, over-lapped, and branched out. Everyone who was approached for records or testimony, whether it was a key player or a file clerk, had a lawyer. Although it was not obvious, it was clear that many of the lawyers were being paid with political funds. And when you have lawyers, you have delays. Delays in getting testimony and records. Subpoenas had to be issued, interviews scheduled and rescheduled, disputes over records resolved by judges, appellate courts, and even the Supreme Court. The investigation was halting, with little traction or momentum. All of the reports were made public, which provoked a deluge of media to track and respond to. Everyone was spread too thin, and the independent counsel found it harder to control and direct the investigation.

The investigation plowed new ground in numerous areas. Because Ewing was Starr's deputy and "spoke Southern," he went to the White House to interview the Clintons on five separate occasions. At each of the meetings, there were constitutional law professors present and probing discussions about which areas of inquiry were valid, which were privileged, and which involved national security.

Starr was not a prosecutor and did not have much experience with undercover investigations, which meant he moved more cautiously. He also utilized a cooperative management style that favored getting everyone's input. While this helped to build a tight-knit team of U.S. attorneys, it also took longer to get things done. This had a direct consequence on the timing and course of the investigations. Every investigation has its own rhythm, its own pace. There are times you have to be patient and times you have to move, as Dawson said, "with deliberate speed."

The slower pace prompted by this cautious and collaborative style as well as the constancy of defense lawyer delays allowed the White-water suspects to regroup and contact witnesses. The news investiga-tions also added potential leads that needed to be followed by Starr's office. This also caused the loss of surprise that prosecutors count on to leverage their case. Some witnesses had to be scrapped because of credibility problems, as they were interviewed by or sold their stories to the media.

The Office of the Independent Counsel also had no infrastructure in this new jurisdiction. Starr's team replaced the entire Little Rock division of the Department of Justice. They needed to get FBI and IRS agents allocated from a new and thinly stretched administration. Some agents needed to be brought out of retirement. They didn't have an office with pencils, paper clips, or computers. They dealt with delays in issuing subpoenas and production of records, the claims of privilege stamped on every document subpoena. They started the office from scratch and everyone was scrambling.

Starr, Ewing, and Dawson held meetings in Colorado and Illinois. They noted that they had convictions on the McDougals and Tucker, and had the tax case against Tucker in the pipeline. However, they were looking for direction on the investigations into the Rose Law Firm and Bill Clinton's involvement in the $300,000 Hale loan, the White House travel office scandal, and Foster's suicide. Tucker had to have a liver transplant, so his tax trial was delayed again. This and delays in the other investigations allowed the White House to regroup and to develop an offensive media strategy.

Even though the actual allegations of presidential misconduct were slight—that he had somehow pressured Hale to give McDougal a loan and the fact that the First Lady had done some legal work for the McDougals—the public's interest was so great that the press kept looking into new stories to feed a hungry public. It became a secondary justice department, following leads and making claims. Congressional committees, also hungry for political fuel, seized on every new detail. Among these, new details about the president's personal life emerged, including a rumor about an incident with Paula Jones.

In the past, the dalliances of presidents and would-be commanders in chief were simply out of bounds. Although rumors of the affairs of President Kennedy and numerous other presidents were acknowledged in hushed whispers, they did not make the front page. We wanted our leaders to be faithful to their wives because we wanted them to be faithful to us, so the media did not substantially report rumor, innuendo, or even substantial facts related to the personal lives of politicians aside from the *Life* magazine profiles, which featured idealized versions of their true selves.

The reported affair between Democratic senator Gary Hart and Donna Rice changed that, ruining Gary Hart's presidential run and opening up a new set of journalistic rules about reporting on a candidate's extramarital relationships and sexual appetites.

During his 1992 presidential run, Clinton had dealt with claims from Gennifer Flowers, a Penthouse model and sometimes actress, that she had a twelve-year affair with then-governor Clinton. Paula Jones, a minister's daughter in the Church of the Nazarene, filed a sexual harassment lawsuit against Clinton on May 6, 1994, just before the statute of limitations for her suit ran out. She alleged that in 1991 she was escorted by Arkansas state troopers to Clinton's hotel room in Little Rock, where the presidential candidate propositioned her and exposed himself to her. She had kept quiet about the alleged incident until 1994 when a story about the harassment appeared in the *American Spectator*, a conservative Republican publication funded by Richard Scaife, a Republican billionaire who was a vocal critic of Starr's handling of the Whitewater affair. Critics on the left also claimed that three Federalist Society lawyers played a part in bringing the lawsuit. In the suit, Jones sought $750,000 in damages. Her spokesperson, a California conservative named Susan Carpenter McMillan, vilified Clinton on *Meet the Press*, *Larry King Live*, and numerous other shows.

So, during the 1996 presidential campaign, the media circus stayed in town, putting Whitewater, the Foster suicide, and Flowers/Jones in three separate rings, complete with jugglers, clowns, and a high-wire act. The White House had also managed to turn the spotlight around and place Starr's Office of the Independent Counsel in a separate ring, titling that act the "Vast Right-Wing Conspiracy."

As Tucker had recovered from his liver transplant surgery, his second trial on tax evasion charges was pending. Because of the intense scrutiny that Starr's investigation was getting, he felt it was important to see how this might affect the Little Rock jury pool and whether they felt the continued prosecution of their politicians was indeed a vast right-wing conspiracy.

Dr. Paul Lisnek, who had done a great deal of training for the Department of Justice, was recommended. Lisnek was an assistant dean at Chicago's Loyola University Law School, a two-time past president of the American Society of Trial Consultants, and a prolific and incisive author on trial strategy, holding a PhD in communications. Lisnek was teaching in a summer program down in Austin at the University of Texas, so Dawson decided to fly down to meet with him.

I had worked with Lisnek for years, and he invited me along because of the experience I had in high-profile cases and in conducting jury research in small rural areas. I had to smile when I got the call, because I was raised a West Coast liberal and had voted Democratic for as long as I had been registered, including casting a ballot for Clinton. But I learned a long time ago from my mother the judge and my father the psychologist that understanding your own biases can be a useful tool for your clients. Over my years in the profession, I had learned to use my upbringing and beliefs when representing mostly conservative and corporate clients.

While the U.S. attorneys wanted to know how jurors in Little Rock felt about the Tucker case, Little Rock was a small town, and they didn't want to risk the defense finding out about the research or, even worse, prospective jurors in court talking about how they had been involved in a mock trial or focus group. After all, the entire population of the capital of Arkansas was less than two hundred thousand.

We decided on conducting a community attitude survey. Because we knew that Tucker had a great deal of political reach and community ties, we were concerned that the defendant would accuse us of trying to taint the small jury pool. So we decided to do a matched venue study. These are tricky because you have to go to surrounding counties to conduct the survey. However, you want to make sure that you are not only capturing the demographics of the venue you are trying to poll but also trying to approximate the attitudes and lifestyle of the people in that community. We had to conduct the polling close enough to Little Rock to capture the exposure that citizens in the political center of the state would have to the Whitewater investigations. And the polling sample had to reach the kinds of jurors who actually showed up for jury service in Little Rock to ensure that the results would be truly representative of a Little Rock jury.

We ended up cobbling together different sections of the surrounding counties to create a compilation of what a Little Rock–like jury pool would look like, and we conducted a telephone survey, disguised as a political poll, on a number of trial issues. First, we wanted to test juror attitudes toward Starr and his investigation, including whether prospective jurors thought that Starr's investigation was more motivated by politics than wrongdoing. Second, we wanted to test jurors' attitudes toward Jim Guy Tucker both as a governor and a convicted felon. Third, we needed to understand juror attitudes toward the Clintons, even though technically they were not a part of the case. We knew their time in Little Rock and their ascension to national power would be a powerful magnet in the case for anyone associated with the president and the First Lady. A juror's positive or negative attitude toward them could be predictive of how they saw ex-governor Tucker's case.

We, of course, were concerned that overwhelming support for the Clintons and a strong resentment toward Starr would make it very tough to try a second case against Tucker. We were also concerned that jurors would believe that he had been convicted and sentenced already so a second case would be piling on. Finally, we were concerned that juror awareness of Tucker's poor health would make them sympathetic to the governor, making it difficult to obtain a conviction.

Starr's team was under increasing political and media scrutiny, so a good result was imperative. That meant we had to identify those jurors who would acquit or hang the jury, no matter the evidence in the case. We also wanted to find out how much of a credibility hit the Office of the Independent Counsel had taken as a result of all the negative publicity and the media offensive undertaken by the White House. The survey brought back interesting results.

In order to get a baseline reading of how each of the potential players in these cases was perceived, we asked questions to gauge how the community thought about the "power" and "goodness" of the Clintons, Starr, Tucker, McDougal, and Newt Gingrich. When we normally use these measurements, we have found it is desirable for a client to have a high goodness and low power rating.

Not surprisingly, the respondents we polled perceived President Clinton and the First Lady as powerful but were mostly neutral about Independent Counsel Starr. On the issue of "goodness," the respondents split on their perception of the Clintons. They perceived Starr as neutral with an inclination toward the "bad" end of the scale. Most importantly, they perceived Newt Gingrich, the McDougals, and Tucker as "bad." Tucker had suffered a serious loss of esteem as a result of his prior conviction.

We also asked participants about whether various organizations abused their power. We were concerned that the Office of the Independent Counsel, the IRS, and the FBI, who were all involved in investigating Tucker, would be seen as abusing their mandated power as puppets of political interests. Interestingly, the IRS, the White House, and big business were seen as the most abusive of their power. However, the community did not feel that the IRS particularly targeted political figures. There was a mixed opinion on whether the Office of the Independent Counsel, FBI, and Congress were abusive of their power.

We also wanted to track whether people in Little Rock would think that the investigation of Tucker was politically motivated. Our survey participants agreed that political figures are targeted for investigations for political reasons but also thought that political figures used their power for unfair advantage. In the most directly applicable finding, most people in the Little Rock area felt that the Office of the Independent Counsel served an important function, but they were also clearly split about whether the Whitewater investigation itself was justified or politically motivated. This was also one of the core attitudes that clearly distinguished pro-prosecution from pro-defense jurors in the case, and these jurors would obviously need to be identified in jury selection.

On specific case-related attitudes, most in the community thought that it was inappropriate to misrepresent or falsify facts to obtain a loan, or to fail to report income from a corporate sale, things Tucker had done. In a related attitude, many felt that businesses' avoidance of taxes ultimately hurt the average taxpayer. Importantly, some of these attitudes came from the community's actual experience and values. Of those in the community, 83 percent had applied for a loan, 86 percent said they promptly filed their tax returns on time, and interestingly, 30–40 percent of the respondents had been audited by the IRS, had been cheated or defrauded, and had investments. This told us that jurors knew what the rules were when it came to investments, taxes, and the IRS.

We then presented a brief scenario of the case to our survey respondents. Based on the scenario, most respondents clearly indicated a belief in Tucker's guilt. But there were some that were strongly convinced of his innocence. This told us we had to be careful about the lone holdout juror with a hidden agenda trying to get on the jury, believing Tucker's prior conviction was improper. However, most felt that Tucker should still be prosecuted, despite a prior guilt conviction. Most felt that he intended to defraud the government rather than made an inadvertent mistake in his tax planning.

When we looked at the significant differences between those that would be inclined to convict rather than acquit Tucker, a few characteristics emerged:

1. Not surprisingly, Republicans and Independents were more pro-prosecution than Democrats.
2. Jurors in the age class of 35 to 44 and 55 to 64 made better prosecution jurors.
3. Prosecution jurors were more likely to be men, married, and to have served in the military. We sometimes call these "rule-oriented" jurors.
4. Prosecution jurors were more financially savvy and actively involved in investments and financial planning. Again, these jurors understood the rules, followed the rules, and knew the consequence of breaking these rules.
5. Defense jurors had a strong bias against the IRS and the Whitewater investigation, or had a favorable opinion of the ex-governor.

Overall, we felt encouraged by the findings. Despite the daily spin about the political motivations of the Starr investigation, jurors in the area did not seem to have been negatively influenced by the media coverage. Although there was strong support for the Clintons, this did not carry over to Tucker. His prior conviction and his subsequent refusal to leave office had colored the public's view of his probable culpability in this case. And, most importantly, jurors seemed to believe that fudging on financial documents or avoiding paying taxes was a clear violation of the law. You follow the rules. If you break the rules, you pay the price.

To back up our findings as we got closer to trial, the *Arkansas Democrat-Gazette* did a statewide poll that demonstrated that only 19 percent of the state believed that Tucker was telling the truth about his claims of innocence. More than 50 percent thought the ex-governor was outright lying.

Our research gave us a profile of pro-government and, most importantly, anti-Starr jurors for jury selection. We had to be selective since we only had a limited number of peremptory strikes in federal court. Dawson and the independent counsel team felt much more comfortable going into trial based on the results of the community survey report.

Arkansas ranks forty-ninth in median household income and forty-fifth in per capita income out of fifty states. Tucker made $11.75 million on the sale of Plantation Cable, one of his Florida companies. Instead of paying taxes on all of his capital gains, he spun the gains into a sham Texas company, which then declared bankruptcy so he could avoid $3.5 million in federal taxes. We found that the average Arkansan did not have a lot of sympathy for a politician convicted of bank fraud who then avoided more than $3 million in taxes. And although citizens in small communities want to believe in their politicians, many know about the backroom deals and graft that grease the wheels of the political machine. Although everyone on Starr's team was sensitive to the media onslaught taking place in Washington and on the national news, many in the smaller communities in Little Rock simply weren't paying close attention to every twist and turn in the sordid Whitewater saga. The press also did not seem to take the independent counsel to task for the Tucker prosecutions. The research had given us our jury profile, and as we got closer to the trial date, I was preparing to come out to Little Rock for the jury selection.

In Tucker's first trial, he didn't take the stand. And in this case, Dawson knew he had a bogus SBA document where Tucker had forged his wife's signature. If Tucker took the stand, he knew he would face a blistering cross-examination on this and many other issues. Tucker had also seen the public opinion polls done by news organizations. He knew he had lost the trust and faith of his constituents by refusing to step down after the first conviction. On the first day of the trial, before jury selection, the government brokered a plea agreement with Tucker. Dawson knew that Tucker would be unlikely to get jail time anyway because of his liver transplant and frail health. McDougal had died in jail, and the judge was not going to do that to Tucker. As part of the deal, Tucker would pay a one-million-dollar fine and agree to cooperate with the Whitewater investigation into the Clintons, although it was unclear what he could add to that inquiry. Dawson called me as I had one hand on the doorknob on my way to the airport and told me the case was done and they were satisfied with the deal. I put my bag away, sat down, and had another cup of coffee.

THE PR BATTLE

Corruption and hypocrisy ought not to be inevitable products of democracy, as they undoubtedly are today.

—Mahatma Gandhi

Although journalists pride themselves on the opaque concept of objectivity, they choose sides whether they mean to or not. They decide the narrative they want to use in the story, then investigate and cover *that* story. In this, they are no different than any law enforcement or prosecutorial agency. And when you have high-ranking officials from two branches of government, the judicial and the executive, on either side of the field, they are inevitably battling in the court of public opinion as much as in an actual courtroom. Public opinion is political. And the political creates pressure, risk, and potential tactical advantage for all parties. Predominantly, prosecutors have the advantage on this field. They control the case information and the timing of its release. They have the element of surprise. But the media can level the field for a defendant in a high-profile case.

Dawson recalls the press wars against the president and White House as being particularly brutal. In his experience, the order of attention in conducting a high-profile investigation was: 1) the law; 2) politics; and 3) the press, with the last two being distant concerns. However, in the post–O. J. press era, media competition, new technology, and the 24/7 news cycle demanded a new formula, especially with a story this scandalous and "newsworthy." In this new era of media power, the formula was reversed and the order of priority became 1) press; 2) politics; and, finally, 3) law.

The Office of the Independent Counsel was also put in the uncomfortable position of making statements to the press about their investigation, despite most prosecutors' instincts to "let the facts speak for themselves." In a matter of national importance, it is unwise to simply state, "No comment." In this forum, the press and the public act as police investigators interrogating suspects, interpreting their silence as stonewalling or culpability.

Dawson's view was, "You never have to explain something you don't say." But when you are forced to make a statement, it raises your profile, it raises expectations, and it makes you defend your remarks. You become the defendant. So the statement better be good.

Starr's office had a clipping service that provided them with a running list of stories to keep tabs on the spin in the press and the resulting public opinion. As the White House PR machine moved into high gear, the office tracked the media narrative and the change in the tide of public opinion.

Michael Isikoff was a member of the press whose investigation for *Newsweek* of the Paula Jones suit prompted continuous responses from both the White House and Starr's office. While rumors of Clinton's affairs and even accusations of his alleged sexual harassment made the press notably nervous about the line between lurid supermarket tabloid stories and journalism, Isikoff kept doggedly following leads, even when *Newsweek* held it and let Matt Drudge scoop Isikoff's story. Indeed, Isikoff's name appears ten times throughout Starr's final 453-page report on Whitewater, and numerous times in the 4,610 pages of grand jury testimony. This illustrates the press's multiple roles as both prosecutor and public scribe, affecting the course of criminal investigations and crisis management strategies at the White House.

AFTERMATH

In 1997, the president's lawyers resisted the efforts by Paula Jones's lawyers to take Clinton's deposition in Jones's civil case. His lawyers argued that a sitting president should not have to be tied up in civil litigation while running the affairs of the country and urged them to force the suit to be continued after the president left office. The case went up to the Supreme Court, and they unanimously ruled against the president, stating that the president was a citizen who had no immunity against civil actions.

Also in 1997, a twenty-two-year-old White House intern from Brentwood, California, started talking to a co-worker, Linda Tripp, about the affair she had been having with President Clinton. Tripp had told that intern, Monica Lewinsky, to save gifts that the president had given her and to not dry-clean the infamous blue dress that apparently had Clinton's semen on it. Tripp contacted a literary agent, Lucianne Goldberg, who told Tripp to secretly tape her conversations with Lewinsky.

Tripp had approached Goldberg about a book on sex in the White

House, which never panned out. Tripp had also become aware of another White House volunteer, Kathleen Willey, who had also allegedly been sexually assaulted by the president.

Lewinsky was contacted by Jones's lawyers about her relationship with the president. She provided them with an affidavit in January of 1998, where she denied having a physical relationship with the president. She then contacted Tripp and urged her to lie about the affair, since Tripp had also been subpoenaed in the case. Instead, Tripp turned over all of her recorded conversations with Lewinsky to Starr.

Clinton's proclivities with women were well known. But in the puritanical moral universe of public office, affairs, or at least public affairs, were considered political suicide. This was before Eliot Spitzer and before Anthony Weiner. This was the president of the United States.

Dawson told his colleagues he would bet a paycheck that Clinton would not show up for the deposition in the Jones case, using the handy excuse, "Sorry, today is not good for me. I have to handle a situation in Libya." It would have been easy. And the Supreme Court could not have enforced the mandatory appearance of the president at a deposition. A state court judge could have sanctioned Clinton for not showing, but that was all. But the White House, also dealing with an unprecedented public relations crisis, decided that the political cost of not showing was too great.

On January 18, 1998, President Clinton gave his deposition in the Jones case, stating on the record that he had not had "sexual relations" with Lewinsky. Also revealing his legal training, Clinton responded to a line of questioning in the deposition with his famous line "It depends upon what the meaning of the word 'is' is." It surprised all of the U.S. attorneys that Clinton showed up for the deposition, and Dawson lost his bet.

When Starr received the taped conversations between Lewinsky and Tripp, he did not want them. Another U.S. attorney working with

Starr, Jackie Bennett, took this taped evidence of Clinton's perjury and met with U.S. Attorney Janet Reno and Deputy U.S. Attorney Eric Holder. They told her that they would not take the investigation and that it was up to Starr's office to pursue the matter. Starr went to the special division judges and told them of his reluctance to pursue the matter as it was so far afield from his mandate in the initial Whitewater investigation. Starr had already tried to resign once, having delayed a position that he was offered as dean of Pepperdine Law School. The special division judges instructed Starr to pursue the Lewinsky matter.

Starr flew down to Little Rock, where he called Ewing and Dawson into a cinder block room in the basement of the Federal Building. They carefully examined the ducts in the room, paranoid about secrecy. Starr turned to Ewing and Dawson, asking, "How do we proceed with this?"

As a result, the Office of the Independent Counsel looked into whether Clinton and his close friend Vernon Jordan encouraged Lewinsky to lie about her affair with the president. Again, in a law enforcement investigation, sometimes the reaction becomes the crime. The attempt to cover up becomes obstruction of justice, and a little white lie or a shading of the truth becomes lying to a federal officer. So the personal, the moral, and the ethical become the legal under the color of the law.

According to campaign advisor Dick Morris, the president called him before the Lewinsky scandal became public and said, "I have messed up with an intern." He wanted to find out how much trouble he would be in with the American public. Morris originally told him that the people were forgiving and that he could weather the storm. Later, Morris would tell the president that he had been wrong, saying, "You can't survive this."

Most prosecutors agree that in a white-collar case, the longer it goes, there is a law of diminishing returns for prosecutors. The public, although mixed in its opinion of Starr's investigation, detested the steamy revelations of the president's affairs and his subsequent denials. These stories sullied the dignity of the president's office. It made their commander in chief common, no different than a cheating co-worker. It made it harder to put their leader, their president, on a pedestal. To them, his "crime" was being caught, and the incriminating evidence were his reactions as much as his actions.

Clinton's luck came in the form of attorney William H. Ginsburg, the original lawyer for Lewinsky. Ginsburg was a medical malpractice lawyer who was a friend of Lewinsky's parents in California. Ginsburg was mesmerized by the publicity in the case and treated it like a civil instead of a criminal case. Lewinsky had clearly lied under oath in the Jones case. Yet Ginsburg dragged the negotiations out over her plea deal for a long time, which allowed the White House to regroup and turn the tide of public opinion.

According to Dawson, Lewinsky was faithful to her president and actually saved him through these delays. Ultimately, she fired Ginsburg and hired an experienced white-collar attorney, Jake Stein, in Washington. Within a week, Lewinsky had a plea deal and the blue dress was turned over to Starr. Later, when the president testified in front of the grand jury about his statements, he would say that he did not consider oral sex to be "sexual relations," and therefore had not perjured himself. Not surprisingly, the U.S. attorneys in Starr's office saw it differently.

Dawson and Mark Barrett, another senior U.S. attorney in the independent counsel's office, reviewed the investigative reports and suggested to Starr how the information should be pieced together for the articles of impeachment, editing carefully to get it into shape to submit to Congress. They struggled with the question about whether it was even within their mandate to draft these articles. They wondered how to bring the charge and wrestled with the difficulty of the statutory language. Is perjury a high crime or a misdemeanor? What constituted a misdemeanor? Is lying about sex obstruction of justice?

In the end, Starr's office sent eleven articles of impeachable offenses, accompanied by the 453-page Office of the Independent Counsel report and a fleet of U-Haul trucks with supporting documents from their offices at 1101 Pennsylvania Avenue to make the five-block trip up to Capitol Hill.

Article II, Section 4 of the United States Constitution states, "The President, Vice President and all civil Officers of the United States, shall be removed from Office on Impeachment for, and Conviction of, Treason, Bribery, or other high Crimes and Misdemeanors."

In fact, there was a great deal of debate at the Constitutional Convention in Philadelphia in 1787 about the validity and scope of the impeachment process. In notes from the convention where the impeachment process was hotly debated, James Madison, the fourth president of the United States and principal architect of the Constitution and Federalist Papers, thought it indispensable that some provision should be made for "defending the community against the incapacity, negligence or perfidy of the Chief Magistrate." The thought was to protect the public from an official that "might pervert his administration into a scheme of peculation and oppression" or betray his trust to foreign interests or for bribes. "Besides the restraints of their personal integrity and honor, the difficulty of acting in concert for purposes of corruption was a security to the public." If a public official in the executive, legislative, or judicial branch were compromised, the impeachment process would help to separate that official from the body politic before infecting and proving "fatal to the Republic."

Benjamin Franklin noted that "obnoxious executives had traditionally been removed from office by assassination" but that a procedure for removal would be preferable.

Rufus King, a lawyer and delegate for Massachusetts to the Constitutional Congress, argued, "Under no circumstances ought he [the official] to be impeachable by the Legislature. This would be destructive of his independence, and of the principles of the Constitution."

However, Edmund Randolph, the first U.S. attorney general, stated, "Guilt, wherever found, ought to be punished. The Executive will have great opportunities of abusing his power. . . . Should no regular punishment be provided, it will be irregularly inflicted by tumults and insurrections."

But Madison and James Wilson (who was one of the first justices appointed by George Washington to the Supreme Court) anticipated the inherently political nature of the impeachment process in that it would allow "intrigues against him in States where his administration might be unpopular, and might tempt him to pay court to particular States whose leading partisans he might fear, or wish to engage as his partisans." Or, ". . . enable a minority of the people to prevent the removal of an officer who had rendered himself justly criminal in the eyes of a majority."

Both Madison and Wilson were skeptical of the process and found it susceptible to political influence. Some at the convention did not feel that the legislative branches would have the strength of will to oppose the president. Some saw it as a threat to the authority of the office. The Congress could not reach substantial agreement, thus compromised, leaving the final wording intentionally vague.

On December 19, 1998, William Jefferson Clinton was impeached by the House of Representatives on charges of perjury and obstruction of justice. The Senate trial of Clinton started on January 7, 1999, with Chief Justice Rehnquist presiding, the same justice who had chosen the special division judges that had directed Starr's investigation. A fan of light opera, Rehnquist added four gold bars to each sleeve of his robe to match the Lord Chancellor, a character in the Gilbert and Sullivan opera *Iolanthe*. On February 12, 1999, the Senate voted on the impeachment charges with forty-five senators voting guilty and fifty-five voting not guilty. Later, Rehnquist would quote *Iolanthe* about his participation to interviewer Charlie Rose, "I did nothing in particular and I did it very well."

As the press is bipartisan in their selectivity of scandal coverage, during the impeachment proceedings, it was revealed that Newt Gingrich and other prominent Republican senators who had voted for impeachment had also engaged in affairs and infidelities. These included Dan Burton of Indiana, Helen Chenoweth of Idaho, and Henry Hyde of Illinois, who was the chief House manager of Clinton's trial in the Senate. Larry Flynt, the publisher of *Hustler* magazine, offered one million dollars for information about these infidelities.

The evolution of the Office of the Independent Counsel statute along with the history of impeachments bring into sharp focus the strange marriage between the judicial and legislative branches of government. The investigation is borne out of political necessity by appointment of the Office of the Independent Counsel, then resembles a criminal investigation, then reverts to a purely political process as Congress becomes the court.

On June 30, 1999, the Independent Counsel Reauthorization Act of 1994 quietly expired.

CONCLUSION

Where does a public official's fraud and corruption come from? Desperation? A "survival of the fittest" instinct? A hunger for power? Entitlement? All of the above?

Four of the last seven governors of Illinois have ended up in prison, three of them directly connected to corruption when they were in office. And despite the parade of politicians that have been indicted for fraud, extortion, racketeering, or bribery, it's not limited to Illinois. Across the country, aldermen, city council members, and even members of Congress are routinely arrested on corruption charges.

What is it about politics that attracts this unethical and illegal behavior? Politicians have spent the better part of their careers making the rules. Maybe the smooth, cash-contained handshake of private influence and political connections and the power of public office make them feel invincible. Maybe they think their popularity and larger-than-life personalities shield them from scrutiny. Hubris is a symptom of denial, and it is a disease that all high-profile, white-collar defendants carry. However, there are more subtle psychological influences such as self-deception and what one group of researchers calls "ethical fading," in which corrupt officials actually rationalize their behavior as helping the exact constituents that they are defrauding.

Dawson, over his decades of service with the U.S. Attorneys Office, pinpoints a single trait in criminal defendants: their inability to see how their conduct will affect them down the road. When arresting drug dealers and politicians, the most frequent comment he receives is, "This is really going to screw up my weekend."

For most politicians, it starts small. A gift here, a favor there. But the more you do it, the easier it becomes and the more you justify it. You tell yourself you deserve it because of how hard you are working and how much you are doing for others. You tell yourself it is not really illegal. You feel the power. And it is easier to bend people to your will. Because you have the power. And you use the power. You use it for yourself.

For white-collar criminals, they are also the risk takers who push up to the edge of the line with bank loans, tax shelters, or inside information. Risk takers are usually rewarded for this risk so they push further, toeing just a bit over the line. They are again rewarded for their risk and, more importantly, they are not caught. They start to feel invincible and with this newly felt risk-and-reward power, they start to make their own lines, arguing to themselves that they have not broken the law at all, just bent it a little. They finally utter the great self-justification for misconduct in politicians, "It benefits me, and I benefit the public."

There is a question that often arises from these cases when a prominent public official is hooked by another scandal. Were they corrupted by success, the lure of money, fame, power, or sexual prowess? This question applies to politicians, the press, defendants, witnesses, and even judges as they struggle to distinguish the difference between business, rumor, facts, allegations, political gain, stories, innuendo, and crime.

Dawson recalls a time during the Lewinsky matter when he and Kenneth Starr had to make an appearance in a Little Rock courtroom. They emerged from the hearing and encountered the press corps, standing six feet deep on the courthouse steps. They immediately started peppering Starr with questions, and after fielding a number of inquiries, he calmly stated that it was important that law not become politics by another name.

But law in the public forum is politics. In the end, the politicians, the press, the judges, the lawyers, and the witnesses are all both fish and fisherman, depending on which way the stream flows.

United States v. Rex Shelby, et al.

| | | | | | | | | | | | | | ENRON BROADBAND | | | | | | | | | | | | | |

I don't understand a single thing you are telling me. And I don't
know anything about your industry.

—John Kroger, assistant U.S. attorney and prosecutor
of Enron Broadband defendants, in
his autobiography, *Convictions*

In 2000, *Fortune* magazine rated Enron the most innovative large company in America. In December of 2001, only one year later, Enron declared bankruptcy, put twenty thousand employees out of work, and left behind sixty-seven billion dollars in debt, destroying the retirement portfolios of millions of people. With the United States still reeling from the recent attacks on the World Trade Center, the cries of confusion, fear, and outrage at Enron's collapse made their way up to the ears of Attorney General John Ashcroft. Our illusion of physical safety had been shattered on a clear September morning, and now our illusion of financial safety was gone as well. On September 18, 2001, Congress passed a joint resolution, later passed as Public Law 107-40, which is still on the books. It states that "the President is authorized to use all necessary and appropriate force against those nations, organizations, or persons he determines planned, authorized, committed, or aided the terrorist attacks that occurred on September 11, 2001, or harbored such organizations or persons, in order to prevent any future acts of international terrorism against the United States by such nations, organizations, or persons."

President George W. Bush had taken action to restore our confidence in our military might, and now similar action needed to be taken to restore the public's confidence in our financial system. In 2002, Bush held a press conference to announce a Corporate Crimes Task Force, holding white-collar criminals accountable for their crimes. At that moment, although the joint resolution was specifically geared toward terrorism, it changed the nature of law enforcement in general from reactive to anticipatory. It opened the door to new avenues of preventative safety, presumptive guilt, and suspension of habeas rights. The message went out to the world, and it was not lost on federal and local law enforcement and prosecutors: there was a new sheriff in town.

In the early 1980s, the natural gas industry noticed that some of the biggest industrial customers were switching to coal and other forms of energy for power production of their plants. As a result, several pipelines instituted a special program to allow customers to switch suppliers and use other pipelines to transport their natural gas. In 1985, the federal government deregulated natural gas pipelines, which established a voluntary framework where interstate pipelines could act solely as the transporters instead of merchants of natural gas. As companies scrambled to accommodate this new economic and business model, natural gas companies lost significant amounts of money, thus prompting mergers and consolidation in the industry. It was a new day in the energy business and companies had to scramble to find new ways to stay profitable and competitive. Ken Lay, a federal energy regulator and undersecretary for the Department of the Interior in the 1970s before becoming the chief executive of Houston Natural Gas, became the CEO of one of these mergers. The company he was in charge of was Enron.

When large companies are in trouble or are looking for ways to become more profitable, they hire management consulting companies to help them analyze their problems and come up with new strategies. Lay hired McKinsey & Company, a consulting firm founded by accounting professor James McKinsey in the 1920s, which was widely considered to be the originator of managerial accounting. This firm has been a leader in its field for decades, counting many major corporations as its clients. Today, McKinsey has about nine thousand consultants in fifty-five countries, working with more than ninety of the one hundred leading global corporations.

McKinsey assigned a relatively new consultant, Jeffrey Skilling, to the Enron account in 1987. Skilling had a strong financial background and came up with an entirely new model that would solve Enron's problems in the natural gas marketplace. Since pipelines themselves were now deregulated, Enron would become an energy broker, buying gas from suppliers and selling it to consumers. They would guarantee supply and price and would make money by charging a transaction fee.

However, energy is dependent on weather, and thus is more volatile and less predictable than most other products and commodities. Regions of the country could need last-minute purchases to deal with a blizzard or a heat wave. And deregulation also meant that local utilities had to cut prices by 10 percent and were now required to purchase large supplies, sometimes at the last minute, from one of five existing unregulated generating companies, who could withhold supplies and escalate prices.

In 1990, Enron hired Skilling away from McKinsey and developed a division called Enron Finance Corporation, which led the market in natural gas contracts. With this new gas brokerage model, it had the inside scoop on energy futures. It knew about and could control the supply and demand in the natural gas market, and it got a piece of both as a middleman in the transaction.

Skilling, who had started his career as a bank analyst at First City Bancorporation of Texas, changed Enron's corporate culture from energy to finance. In 1990 he hired Andrew Fastow, who had experience in leveraged buyouts of companies and had started working on a new-at-the-time financial instrument called "asset-backed securities" at Continental Illinois National Bank and Trust Company in Chicago until its failure in 1984. Continental was the largest bank to fail in U.S. history, until 2008. This new instrument of asset-backed securities was able to take assets on a bank's balance sheet, such as their home or auto loans, and bundle them into a security, which they could then sell off to a larger bank, foreshadowing the credit meltdown nearly twenty-four years later.

Together at Enron, Skilling and Fastow implemented a corporate culture that was driven by profit. Employees were encouraged to be predatory, hungry, and "kill or be killed." In this Darwinian culture, 15 percent of the workforce was replaced every year, and those that survived were lavished with bonuses and corporate perks.

Before Skilling and Fastow had come to Enron, the movie *Wall Street* was a hit in 1987, a modern cautionary tale of excess with the signature line from its antihero Gordon Gekko, "Greed, for lack of a better word, is good." While many critics saw the movie as a cautionary morality tale, many looked at this natural economic selection and predatory simplicity with admiration. Years later, Oliver Stone and Michael Douglas would be approached by people who said the movie prompted them to launch a career on Wall Street.

The 1990s saw the longest bull market in history. Following the savings and loan crisis in 1989, inflation, high interest rates, and Congress's Budget Reconciliation Acts of 1990 and 1993, along with the dot-com bubble, created a surge in investment and prosperity. New technology and start-ups created an economic promise, a hopefulness in the financial markets. Everything seemed possible. The boundaries of traditionally conservative business and economic models were being pushed. Hundreds of millions of dollars were being invested in companies with no visible product and no defined market. Investors became so used to this bull run that they demanded profits, and double-digit ones at that. An 8 percent return was for suckers. A 5 percent return was for losers and weaklings, mattress-stuffing cowards. A national bravado, an arrogance fueled by optimism, innovation, and greed, emerged.

Part of this revolution was ignited by an unassuming British scientist named Tim Berners-Lee, who invented the World Wide Web in 1989 as a global network for access and exchange of information. The concept that digitally compressed information could be instantly shared throughout the world had tremendous cultural, political, and business implications. Although computers had been around for decades, the Golden Age of Information had finally arrived.

Over the next ten years, a number of innovations would accelerate the access and availability of information that we now accept as commonplace. In 1993, Intel made the first Pentium processor, which made computers powerful enough for everyday consumers. In 1995, the Java programming language was invented, which made the creation of web applications easier. In 1998, the now-ubiquitous Google came into existence, and Apple released its first iMac. BlackBerry launched its first mobile device in 1999.

Remember that in 2000, only 51 percent of households in the United States had computers, and only a little more than 40 percent of those households had a person who had accessed the Internet even once that year. Of this small percentage of people who had access, most had dial-up connections, with only 6 percent having broadband access.

With the advent of the World Wide Web, the whole concept of *networks* as a marketing and business model took off, cellular telephones and cable television being two primary examples. The business model is that customers no longer buy a product, they buy *access* to the product. Cellular providers don't make money by selling cell phones; they make money on the plans for the calls, texts, and data that customers use.

With deregulation, Enron became more like a cell phone company. It no longer solely relied on directly sold natural gas; it provided access to and brokered deals for the gas. The deal became the product. Enron didn't just sell energy anymore. It traded it as a security, reflecting the junk bond markets of the 1980s and foreshadowing mortgage-backed securities that became the hallmark of the 2008 crash.

In the natural gas world, Enron was the Titan, and it held its standing with swagger. Enron bought Portland General Electric for two billion dollars, and developed Enron Capital & Trade as the nation's largest buyer and seller of natural gas and electricity. And with Lay, Skilling, and Fastow in the driver's seats, Enron took that showroom-new, American-made, twelve-cylinder, turbo-charged capitalism out on the street to see how fast it could go. It turns out it went quite fast indeed—Enron grew from two hundred employees to two thousand, and from two billion dollars to seven billion dollars in revenue.

In 1999, Enron established EnronOnline, an electronic commodities trading site. This essentially gave the company inside information on every transaction in the natural gas markets. Enron's credit rating became crucial to giving traders confidence that Enron had the financial stability to handle these transactions. In 2000, EnronOnline handled $335 billion in trades.

Skilling understood the future value of online business, and in January of 2000, Enron announced plans to build a high-speed online network for trading capacity, like natural gas futures. He had also seen the promise of online video on demand on high-speed Internet lines and appreciated the potential of a global information network controlled by Enron. Enron's stock traded at an all-time high of $90.56 in August of that year.

The more Enron fed, the bigger it got and the hungrier it became. Its investors were hungry as well. Billions were being invested in dot-com companies with hundreds of employees and no customers. For investors at that time, the appearance of profitability was as important as actual profitability. Enron was forced to comply with pressures from Standard & Poor's and Moody's, all looking to rate Enron's investment risk for investors. Skilling and Fastow, both with financial backgrounds, developed creative accounting measures to construct the appearance of profitability and growth. They created thousands of special purpose entities (SPEs) to shuffle assets like pipelines in order to keep them off the books. They used a legal but limited technique called "mark to market" accounting, which allowed companies with energy or other derivative contracts to adjust those contracts to a fair market value in order to book unrealized gains and losses. Traditionally, most energy companies had specified contracts so they could book *actual* gains or losses. But because of the deregulated market, there were no quoted gas prices so nothing upon which to base that valuation. Enron was free to "estimate" its gains and losses in order to bolster its earnings for investors.

The year 2000 was bad for energy. There was an extended drought in the Pacific Northwest, extremely low gas storage supplies, and exorbitantly high power prices as a result of the deregulated market. Anticipated new power plants were put on hold, energy efficiency programs never materialized, and surplus power supplies were depleted.

By late 2000, the dot-com bubble was about to burst, and investors were weary of false hope and empty optimism. There was growing skepticism in the investment community about Enron's earnings. But Skilling was committed to the stock sales spin. He became defensive at one analysts' conference and claimed that Enron's stock should and would soon be at $126, even though at the time it was at a healthy $80 per share.

In 2000, an energy crisis in California resulted in a heavy spike in energy prices and a nine-billion-dollar loss for the state. The resulting taped telephone conversations of Enron energy traders laughing about "Grandma Millie" and how "she wants her fuckin' money back for all the power you jammed up her ass for fuckin' $250 a megawatt hour" prompted public outrage, which in turn prompted regulators' scrutiny. The regulators found a mixture of causes for the crisis, including market manipulations where companies like Enron and Duke Energy were accused of creating artificial shortages to raise prices. Soon after, regulators started looking at reregulating the energy market. To preemptively protect their market and the current legislative agenda, Lay and other energy executives started meeting with Arnold Schwarzenegger, who was already being groomed to challenge then-governor Gray Davis, a proponent of the new regulation measures.

In April of 2001, Pacific Gas & Electric, the source of electricity to all of Northern California, declared bankruptcy, leaving thirteen billion dollars in debt and 4.5 million customers figuratively in the dark.

In August of that year, Enron's stock started falling, and a company vice president, Sherron Watkins, issued a memo about Enron "imploding under accounting scandals." Fastow notified Enron's law firm, Vinson & Elkins, and the company's accounting firm, Arthur Andersen, about some of the adjustments that had to be made to its earnings report.

On September 11, 2001, two planes hit the Twin Towers in New York, one plane hit the Pentagon, and another crashed into a field in Pennsylvania. The world changed.

On October 16, Enron announced losses for the first time and a billion-dollar restatement of earnings. On October 17, the company froze its 401(k) plan, stopping employees from selling stock in the company. On October 22, Enron issued another restatement of its earnings, going all the way back to 1997. Fastow was fired on October 24. Enron had burned through five billion dollars in cash in just fifty days.

On November 30, Enron traded at twenty-six cents a share. The company declared bankruptcy on December 2, 2001.

ENRON BROADBAND

Rex Shelby is the only son of an air force sergeant who was a veteran of the Berlin Airlift and earned a Silver Star, Bronze Star, and Purple Heart in World War II. He had a knack for electronics and hard work, which he passed on to his three daughters and his son.

While he excelled at sports, Shelby was a nerd at heart, working his way through college and receiving an engineering research assistantship at the Arnold Engineering Development Center (AEDC). Among other things, AEDC is where NASA kept fully operational replicas of various space vehicles so that it could simulate what was occurring during space missions to anticipate and solve potential problems.

He used his work at AEDC as the basis for his master's thesis, involving the creation of a computer program that modeled the behavior of light from a "cylindrically symmetric radiating source." Much of his work applied to the behavior of light in fiber-optic cable, although, at the time, he was more focused on cylindrically shaped plasma streams because of AEDC's space program connections.

Shelby joined the U.S. Air Force, where he was stationed at Bolling Air Force Base in Washington, DC, and spent a large portion of his working time at the Pentagon. Even though the Pentagon wanted to retain him, he decided on a private sector path.

He joined Arthur Andersen, one of the "Big Five" accounting firms, which later would also become embroiled in the Enron accounting scandal, and worked for a short time in the firm's consulting division, focusing almost exclusively on large information technology projects for Fortune 500 companies. He also briefly joined McKinsey & Company and helped to create their worldwide IT consulting practice.

Shelby always thought of himself as an entrepreneur, and despite his stints at the two large consulting firms, he decided to join Modulus Technologies in 1994, a small start-up in a windowless room in an old office building in Houston.

Modulus had a software technology called InterAgent that could be used by programmers to build software applications needed to operate over networks. Like all new technology ventures, the success of Modulus was a long shot. But, over the next five years, working pretty much seven days a week, the Modulus team of eight people grew the company from nothing to a business with a market value of tens of millions of dollars.

In 1998, Enron started a brand-new communications start-up venture called Enron Communications Inc. (ECI) with only a few dozen employees and a new approach to the communications business. It was launched as a spin-off from Portland General Electric, a utility company in Portland, Oregon, that had been recently acquired by Enron. Originally, Enron had planned to shut down ECI, but a successful fiber-optic network deal, called the "Western Build," convinced Enron management to pursue building the broadband business. This deal, where Enron sold a small allocation of fiber-optic lines for the cost of the entire project, told Skilling that broadband had a real future.

So Enron, in effect, served as the venture capital supplier to ECI even though, at the time, Enron considered ECI to be a side venture with no direct connection to its core energy, trading, and financial businesses.

ECI was in Portland and started laying the groundwork for an extensive broadband network, rarely used by the public at that time. This involved laying tremendous amounts of fiber-optic cable and developing software. Because of the scarcity of available cable and the necessity to have the bandwidth to transmit the Holy Grail of Data, the now-commonplace streaming video, ECI's Houston office would leverage the use of bandwidth, essentially ensuring that the pipeline would be big enough to stream the kinds of data that clients would want.

ECI was building the infrastructure for the network and ways to provide access to that network. Now it started looking for content to fill that network. Atom Films had the idea in 1999 to stream independent movies digitally while metering and measuring audience responses and billing. This early conception of Netflix caught the attention of ECI as a content provider. This way, ECI could not only rent out the movie theater and sell the popcorn, it could also make the movies and sell the tickets.

In early 1998, Shelby, David Berberian, and Larry Ciscon developed a presentation titled "Changing the Industry: It's the Applications, Stupid." It was about cloud services and applications, software for services and products embedded into the network for on-demand users. This was 1998, when President Clinton faced impeachment in Congress, *Titanic* became the highest-grossing movie of all time, and the FDA first approved Viagra. Modulus's middleware solution, a full decade ahead of its time, would essentially allow any ISP user to drive onto the on-ramp of ECI's information superhighway through high-end servers and then drive to all of ECI's partnered providers, something we now do to access Facebook, YouTube, Skype, Google, or play games on our phones, tablets, and computers.

And that's where Modulus's InterAgent solution caught the eye of ECI. Modulus was in negotiations to be purchased by Sun Microsystems at the time, when ECI swept in and offered Modulus thirty million dollars for their company. This stunned Sun as an ungodly sum for an eight-employee shop. But the Modulus purchase, with Shelby, became a critical piece for the ECI broadband vision of a national network. The marriage of ECI and Modulus was promising to both companies. Both companies looked at ECI as a start-up, which would eventually be spun off from Enron via an IPO to become its own independent company.

ECI had envisioned two fundamental components of their designed system. The Enron Intelligent Network (EIN) encompassed this massive fiber-optic network that would run across the United States and include applications, services, and streaming media. The Broadband Operating System, or BOS, was the operating system that would run the network, similar to Windows on PCs or iOS on Apple's iPhones.

Skilling, with a keen eye for new business, saw the glint of new revenue streams and new ways to allocate assets in ECI. Although his expertise was in energy trading and pipelines, he also saw a huge imbalance of supply and demand in the developing technology. Enron management had apparently become enamored with the shiny new promise of the communications industry, and at the end of June 1999, they announced that ECI had become a "core Enron business." But, unlike energy, they didn't understand the infrastructure for technology.

There are unseen lines in our lives, a confluence of interconnected events, circumstances, and choices that subtly direct our triumphs and tragedies. On one line, we meet a lifelong love. On another line, we have an exciting career traveling the world. On another line, we get hit by a bus.

Enron's decision to make ECI "core" was the bus. In January of 2000, Enron had its annual stock analysts' conference and around that time, Enron changed ECI's name to Enron Broadband Services (EBS). This meant the new EBS would get more attention and "help" from Enron. EBS soon received an overwhelming influx of Enron employees who transferred to EBS from other Enron businesses. In particular, the management ranks of EBS quickly became dominated by people from Enron's various commodity-trading businesses. In addition, all former ECI employees lost their stock and received, in its place, Enron common stock or stock options. All the promise and entrepreneurial culture of the independent high-tech start-up, which had been the origin of ECI, was lost when the company became "core" to Enron.

With shareholder confidence slipping, there was a push by Enron management to the broadband division to make it profitable as quickly as possible. While Shelby and his team at EBS were trying to develop the hardware and software infrastructure, Enron's businesspeople kept trying to push the team into developing quick-money projects like content delivery, which the system was not fully prepared to accomplish. Unfortunately, this is one of the cyclical contretemps in American business—to stifle new innovation with attention. To take a good idea and make it "better," "bigger," and "faster." To make it more than it is.

It is tremendously ironic and sad that, while Enron was crumbling in 2001, the EBS team was developing platforms, networks, and software that would later be used by Google, Sun, IBM, AT&T, and all of us today.

S helby was a former officer in the U.S. Air Force and had always felt a kind of protective kinship with the government. So, when federal agents knocked on his door on August 15, 2002, and wanted to speak to him about Enron, he was more than willing to oblige, spending three hours with them discussing EBS and the network he had been building.

This is a defense attorney's nightmare. A prospective client calls to hire you and tells you he has spent three hours giving a statement to federal agents with no lawyer present. But Shelby was unique. When Shelby spoke to the agents in this meeting, he forthrightly tried to explain to the agents how the BOS, his operating system, worked in

EBS's network. When they asked Shelby why the system "didn't work," he calmly explained that it *did* work, but that network and software systems were constantly being upgraded and expanded.

When a friend told Shelby the FBI had also interviewed him, and Shelby was indeed a target of a fraud investigation at EBS, Shelby was alarmed and contacted another attorney friend. He made an offer to John Kroger, the lead government lawyer in the case, to bring Shelby in to the U.S. Attorneys Office and explain the software in a white-board session. Kroger refused and said that he did not need any explanation, because he had already made up his mind. This offer was repeated later to the U.S. attorneys and was again refused.

This was a telling reaction by the government lawyers. Normally, in a white-collar investigation, the Department of Justice is used to suspects clamming up and asserting their Fifth Amendment rights at the elbows of their bespoke-suited, nine-hundred-dollar-an-hour lawyers. Prosecutors usually salivate at the promise of defendants giving additional testimony to create contradictions or misstatements that they can later use in trial. More importantly, in the investigative phase, law enforcement and prosecuting attorneys are supposed to follow the evidence wherever it takes them, even if it leads to a dead end. For example, in the Whitewater case, the Office of the Independent Counsel spent years investigating the Clintons' illegal participation in the McDougal, Tucker, and Hale bank frauds before concluding they did not have enough evidence to charge them with a crime. For Kroger to refuse the opportunity to learn about EBS and the BOS system meant that they had a different agenda. They had marching orders and were not interested in exculpatory evidence distracting them from their chosen path.

There is a constant challenge for prosecutors in how they define their role in a case. At what point do you investigate the facts of a case to find out whether there has been illegal activity and at what point do you presume illegal activity *has* occurred and investigate to support that presumption? Prosecutors are also mindful that they have to make a case in court, and as advocates for the government, they have to try to win that case. But they are also charged with an investigator's impartiality, which means they have to objectively follow the evidence, even if it leads toward exonerating the very defendants they are trying to prosecute. It can be a difficult balance for prosecutors to strike.

However, when Washington weighs in and wields its political influence, that balance is tipped strongly in the direction of win-at-all-costs. Measured impartiality gets the tap to leave the interrogation room, and brass-knuckled advocacy enters to produce results. It's bad cop all the way, and it doesn't care if it leaves a mark.

The tap in this case were meetings between Ken Lay and Dick Cheney's Energy Task Force on February 22 and April 17, 2001. Lay went to Washington to lobby the task force against investigating Enron and to defeat new regulation measures. A memo outlining Lay's recommendations to the Energy Task Force ultimately surfaced and reflected several of the task force's ultimate recommendations.

When Enron came tumbling to the ground, less than three months after the Twin Towers fell, the shock waves were felt in the economic and political communities. At that tremulous point in 2001, with America vulnerable and questioning its military might, it could not afford to question its economic authority as well. Never had a top ten company gone from the pinnacle of value to the chasm of bankruptcy in such a short period of time, and the fear of a Great Depression domino effect gripped the business and political Pantheon.

When such fear runs rampant, a quieter, more meaningful inquiry about the causes of failure are drowned out by the howls of blame and vengeful cries of punishment. In the ensuing tumult of the Enron bankruptcy, there were demands for the disclosure about Lay's ties to the White House and the Energy Task Force. The Bush administration, already dealing with an unprecedented international situation and the looming prospects of war, formed the Energy Task Force to show that it would not show favoritism to Lay. And politically, once a task force is formed, arrests and prosecutions follow. The investigation will prove the crime.

The Department of Justice formed its task force with attorneys in Houston, New York, and San Francisco. The entire Houston DOJ office had to recuse itself because of ties to Enron and to avoid the appearance of impropriety. It is no surprise that in any investigation, the bigger the target, the bigger the trophy, so Lay, Skilling, and Fastow were already in the sights of the government. And in the government's mind, it could not imagine how a crime had *not* been committed. After all, it was a seemingly incomprehensible failure. How, in our highly scrutinized financial system, could the seventh-largest company in the United States go from boom to bust in a matter of months without metastasized fraud?

In the initial investigation, the Department of Justice knew that the Broadband unit was liked by Skilling and made a core product toward the end of the empire. So the DOJ's initial thinking was to get some of the executives from this unit to cooperate with the government and testify against the top executives at Enron. EBS was initially thought of as a DOJ stepping-stone instead of a primary target. Additionally, in this politically charged environment, there was a kind of competition among the DOJ prosecutors to see who could get the brass ring, i.e., Skilling or Lay.

However, the prosecutors were surprised when the EBS executives they confronted did not take the proffered plea deals, insisted on their innocence, and hired lawyers to defend them against the charges. Instead of accepting that these witnesses were honestly telling the truth, the prosecutors felt this was further evidence of a cover-up and decided to pursue the EBS defendants even more strongly.

Kroger was primarily a Mafia and drug gang prosecutor with the Department of Justice. Organized crime prosecutors take a fundamentally different approach than white-collar prosecutors in criminal cases. As the old saying goes, "When you are a hammer, everything starts to look like a nail." So Kroger, the lead prosecutor in the Enron Broadband case, saw alleged securities fraud as organized crime. And in a mob case, all of the players in the criminal organization are accused of conspiring to commit illegal acts. So Kroger was already thinking that the alleged conspiracy in Enron was a wide-ranging one and that most, if not all, of the executives were engaged in furthering their criminal scheme.

In his autobiography, Kroger has said that business attracts greedy people that are prone to fraud. It is a lazy and faulty conclusion, but very convenient for prosecutorial purposes as it has great populist jury appeal. So, in Kroger's mind, he was already equating business profit with some type of illegal activity. The market value of Enron before its plummet was vast compared to most crime organizations, making the criminal conspiracy in his mind more likely. Experienced white-collar prosecutors are keenly aware that only certain executives may actually cross the line from legal to illegal activity in a business context, and it is rarely a pervasive company-wide conspiracy.

As opposed to gang prosecutors, federal white-collar prosecutors also put little credibility in what people say. In a gang case, a cooperating witness will say, "Joe told me to kill him," and the prosecutor will rely on a witness's recollection of conversations, even though their memory may "change" depending on the deal they strike with the government for immunity or a reduced prison sentence.

White-collar cases are paper cases—they rely on documents. Experienced prosecutors in these cases look at the documentation because that is a clearer indicator of what happened at the time of the events in question: emails, faxes, and financial transactions such as the selling of stock options. In a paper case, the paper is either there or not there. And you had better know what the paper says.

But with a Mafia mind-set, the Department of Justice in the Broadband case relied on people that had no actual involvement with the

Broadband unit and their opinions and guesswork about the viability of the BOS system. And because the Department of Justice had already concluded that this alleged fraud could not have happened without a wide-ranging scheme, it also used a common trial tactic called "the unindicted coconspirator." These are people that prosecutors threaten with indictments but agree not to charge in exchange for favorable testimony. They convince these cooperating witnesses that, even though they may not have intended to defraud investors, the statutes are clear, and the prosecutors have enough to technically find the witnesses guilty of a crime. The witness agrees to cooperate out of fear of prison or because they do not have the money or emotional resolve to defend themselves through years of harrowing litigation.

In the eventual DOJ case against Skilling and Lay, they listed over one hundred unindicted coconspirators. In the Enron Broadband case, they listed twenty-four, most of whom Shelby had never met and half of whose names he did not even recognize. The government named over two hundred coconspirators in all of their cases against Enron defendants, showing the DOJ's tactical leverage and belief in the massive company-wide scheme. F. Scott Yeager, who was a business executive with Enron Broadband, said, "I was told [by the Department of Justice] I might get five years if I would make up lies about people, or I could fight this and go to prison for life if I lose."

As the government was still trying to build its case against Skilling and Lay, it decided to pursue a few smaller fish on its way to the big Enron trophy executives.

Jamie Olis was a midlevel tax expert at Dynegy, an energy firm that followed Enron's example in the new deregulated energy economy. Olis, his boss, and his colleague used a special purpose entity to temporarily write off a loss on their books, a similar accounting trick that Skilling and Fastow used at Enron. Although the use of SPEs was deemed legal in general, the government declared Dynegy's particular use to be illegal. Olis's boss and colleague pled to one count and got no more than five years. Olis pled innocent and was convicted in trial and subsequently sentenced to more than twenty-four years in federal prison for this miniscule infraction compared to Enron's use of SPEs.

Federal judges use a complex sentencing formula under the *Federal Sentencing Guidelines Manual* that includes the amount of the loss attributed to the fraud and the number of victims. If on the day of the SPE adjustment the stock of the company dropped five cents, a judge could attribute that loss to the fraud. If a company has ten billion shares, that five-cent drop could result in a life sentence for a defendant. Hence, the twenty-four-year term for Olis.

This verdict sent fear through the Enron community as the FBI and the government pursued its investigation, prompting cooperation from a number of ancillary witnesses. The Department of Justice settled on three main witnesses in its case against seven Enron defendants: Shawna Meyer, John Bloomer, and Bill Collins.

Collins was a director of business development at ECI, a salesman who was fired by Yeager, one of the defendants. He had no hands-on technology background and seemed to have some psychological issues, prompting DOJ prosecutor Lisa Monaco to say, "That guy carries more baggage than a freight train."

Meyer was a customer engineer who was a psychology major in college and had no background in engineering. During the trial, Yeager's attorney, Tony Canales, said to Meyer during cross-examination, "Ms. Meyer, if you had left me with the impression that you actually had an engineering degree, I would be wrong, wouldn't I?" Meyer left EBS to join a company that Collins had joined after he was fired. That company was desperate for business and tried to get Kevin Hannon, another Broadband defendant, to agree to give it some work. In an email, Hannon wrote, "I would not work with those losers if they were the last people on earth."

Bloomer started as an internal consultant at EBS and then, in early

2000, Ken Rice, the co-CEO of Enron Broadband and the lead defendant in the case, appointed him as vice president of product management. Bloomer had the most legitimate technology role of the prosecution witnesses. However, he had arrived relatively late at EBS and played no role in defining the network, or the offered services and products. Additionally, he played no role in the initial network and services implementation. Bloomer was fired by Rice and Hannon, both Broadband defendants. Bloomer, Collins, and Meyer were all friends at EBS.

Armed with their witnesses, the government was finally ready to move against Enron. On April 29, 2003, in the U.S. district court in Houston, the Department of Justice indicted seven defendants from the Broadband unit, including Shelby. In this indictment, the department accused the defendants of conspiring in a scheme to defraud investors by making false statements to investors and analysts about EBS and failing to disclose material information about "EBS's poor business performance."

They claimed the defendants issued misleading press releases telling investors and analysts that the Enron Intelligent Network was operational and ready to deliver streaming media and large files as well as measure usage and billing. They also alleged that at the January 20, 2000, analysts' conference, Shelby and the other defendants said that the BOS, or operating system for the network, was built, operational, currently able to control the network, and successfully capable of providing all services to their customers. The government said these false claims caused the stock price to rise, misleading investors. They also claimed that Enron misled Blockbuster about a deal to stream video through their network. Finally, they claimed that the defendants traded their Enron stock and made millions of dollars based on these false and misleading promises.

All of the defendants hired their own lawyers. Shelby hired Edwin Tomko, an esteemed Dallas lawyer who was a former U.S. attorney with the Department of Justice and the Securities and Exchange Commission, and was an ex–assistant district attorney in Pittsburgh. In the Department of Justice, Tomko prosecuted Burt Lance, President Jimmy Carter's director of the Office of Management and Budget for corruption while he was chairman of the board at the Calhoun First National Bank of Georgia. Lance is credited with originating the phrase "If it ain't broke, don't fix it."

Tomko brought a sage perspective to Shelby's case. He knew that the Department of Justice focused on different kinds of white-collar fraud over the years, depending on the political environment. In the 1970s, the Securities and Exchange Commission focused on foreign corrupt practices. In the 1980s, following the savings and loan crisis, the government's focus was on insider trading and junk bond fraud. The 1990s brought a focus on government contractors, the 2000s on Medicare and Medi-Cal fraud until the Enron debacle and then back to corporate practices and accounting fraud. Tomko's view was that government prosecutions were cyclical, depending on the political environment and which definitions of the vaguely written statutes were being tested by bankers, brokers, and businessmen.

Jason Ross was working with Tomko on Shelby's case and had devoted his law career to white-collar criminal defense since he graduated from law school at the University of Texas. The summer after his first year of law school, he worked in a boutique defense firm in Baton Rouge that was defending the son of Governor Edwin Edwards in a federal racketeering investigation. So Ross was also extremely experienced with arcane white-collar laws.

Capitalism and the white-collar justice systems have always had an ambiguous and uneasy relationship. Our system glorifies both pioneers and profiteers. They become celebrities, whispering in the ears of presidents and appearing on their own reality shows. We reward both of these traits, and we trust them with investors' money. On the one hand, we want them to push the boundaries and innovate. But we also develop arcane statutes about corporate information, disclosure, and accounting practices to keep them in check. We expect them to be ruthless, and we admire cutthroat practices when they result in dividends and share price rises. But that same promise of reward also tempts these risk takers ever closer to the legal and ethical borderlines, which at times are hard to define.

CHANGE OF VENUE

Houston was originally designed in 1836 to be a commerce and government center. It developed as a port and early railroad hub for east Texas. The Galveston hurricane of 1900 was the deadliest hurricane in U.S. history, causing by official reports eight thousand deaths and unofficially up to twelve thousand. It flooded the entire island of Galveston and scared all of the investment money out of the area and up to Houston.

Oil was discovered in Beaumont in 1901, setting the stage for a huge Texas oil boom that continued through most of the twentieth century. By 1913, there were twelve oil companies in Houston as it became a more reliable port and hub weather-wise for oil transportation. In the 1940s, many of the oil companies in Houston expanded from basic oil refineries and developed petrochemicals, spurred by wartime investment and need as the Houston population continued to grow.

There was a huge population explosion in the late 1970s as a result of the Arab oil embargo, as motorists across the country lined up for hours to fill up their cars, and America became extremely dependent on domestic oil supplies. As Japanese car sales surged during this time and Detroit automakers started laying off workers, many headed down to Houston to find jobs in the oil or aerospace industries. It was estimated at its height that up to one thousand residents a week crowded into Houston in search of jobs.

Business continued to boom in the early 1980s, but suffered in the middle years as another massive hurricane struck both Galveston and Houston in 1983, causing two billion dollars in damage to the two cities and affecting many production facilities. While recovering from that damage, oil prices sharply dropped in 1986, which triggered a local recession in Houston that, exacerbated by other factors, lasted for a number of years.

Enron's spectacular fall was recorded and amplified by the media, echoing in television, radio, and newspaper stories. The din was loudest in Houston where the *Houston Chronicle* shouted daily stories about Skilling, Lay, the Fastows, Cheney, and numerous other Enron players. Scathing editorials appeared, investigations were demanded, and the reverberant fallout of the bankruptcy began. In Houston alone, 4,500 workers were immediately laid off from Enron's headquarters with $4,500 in severance pay, no matter how many years they had worked there, their pensions and retirement accounts frozen. School districts, municipalities, and mutual funds saw an immediate plummet in their portfolios. Charities, churches, florists, and caterers all saw precipitous drops in donations and business. Enron Field, home of the Houston Astros, would have to be renamed.

I received a call from Tomko, Shelby's lawyer. He originally wanted to know if I could give him the name of a market research firm in Texas to conduct a change of venue survey for the Enron Broadband trial. Change of venue is when a party, usually a defendant in a criminal case, believes they cannot get a fair trial in the community where the case has been filed. They want to poll the community to demonstrate to the court that there is prevalent bias against the defendant or defendants.

Most of the time, these motions occur when there is both pervasive and prejudicial publicity such that a jury pool has been tainted to the point where seating an impartial jury is so difficult, it would be better to move the case to another jurisdiction. I explained to Tomko both the benefits and the risks of doing such a study. First, the press's vilification of Enron executives had been apparent, making such a motion important to preserve an appellate issue in the case. I believed, based on my experience, that a majority of jury-qualified citizens would already have judged the EBS executives to be guilty, simply because they were branded with "Enron," despite the fact that they did not have the name recognition of Lay or Skilling.

I also explained to Tomko that I would take a slightly different approach to the change of venue study. Traditionally, you conduct a telephone survey in which you ask people in the community about the news they have seen about the case and how they feel about the defendants, based on the media coverage. However, there have been cases where the Supreme Court has dismissed these arguments, citing that jurors "need not be wholly ignorant" of the matter they would be judging. In addition to measuring the extent and effect of the media jurors had been exposed to, I also wanted to look at the direct economic and social impact on their lives. Because of the wide-ranging repercussions of the Enron bankruptcy, I thought it would be a better argument to establish that jurors had friends and family that had been laid off and closed businesses as a direct result of the bankruptcy. Thus, the community would have a personal and retributive motive to see a guilty verdict in the case. This would make it more important to move the case to another venue.

However, I also warned Tomko that, if an individual judge wanted to keep a case in their courtroom, he or she could easily find excuses to deny a change of venue motion. First, in a jurisdiction the size of Houston, they could argue that the jury pool was large enough to find twelve impartial citizens. Judges do not seem to appreciate that even though the jurors themselves can try to be impartial, their friends and family can exert pressure to convict a defendant in subtle ways not apparent to a juror. These subtle pressures can easily affect their impartiality. After all, they have to go back and live with their family and work with their fellow employees, all of whom may have strong negative opinions toward the defendants. I also told Tomko that I could not tell him what the results of the survey would be. If, for some reason, the community was *not* predisposed toward the guilt of the defendants, we could not argue that they couldn't get a fair trial in Houston.

Tomko got approval from the other defendants to retain me, and I started to put together a plan for the study. First, I asked Tomko to retain Dr. Jon Krosnick, who was a professor at Ohio State University but was in the process of moving to Stanford University. Krosnick had written three books, eighty-five articles, and 120 research presentations at conferences on survey research methods and sociology. He had won several awards for his work and was a coprincipal investigator of American National Election Studies, a preeminent academic research project studying voter decision making and political campaign effects. Krosnick had been deeply involved in analyzing the 2000 presidential election outcomes in Florida. I knew that the DOJ attorneys would be strongly challenging any study we did, so I wanted to have the strongest credentials and methodology behind the study.

I discussed with Krosnick my experience that exposure to pretrial publicity alone would not be enough for the courts to move the trial out of Houston. However, when the impact of an accused crime is felt community-wide, it is difficult to see how that community can truly be impartial in judging a defendant. I saw this in the case of Scott Peterson, a fertilizer salesman who was convicted and sentenced to death for killing his wife and unborn child. His case was moved out of Modesto because of the pretrial publicity as well as the community's participation in vigils and searches, and its strong ties to the case.

Krosnick retained a New York polling firm to conduct the surveys. We periodically monitored the calls to make sure they met the calling criteria and there was no bias in the way the surveys were being conducted.

In his report to federal court supporting a change of venue, Krosnick wrote, "Of the 503 people interviewed, 81.4 percent said they thought these executives were guilty, and 7.8 percent said they thought these executives were not guilty. 8.7 percent of respondents answered this question by saying, 'Don't know.'" In other words, only 16 percent of Houston met the criteria for an impartial jury.

In his report, Krosnick explained that such a large agreement on any individual issue in survey research is rare, cutting across all demographics. This, in his mind, created an overwhelming presumption of guilt against the defendants in the case. With more than 80 percent of likely jurors in the Houston area already believing that the defendants were guilty, the burden had already shifted to the defendants to prove their innocence. This creates an impossible and unconstitutional standard for a defendant. While many people believe that a criminal defendant is probably guilty of something or they would have not been investigated and charged by the government, the presumption of innocence is supposed to level the playing field, making the government prove their case beyond a reasonable doubt. This is easier to do when jurors have no idea what the case is about and have no interest in the outcome. Given the Houston jurors' presumption of guilt, we would have a tough challenge in jury selection if the judge denied the venue change.

Further, half of those polled had read fifty or more stories about the case. This indicated that prospective jurors did not have a mere glancing familiarity with the case, but were deeply and personally invested. This also meant that jurors would likely bring a wealth of information to the case about Enron—information that would likely never make it to the witness stand. We also wanted to show the court that these were not innocuous news stories, but editorials and coverage with a particular slant. Of those that had seen publicity about the case, more than 80 percent had said that most, if not all, of the stories had suggested that the defendants were guilty. To see if the community would be able to readily dismiss these stories as having a media bias,

82 percent thought the stories were mostly accurate. Simply put, the more Houston jurors had read and seen, the more they presumed the defendants were guilty.

Probably most astonishing of all was the following statement in Krosnick's report: "In order to explore whether direct experience of harm caused by Enron influenced respondents' presumptions about guilt, I examined the relation of these presumptions with three measures of perceived harm. 47.2 percent of respondents said they knew someone personally who was harmed by what happened with Enron, 14 percent directly themselves." The courts have long held that if jurors have an implied bias, such as knowing the plaintiff or defendant in a civil case, they should not sit as jurors. This aspect of the study showed that, regardless of what people had seen and read, almost half of likely jurors had personally experienced the harm done by the fall of Enron.

We did not want the judge to dismiss this single study by stating that the national publicity would show similar results in other areas. As a result, we conducted the same survey in three additional jurisdictions: Austin, Corpus Christi, and Albuquerque. While those cities also showed a high presumption of guilt, indicating that the news articles were reaching a nationwide audience, the number of people who had been directly affected by the economic meltdown of the company was significantly lower. Again, this showed how much Houston was invested in a single outcome, the guilt of the defendants.

However, as we expected, the judge denied this motion, deciding to keep the trial in town. We now knew that we had to take particular care in jury selection. The community wanted a guilty verdict to bandage the terrible gash that Enron's downfall had caused to the body of Houston's economic and emotional health. We needed to find jurors who could rise above revenge and understand that Enron's broadband network was real, and the architects of this innovative system had in no way misrepresented its capabilities.

As the government continued to build its case, the fear and anger in the legal, business, and financial communities made it harder for the defendants to get witnesses to testify for them at trial. Kroger and his DOJ team, with the view that the conspiracy was widespread, had also threatened numerous witnesses, telling Ciscon, who had moved from Modulus to Enron with Shelby but was not charged in the EBS case, that it was not "in his best interest" to testify.

The defense also had a hard time getting experts to testify in their case because of the stigma of Enron. No one wanted to be associated with a name now commonly associated with business avarice and greed. The defense was being accused of being apologists for white-collar crime. In his book, Assistant U.S. Attorney Kroger speaks about how hard white-collar cases are to prosecute and how white-collar criminals are more appealing to juries. But in this environment, our research told us that any defendant labeled with the cursed Enron name would have a tough time appealing to a jury.

In another setback for the defense, the government allowed all of EBS's hardware and software to be dismantled and sold off during the bankruptcy. The government was alleging that the technology did not exist to support the allegedly false statements by Shelby and his codefendants. And now they had gotten rid of the primary evidence that the defense could use to show that the technology did in fact exist.

THE REHEARSAL

In most cases of consequence, experienced lawyers conduct mock trials. In civil cases, you try to understand what drives a jury to find liability or contract damages and award money. In a criminal case mock trial, you try to understand what drives a jury to convict or acquit the defendants. We recruit multiple panels of jurors, match them demographically to the kinds of jurors we expect to see in the real jury, and do a condensed dry run of the case. We especially concentrate on the opposing side's case to learn which case issues make the jurors want to vote against our client. And in a mock trial, if we lose, we learn. If we do our work right, we identify the specific arguments and evidence that push jurors in one direction or another. We learn our strengths, weaknesses, and, most importantly in a white-collar securities case, where jurors get confused. Confusion becomes most problematic for a defendant in a white-collar case because jurors become overly reliant on the government's simplified "where there's smoke there's fire" conspiracy theories.

The Broadband defendants hired an experienced trial consulting company called Tsongas Litigation Consulting to conduct the mock trial. The consulting company had been founded by Joyce Tsongas, one of the first trial consultants in the field, and a cousin of Paul Tsongas, a democratic senator from Massachusetts who ran for president in 1992.

Before the mock jurors had heard the presented cases, they confirmed our survey research findings: they already thought the defendants were probably guilty. And after the case presentations, the deliberations, and the verdicts, jurors were leaning toward finding most of the defendants guilty on most of the charges. This validated our concern about prejudicial pretrial publicity. If jurors think you are probably guilty, they will only look at the evidence that confirms their original impressions conditioned by the publicity.

One of the jury panels leaned more strongly pro-defense. So we wanted to know the characteristics of those people who favored the defense case. Most importantly, we wanted to discover the issues that convinced jurors to vote for conviction in order to address their concerns.

The Tsongas report discussed the fact that most prosecution jurors tended to take a more generalized view of the case, while defense jurors focused on the details and evidence that created sufficient reasonable doubt to keep them from finding fraud or conspiracy to commit fraud. This suggested that less educated and "big picture" jurors were conviction prone, and more educated, analytical jurors were defense oriented.

Many jurors carry biases toward corporate defendants, whether it is a criminal or civil case. Jurors will impose a high standard of knowledge and vigilance based on the standing of the company. And Enron had quite a standing. As Tsongas pointed out in their report, "Supervisors know, or ought to know, what is going on beneath them in the chain of command. Notice proves they had knowledge. Knowledge of error creates a burden to correct the error. Knowledge of error without corrective action is conspiracy to commit fraud." And this power equation is often counterintuitive to corporate defendants who want to assert their knowledge and expertise in trial. But the more they emphasize this, the more jurors impose a policeman's duty to catch and correct all errors or misrepresentations in the company. If you don't, jurors don't think you made a mistake. They think you are part of the scheme.

Pro-government jurors in the mock-trial research also believed that the EIN and the BOS never worked in the capacity claimed by the defendants. Consequently, any documentation that some part of the technology was not ready or fully functioning was viewed as proof of conspiratorial, fraudulent misrepresentation, instead of the natural process of working out software or hardware bugs.

One of the problems in all conspiracy cases is when jurors speculate about what certain evidence must *mean*. One of the mock jurors said this about the defendants' PowerPoint presentation that they were putting together for the analysts' conference in 2000: "There were sixty-six versions of the PowerPoint presentation; that's a lot. Something must have been going on. Someone must have been trying to cover up something. . . . Someone kept going back and making different versions until they had the perfect version that made it look like everything was up and running."

Jurors, with this mind-set, infer a malicious mind-set. Anyone who is putting together a PowerPoint for a big presentation understands that you may go through numerous versions of that presentation before it is finalized. But sixty-six versions when you are accused of a crime suddenly become suspicious. Jurors also do not have context to understand how all corporations prepare for the analysts' conference. A company is constantly balancing the realities of their current development of a product with the optimistic and aspirational goals they believe they will achieve. They also place trust in an analyst's ability to analyze their position and be able to make recommendations to their investors about the realities of what they are proposing. Without this context, jurors can easily believe that analysts are nothing more than wide-eyed innocents, believing without question whatever a company is feeding them.

Additionally, in all insider trading and cases involving stock sales, timing is everything. As one mock juror said, "They pumped up the stock price, then they dumped it. A year later it plummeted. This just smacks me in the face as a scheme." Another mock juror stated, "The compelling facts are . . . just the math and the clear evidence of *when* things happened, *when* the stocks moved, the wink and a smile approach to the words they used. It all adds up to conspiracy. But these are highly intelligent businessmen who knew what was going on and there was too much coincidence in the way things shook and moved for them not to have some knowledge of what was going on."

Jurors often apply a series of "shoulds" in a corporate fraud or securities case. Jurors apply their own rules for how corporate defendants should act: "The defendants should have done this if they were being entirely aboveboard." In looking at the evidence, they can then apply the most stringent standard to a defendant's conduct. As one mock juror in our case said, "If there is any one word that is incorrect [in the press release], we have to find them guilty." These jurors also use hindsight bias to decide a case, believing a defendant somehow should have known they would end up defending themselves against criminal charges years later when they were writing press releases or developing technology for a company.

Finally, in the mock trial, the EBS defendants could see the powerful tides of public opinion. There was an apparent belief among these jurors that a guilty verdict was needed to right a social wrong, despite the evidence in this case. These jurors believed that no one should make so much money, especially in light of thousands of employees who had lost their jobs and pensions. This pervasive belief in what is right and wrong, what is fair and unfair, is a powerful force in how jurors interpret the evidence in a case.

There is some speculation that Rice got so scared by the mock trial that he ultimately decided to take a plea deal from the government in exchange for testifying against his former codefendants. This added another twist to an already difficult case. As a defendant in a multiple-defendant case, you are constantly looking over both shoulders. You may not have the exact same recollection of events as your fellow defendants. You may have a different interpretation of facts or personality differences. And you do not know whether, at any minute, one of your brothers in arms may turn on you for self-preservation. Initially, there were seven Broadband defendants, Ken Rice, Joseph Hirko, Rex Shelby, F. Scott Yeager, Kevin Hannon, Kevin Howard, and Michael Krautz. Now there were six.

There were bright spots in the mock trial for Shelby. He received the most "not guilty" votes on the conspiracy to commit securities fraud. While some cut him no slack, thinking he was too smart to not have conspired in the fraud, others saw his testimony as an indicator of his overall character. As one juror stated, "He's not a big corporate man, he's a small-business guy. His conditions of the buyout said he had to work for two years. He's just a worker bee. Shelby was the big start-up guy. When he was bought out, he was not as interested in monetary gain as much as he was creating a great product." Many saw him as a follower and not as an active driver of the scheme. Jurors will use their perceptions of a witness's character to explain their actions.

So the lawyers learned a series of key educational points from the mock trial in preparing for the actual trial:

1. Explain the EIN and BOS technology so jurors understand it as a developmental product in progress, not an assembly-line finished-and-done-with product.
2. Help jurors to understand the thought process behind the press releases and the presentations at the analysts' conference so they know the difference between the current state of the broadband network and what EBS anticipated it would become.
3. Explain the timing and limitations of the defendants' stock sales.
4. Try to eliminate as many jurors as possible who had already predetermined guilt.
5. Try to find a smart and detail-oriented jury who would not be swayed by emotional arguments and the fictitious constructed reality of the prosecutor.

JURY SELECTION

Since our survey and mock-trial research showed strong juror bias against any executive affiliated with Enron, we had hoped for an extensive jury questionnaire and voir dire to weed out jurors who had a hidden agenda and those that had already made up their mind about the case. As a result, we submitted a proposed questionnaire and the DOJ attorneys proposed their questionnaire. The judge decided to use her own eleven-page questionnaire and it was sent out to four hundred prospective jurors in Harris and thirteen surrounding counties. It was pretty basic and while it did ask whether the jurors had seen or read anything about the case, it also asked numerous times whether the juror could be fair and impartial and decide the case only on the evidence and the law he or she was given. And of course, most said yes, they could be fair. This question made it extremely difficult to eliminate jurors for cause—jurors who had exhibited a bias and would be excused by the judge—without our having to use precious peremptory challenges.

We read and rated four hundred questionnaires of prospective jurors. Some jurors were extremely candid about their opinions of Enron and their ability to be fair. Some seemed cagey about their views and we tried to gauge their true feelings about the company and their ability to understand the complex case. One juror said, "I don't give a shit," eight times in his questionnaire, and when asked whether there was any reason that he could not be a fair and impartial juror in the case, he stated twice, "Yes. I don't like black people and Mexicans."

This was bizarre as there were no African Americans or Mexicans involved in the case at all. What the juror did not know was that Judge Vanessa Gilmore, our judge, was African American. Judge Gilmore was appointed by President Clinton in 1994 and was the youngest sitting federal judge in the United States at the time of her appointment. She got nominated to her position after being noticed for her work in a lot of charity groups like the YWCA, End Hunger Network, and Houston Ballet. She also taught election law and was the first African American on the Texas Department of Commerce Policy Board. So our juror's comment probably did not go over too well.

We showed up for the first day of jury selection promptly at 8:00 a.m. on April 19, 2005. Dennis Brooks, a thoughtful, insightful, and extremely experienced consultant from Tsongas, and I would be assisting in selecting the jury. The courtroom was arranged with five separate counsel tables for each remaining defendant and a table for the

DOJ attorneys. We had at least two to three attorneys per defendant, eighteen in all.

Judge Gilmore announced that she usually questioned all of the jurors herself but would allow the attorneys to question jurors in this case. She also declared that the jury would be chosen that day. This began a very long day, with the prosecution starting their questioning, and then an attorney for each of the defendants was allowed to question the jurors. Some of the questions were pointed and insightful. Some of the questions allowed jurors to explain their knowledge of Enron, their impressions of the guilt or innocence of the defendants, and their knowledge of technology. Some questions were not questions at all but speeches to the jury.

Jim Lavine, attorney for defendant Kevin Howard, got up and asked the jurors whether anyone on the panel had formed a negative opinion of Enron executives as a result of what they had seen, read, or heard about in the media. A few hands went up. He heaved a deep sigh and tried again. He looked at the jurors, and with a smile on his face asked them if really, after the years of publicity and all that happened to Houston as a result of the Enron bankruptcy, if only a few of the jurors had formed a negative impression of our defendants. He looked at them and said, "It's all right, you can tell me." You could see the jurors relax a little and almost everyone's hand went up. This allowed him to address the proverbial elephant in the room and have a meaningful discussion with jurors about their true feelings about the case. It also allowed us to distinguish those jurors who had a fleeting negative impression from those that had deep-seated animus toward anyone affiliated with Enron.

After the strongest anti-Enron jurors had been eliminated with cause challenges, there were some venire members left who clearly knew people who had been affected by the Enron collapse. However, these remaining jurors did not seem to have strong negative opinions of the company based on a personal investment in the case. Additionally, these jurors seemed to be strong, independent, and smart. This was important in order to have a jury that would not just follow the authoritarian prosecution's arguments like sheep, but would be able to probe meaningfully into the government's evidence and their motive.

After starting with a panel of ninety-five jurors, more than forty were struck from the panel for cause and hardship, many having voiced strong negative opinions about Enron that they could not put aside. Judge Gilmore asked one juror to stay until the very end, even though he was very far down in the pool and would never be chosen.

We were instructed to adjourn and were given a half hour to decide on our strikes. Then the melee began. Each defendant's team of lawyers had their opinion of who to strike, their likes and dislikes. Some talked about how they felt they had connected with some jurors, some said that certain jurors had looked at them funny. And no one could agree. No one was asking Dennis or me, the actual jury consultants, whom we thought should be struck and what the final panel should look like. My fear was that every defense team would strike their least favorite juror, and we would end up with a bunch of weak and uneducated jurors who would just follow the prosecutors' easy-to-swallow story of corruption and conspiracy. And we were running out of time. I spoke up and asked the room in a loud, clear voice who the jurors were that were most likely to acquit the defendants in the mock trial. The attorneys and Dennis said it was the more educated and independent jurors. I told the group that this should be our priority—striking jurors who did not fit this profile. At that point, we were able to quickly prioritize our strikes right as the bailiff informed us that our time was up.

We marched back to the courtroom and handed our strikes to the judge. She compared our strikes to the government strikes, excused the struck jurors, and we were done. We had a jury. It was good group, very smart, very involved in their community. It was risky because I knew that if a smart and strong jury goes against you, they go against you hard. But our greatest enemy in the case was confusion. Judge

Gilmore swore them in and we finished at eight that night after a grueling twelve hours of jury selection.

Finally, Judge Gilmore called the man forward whom she had asked to stay to the end. He looked a little pale as he approached the bench. It was the juror who didn't give a shit and didn't like black or Mexican people. Judge Gilmore looked at him with reproach and told him she did not know whether he really meant his words or was merely trying to get out of jury service. She said she would like to hold him in contempt and throw him in jail, but it was late. She asked him whether his son would be proud of his father's response to jury service. The man started to cry as the judge told him, "There's nothing funny about this. This is a serious matter to these men." She told him she would let him off this time but reminded him of his duty to serve and admonished him that racial prejudice, whether pretended or real, was despicable in this day and age.

The attorneys were off to prepare for opening statements, and I went to have dinner with Dennis to discuss our jurors.

THE PROSECUTION'S CASE

Good attorneys rely on simple equations to convince a jury in a trial. The statement "fully operational" plus an internal email doubting the software's capabilities equaled *it doesn't work* in Kroger's world. Couple that with a press release, and you have a *conspiracy to deceive investors*. Couple that with timing of the sale of company stock, and you have a *motive of greed*. Easy equations and surface appearances are the prosecutor's trial tools. Don't look too deep, or you will start to doubt. If you start to doubt, you may acquit. So keep it simple.

The challenge for the defendant in a securities case is to take something that is really quite complicated and make it understandable.

Because if it stays complex, jurors will gravitate toward the simplest explanation. Social psychologists call this the monocausality heuristic bias. Leave it to pointy-headed academics to create a complicated name for a phenomenon that comes down to, "The side with the simplest explanation wins."

The prosecutor's simple equation in the EBS trial came down to:

1. The EIN never existed in the first place. (Never mind that the government allowed it to be sold it off.)
2. If it did exist, it didn't work.
3. EBS defendants knew it didn't work.
4. They misled investors that it existed and worked.
5. They profited off these lies.

In Kroger's conspiracy world, the Broadband Operating System (BOS) was a single magical program when in fact it was ten separate categories including thousands of individual programs. The prosecutors called experts who did not understand the code, the platform, or the network, and those experts reaffirmed their belief that the EIN and the BOS either did not exist or did not work.

Because it was brand-new technology, there was tremendous confusion even within EBS about the definitions of that technology. There were heated disagreements in emails between technicians, which the government took as a nefarious sign of deception. In the government's definition of the system, the network was the same as a product like a car: it either ran or it didn't run.

They said the system didn't provide storage or caching, but it did. They said it didn't have directories, but it did. The government said the code didn't exist for the BOS, but it did. In fact, after the bankruptcy, there were prominent businesses that bought various software and code pieces of the BOS. The government called InterAgent, the software that Modulus had developed, "pixie dust." But Enron paid thirty million dollars for it when they bought Modulus. AT&T and IBM also subsequently bought versions of InterAgent, and Sun bought the license for ten million dollars.

And despite the fact that the government had systematically disassembled and sold off the BOS piecemeal, Judge Gilmore prevented Shelby from telling the jury that it had done so. The Department of Justice said that the network control software was only about controlling the routers, but they never mentioned the storage or other capabilities. And they scoffed at Shelby's claim that the BOS would be more operational in the future.

The government called their big three witnesses: Collins, Meyer, and Bloomer, people who were either not involved or only peripherally involved, and pressured them to conform their opinions to the DOJ theory of the Enron Intelligent Network. Meyer told a completely different story at trial than she did to the grand jury.

The government also made a big fuss over the fact that EBS had not made money, ignorantly claiming that if a new product works, it will make money. It didn't make money, therefore it must not have worked. Again, simple equations. Of course, this ignored the entire concept and history of start-up companies. And EBS was a start-up. According to some statistics, 75 percent of start-ups fail, especially in the technology sector. Few are profitable in their first years.

In presenting their case, the U.S. attorneys were counting on the animus in the community toward Enron and the pervasive bias against big business in the wake of Enron, and the ensuing Tyco and World-Com scandals. The *Houston Chronicle*, voicing the outrage of the community, took a clearly pro-prosecution slant in its reporting. Big business was greedy. Greed begets corruption. We need to level the regulatory sword of Sarbanes-Oxley at these greedy, corrupt corporate raiders. Otherwise, who knows which village they will plunder next.

THE DEFENSE CASE

Shelby used to say, "Software is not complete until it is obsolete." He tried to make the point clear to the government that there is an evolutionary process in the development of all technology. Like with most software that we are familiar with, such as iOS updates for iPhones or Windows updates for PCs, there was an iteration of the BOS in operation at the time of Enron's implosion and more versions planned for the future.

Especially in technology, much was unknown in 1999 about capacities and capabilities. So claims about the functions of a new system were necessarily anticipatory and optimistic. A start-up is aspirational— you are hoping and believing that a new product or service will be used and that you will be able to develop that product to the extent of your knowledge at the time. All new products and all great products follow this trajectory. And experienced security analysts knew this about technology companies.

The defense evidence also showed a working system, despite the government's attempts to convince the jurors otherwise. An EBS engineer, Kirk Wright, reported that they had successfully streamed *The Drew Carey Show* over its network in a November 10, 1999, email to his bosses. He wrote, "All of the streams worked and started within the acceptable time frame," proving that the system's scheduling functions had performed properly. The 1999 streaming of the Country Music Awards and Wimbledon also established that EBS could meter the broadband use by its customers, at varying levels of quality.

The defense called real experts as well as those that worked on the system and understood it. Larry Ciscon, from Modulus, was a PhD and a vice president of software architecture at EBS, who held two patents for the BOS and three patents for InterAgent. He was an unindicted coconspirator whom the government was hoping would cooperate with their case. Instead, he testified for the defense about the government threatening him to get him to falsify statements about the other defendants. In his testimony, he also stated unequivocally, "I do not think the technical capabilities were overstated. And comparing EBS to the other software companies I've seen in my fifteen years in the software industry, I did not see anything outside of the standard product-development process." Mark Palmer was the director of applications development and in charge of product development. Ellis Giles was the senior software engineer and lead developer. David Leatherwood was vice president of network construction and head of the group who built the physical EBS network, including all fiber, network hardware, and facilities that the government had permitted to be auctioned off. All testified for the defendants.

While Giles was on the stand, Tomko tried to introduce into evidence some of the actual BOS software code that Giles had written, and which the government claimed did not exist. The government objected to putting it into evidence. Judge Gilmore asked Tomko why he wanted to introduce it into evidence. Tomko answered succinctly, "Because it exists, Your Honor." Unbelievably, the judge did not permit the software code—proof that the BOS actually did exist—into evidence because she said, "The jury won't understand it."

The comparison between these witnesses and the government's witnesses was stark. Both Ciscon and Giles won the top computer science award at Rice University when they were students there, and both have also received various national awards in computer science. Ciscon and Palmer are presidents of their own software firms now, and Giles works for NASA.

Although the prosecution usually tries a document case, the defense proved more proficient at mastering the trial documents, the prosecution stumbling at times to find the document that the defense had readily at hand.

One of the disagreements among the defendants was the concept that there was a present versus a future version of the BOS and that all components of the system had both an "existing" version in operation and a "future" version of improvements in development. That is the way software creation works and what the technology documents and witnesses said. While this was true, this may have confused the jury by introducing that there were two static versions of the BOS instead of a constantly evolving model of the technology.

Shelby was the first witness of any of the defendants. I had spent a couple of days working with Tomko, Ross, and Shelby, knowing he would be testifying in the case. Shelby was a straightforward man, able to explain technology simply and clearly, a rare quality for an engineer. I wanted to make sure the jury got to see Shelby's sincerity and to help prepare him for what we knew would be a blistering cross-examination. Prosecutors rarely get to examine a defendant, and they see it as their opportunity to deliver the knockout punch.

We prepared Shelby to be polite and helpful, no matter how aggressive or hostile the prosecutor became. This was not difficult, as it was a natural part of Shelby's character. The jury was his audience, and his goal was to help them understand who he was and what he had done. It was not his job to defend himself. Like a batter in baseball, all he had to do was stand at the plate, look for the seams in the ball, and wait for his pitch. We then ran him through a few mock examinations to prepare him for the fastballs, the curves, the sliders, the knuckleballs, and the junk that we knew the prosecution would be throwing.

On June 14, 2005, Shelby started his three and a half days of witness testimony. He had been watching the three federal prosecutors—Ben Campbell, Lisa Monaco, and Cliff Stricklin—as they questioned witnesses during the trial. Campbell was the lead prosecutor and was widely regarded as the smartest and most talented of the three. Campbell's nickname among the prosecutors was "Killer Opie"—"Opie" because he resembled an adult version of the character on the classic Andy Griffith television series, and "Killer" because of his aggressive, rapid-fire style of questioning witnesses during trials. Shelby had guessed correctly that, as the first defendant to go to the stand, he would most likely be cross-examined by Campbell.

As he observed Campbell cross-examining other witnesses, Shelby noticed that Campbell had a subtle "tell." When things were not going well for him, a red flush would begin to appear on his neck just below each ear; if things continued to go badly, the red flush would slowly spread forward on his neck and face cheeks. While Campbell was questioning Shelby on the witness stand, he kept tabs on the condition of Campbell's red flush—in effect, he had his own handy "agitation indicator" that confirmed when Shelby was getting to Campbell.

Shelby was courteous and respectful with Campbell most of the time. At one point, the judge chastised Campbell for being too fast in his examination. Campbell grew uneasy asking Shelby any real technology questions because he answered those so easily. When Campbell asked Shelby about the first time the FBI had interviewed him, Shelby pulled out the notes that he had taken after his interview and before he was indicted. He referred clearly and consistently to what he had tried to teach the FBI about the EIN in the early stages of the investigation. Nonplussed and red-faced, Campbell asked Shelby a few more perfunctory questions about innocuous matters and sat down.

During the prosecution's case, the government tried to say the EIN was not "intelligent." The prosecutors sometimes asked witnesses, "Where's the 'I' in EIN?" The defense witnesses had no problem answering this question. Canales, Yeager's lead counsel, got some mileage out of the prosecutors' failure on this issue during his closing when he asked the jurors, "Where's the 'I' in FBI?"

The Broadband trial lasted twelve weeks, concluding with the jury deliberating twenty-four hours over four days. Shelby was charged with twenty counts and was looking at twenty years in prison if convicted.

The jury voted 9–3 for acquittal on most counts, although they did some vote trading to avoid hanging the jury on all counts. Shelby was acquitted of four counts, the judge dismissed six, and the jury hung on ten more counts. Not a single defendant was convicted on a single count.

Later, Yeager took an appeal up to the Supreme Court when the government attempted to re-try him on several charges. He argued that it was double jeopardy to acquit on some counts and then re-try him on others that were based on charges for which he was acquitted. The Supreme Court agreed with him, and the U.S. Court of Appeals for the Fifth Circuit dropped all the remaining counts. Unfortunately, they stopped short of applying this same rule to Shelby's and the other defendants' cases. Three of the other Enron defendants ended up taking plea deals for one to two years. Enron Broadband accountant Michael Krautz was re-tried and acquitted.

Years later, Shelby was out of money when it came time for the government to re-try him for six of the counts the jury originally hung on. At that point, he had been passed through eight teams of U.S. attorneys. The final assistant U.S. attorney who was set to try his case, Peter Katz, told Shelby, "Look, you're not the worst guy in the world." In a stunning admission, Katz said that he didn't know if he would have even brought this case originally. But once the ball starts rolling . . .

Even though he was innocent, Shelby didn't have the resources and didn't want the risk of a long prison sentence. The government made him a deal he couldn't refuse, and he pled guilty to one count of insider trading, even though his only crime was working for Enron on a technology that was ahead of its time. He never served a day in prison.

AFTERMATH

Today, technology and telecommunications produce not only some of the world's largest companies, but the transfer of information through computers, tablets, and smartphones is also at the heart of our global economy and our day-to-day lives. During the trial, one executive at a major computer hardware manufacturer stated, "If they succeed in convicting the Enron developers, anyone in Silicon Valley can be sent to jail."

Lay and Skilling were tried by the government in January of 2006 for securities and wire fraud, insider trading, and an ambiguous charge called deprivation of honest services. The U.S. attorneys had clearly learned from the Broadband trial. They hired Jo-Ellan Dimitrius, my former colleague from the O. J. Simpson trial, to help with jury selection. Ironically, while she was working for the prosecution, our opposing consultants from the Simpson case were working for the defendants this time, Skilling and Lay. The justice attorneys had also changed their theory of fraud, simplified their presentations, and excluded most of the evidence from the Broadband trial. This last change was particularly ironic as they originally thought that the Broadband executives would roll over and testify against Skilling and Lay.

In May of 2006, a jury convicted Skilling and Lay of a majority of the charges. Skilling was sentenced to twenty-four years and had to surrender $630 million, including $180 million in fines. His sentence has since been reduced. Lay's sentence would have been up to forty-five years had he not died of a heart attack on July 5 of that year. Since Lay had died before sentencing and before his appeals could have been exhausted, his convictions were all vacated, making him an innocent man in the eyes of the law.

Enron was the seventh-largest company in the United States when it failed in 2001. Citigroup, Bank of America, AIG, and JPMorgan Chase were in slots eight to eleven on the Fortune 500 list that year, and all received government money that bailed them out in 2008. But for Enron, it was too soon for "too big to fail." Because of the fear and uncertainty that gripped our country in 2001, we needed an enemy to prove that our own system wasn't flawed. The government wanted to prove to a skittish public that a big company can't fail without a committed crime. For time immemorial, the external threat, the displacement of the enemy, has provided us comfort that the enemy is not, in fact, us.

Strangely enough, had Enron been bailed out and had EBS been allowed to continue developing the EIN and the BOS, it would have been a tremendous success in today's market. It had assets, customers, was relatively undervalued, and in on the ground floor of technology that a majority of the planet uses today. While oil and natural gas flowed through Enron's pipelines, data and information would have flowed through cable, an Internet pipeline fueling the world's hunger for information instead of energy.

In the end, had Shelby and Modulus chosen Sun over Enron, who knows when we would have had cloud computing, streaming video, and apps on phones. But Enron had a culture of arrogant, driven personalities hungry for profit to eagerly show their shareholders. The company had no patience for EBS's slow build as a technology start-up. Enron was sitting in a turbocharged sports car at race time in the U.S. economy. Over the deafening roar of revving engines and squealing tires, it couldn't hear the counsel of people who had actually worked in the communications industry. Enron management was as ignorant of the technology as the Department of Justice who prosecuted it. Each had different agendas for EBS: Enron wanted profit and accounting magic, and the Department of Justice wanted political appeasement.

EBS defendant Yeager was asked why he chose to fight all the way to the Supreme Court in order to be exonerated. He replied, "I don't know . . . your upbringing, your sense of justice, honesty. It [the case] was counter to what I was taught my whole life. I'm an American patriot. This is my country. Essentially, I was indicted for being an inventor."

People of the State of California
v. Phillip Spector

|||||||||||||| **SCIENCE AND STORIES** ||||||||||||||||

They cannot scare me with their empty spaces
Between stars—on stars where no human race is.
I have it in me so much nearer home
To scare myself with my own desert places.

—"Desert Places," Robert Frost

You hear the 187 homicide call go out at 5:00 a.m. on February 3, 2003. It is a shooting death. You hear from dispatch that it involves a "celebrity," and an eyewitness claims the suspect said, "I think I killed somebody."

It's a cool, windless morning. You drive through a blue-collar neighborhood with small houses next to a freeway. You arrive at a gated hill in Alhambra with a plaque on the wall marking "Phil Spector's Pyrenees Castle." You drive through the gate on a road winding around the hill and emerge in a large stone courtyard with a roaring fountain. It is a castle—a three-million-dollar home set on a hill overlooking three-hundred-thousand-dollar homes. Your backup also rolls into the courtyard, and you all get out.

When you approach the front door, it opens, and the suspect, a small older man with stringy hair, nods inside and says, "You've got to see this." But he does not comply with your commands to take his hands out of his pockets. He is shot with a Taser and tackled by three LAPD officers. He slurs obscenities at you and is taken into custody.

When you look inside, there is a blond woman slumped in a chair, with a gunshot wound to the face. There is a gun on the floor. Later, you verify that the gun belongs to Phillip Spector. You find a white coat on a bedroom floor upstairs. When inspected closely, there appears to be blood spatter on it. You interview a limo driver at the scene, Adriano DeSouza, who says he was sitting in his car outside the front door when he heard a *pah* sound, then saw Spector walk out of his front door, holding the gun.

At the scene and the station, the suspect protests his innocence, and claims that the woman shot herself. You smile and shake your head. That same day, Pat Dixon, a chief deputy district attorney, arrives at the crime scene to confirm evidence that will obviously be used in the indictment. An Alhambra police officer writes in her report and later testifies to the grand jury that Spector says, "I didn't mean to shoot her." Later, when you do more investigation, you find out the suspect, Spector, has pulled guns on women before. Many times before.

For police and prosecutors, the case seems obvious, even easy. You have an eyewitness that will testify he sees the suspect walk out of the house with a gun in his hand, confessing he killed the victim. You have blood spatter on the coat he was wearing. You have a history of him pulling guns on women. What more do you need? It's obvious. He killed her.

Yet there are nagging details that confound the obvious. The coroner initially concludes that the manner of death was accidental. Seven months and nineteen days later, he changes that conclusion to homicide. The prosecutors finally charge Spector with Lana Clarkson's death. But not for nine months and seventeen days.

D are to be Different" was the theme of Spector's high school prom and, for most of his life, he lived by that theme. Born in New York City, he moved to Los Angeles with his family after his father committed suicide when he was nine. He attended Fairfax High School and formed the musical group the Teddy Bears with two other students. He wrote and performed "To Know Him Is to Love Him," a number one hit in both the United States and the United Kingdom. The title was taken from the inscription on his father's gravestone. Later, in a British documentary, *The Agony and the Ecstasy of Phil Spector*, Spector spoke about the loss of his father, "I miss what I would have been. I might have been a different person." He would say the same thing about his son Phillip Spector Jr. who died tragically of leukemia at nine, the same age Spector Sr. was when he lost his father.

After the Teddy Bears broke up, Spector moved back to New York and produced a string of twenty hit records and was a millionaire by the time he was twenty years old. During this time, he started working on his famed Wall of Sound, which he described as "the Wagnerian approach to rock and roll." He considered himself more of a composer than producer and once said about his work, "Most producers don't create, they interpret. I *create* a sound of what I imagine in my head."

However, he grew impatient with musicians who could not fulfill his musical vision and a public who did not appreciate the lush, soaring scores that he composed. He would become reclusive for periods of time and became combative in some of his recording sessions, famously threatening musicians and firing off guns on occasion. As a prank, he fired his gun off next to an angered John Lennon, who famously exclaimed, "Phil, if you are going to kill me, kill me. But don't fuck with my ears, I need 'em." Apparently, Leonard Cohen, Debbie Harry, and the Ramones all had similar stories. However, rather than immediately firing Spector and calling the police, John Lennon and the others seemed tolerant of Spector's gunplay, threats, and sometimes outlandish costumes, considering it all part of Spector's eccentricity and genius. They felt Spector was more than an engineer, building a signature sound for their record. He seemed to understand their passion and their pain. He once said, "Hurting is a natural phenomenon with art."

A few days after his arrest, Spector hired Robert Shapiro of O. J. Simpson fame and paid him a one-million-dollar retainer. Shapiro, whom I worked with on O. J.'s case, quickly went to his starting O. J. lineup and called Dr. Henry Lee and Dr. Michael Baden, the famous forensic scientist and forensic pathologist, respectively. Shapiro, attorney Sara Caplan (also from Simpson's criminal case), Lee, and Baden toured Spector's home on February 4, 2003. As with Simpson, both Baden and Lee inspected Spector's body to see if there was any discernable sign of a struggle between him and Clarkson. They found none.

At nine thirty that evening, after the police had completed their investigation of the scene, both of the experts spotted missed evidence and noted inconsistencies by LAPD's crime scene investigators. Notably, they found blood on the bannister and other areas of the foyer. This was promising news for Spector as it could call into question the initial investigation or even find exculpatory evidence that could exonerate him.

However, as the investigation dragged on for months, Spector grew unhappy with Shapiro's performance, feeling that he was not working hard enough on the case. He fired Shapiro and asked for most of his one-million-dollar retainer back. Shapiro refused, and Spector then hired Leslie Abramson and Marcia Morrissey of Menendez Brothers

fame, who called Spector "an idol, an icon, and the definition of cool."
Six and a half months later, Abramson and Morrissey resigned after
it was revealed that Spector had also hired Bruce Cutler, unbeknownst
to them. Cutler was the son of a detective turned criminal defense
lawyer who famously gained acquittals for New York Gambino family
head John Gotti in the 1980s. When hired, Cutler immediately set
about to reestablish Spector's credibility, speaking about Spector's
"genius" and his "talent."

It is at this point where celebrity and strategy clash in a high-profile
criminal case. The temptation for a celebrity, whether it is an O. J.
Simpson, a Michael Jackson, a Martha Stewart, or a Phillip Spector,
is to rehabilitate their image. To do this, the client wants the attorney
to reinstate his or her credibility, not only by denying culpability for
the alleged crime but also by reminding the press and the public of the
great things he or she has done. Some attorneys believe this is the best
strategy: to wage a public relations battle in the effort to show that an
important person would never risk their reputation by doing something
like *this*, or to make jurors believe that someone with his or her accomplishments would never commit a crime.

However, what ends up happening in reestablishing the credibility
of the important celebrity is that you subconsciously create a higher
standard of conduct. Celebrities, through supermarket tabloids and
social media, become icons the general public places on a pedestal. The
public then raises that pedestal high enough so that they will not see
the blemishes or the flaws. The public (including the jury) believes
these divine beings will not fall prey to the same follies as us mere
mortals. They are considered more than us, and thus should know
better. In a jury's mind, they carry a moral obligation of higher conduct.
A booking mug shot makes a deified celebrity mortal; they tumble
from that high pedestal and fall into a chasm below us, earning our
derision and contempt, their blemishes now more hideous. Our shin-

ing examples are tarnished and we now become superior to them. In light of the accusations, we then contemptuously see them as arrogant, superior, and thinking they can "get away with it."

So rehabilitation attempts in a criminal case can be counterproductive because they shine a white-hot spotlight on the celebrity and any problematic evidence in the case.

Cutler started assembling his trial team and brought in Roger Rosen, an experienced Los Angeles lawyer who had worked on numerous high-profile cases, including the *Twilight Zone* manslaughter case against director John Landis, and a Hell's Angels case with famed *True Believer* attorney Tony Serra. Spector also hired Linda Kenney Baden to take the lead on the forensic case. Baden, a former Monmouth County prosecutor and active member of the American Academy of Forensic Sciences, was a legal specialist in scientific issues. She had worked on the Jayson Williams case, where the New Jersey Nets star was accused of manslaughter, and the Michael Skakel case, where Skakel, a nephew of Robert Kennedy's widow, was accused of murdering his next-door neighbor when Skakel was a teenager. Linda's husband, Dr. Michael Baden, had discovered the extra evidence when Shapiro was still handling the case.

Linda brought in noted San Diego forensic attorney Chris Plourd to second-chair the forensic part of the case. Plourd, now a California judge, was appointed to the Department of Justice's National Commission on the Future of DNA Evidence as well as appointed by the California Supreme Court to the California Judicial Council Science and the Law Steering Committee. Blasier, whose incisive work greatly clarified the scientific issues in the Simpson case, also worked on the Ted Kaczynski Unabomber case. He was also brought on by Linda to take on the motions for these forensic issues. Like patent attorneys in civil litigation, forensic attorneys are the science geeks of the legal world. They are the pocket-protector litigators who have pioneered the new era of science technologies applied to criminal cases. They study mitochondrial DNA, blood spatter, gunshot residue, and make sure that scientific standards are scrupulously observed in the criminal justice system. They would prove to be essential in Spector's case.

This was the team. And like all teams of highly skilled, experienced, and successful professionals, they had egos. Big but necessary egos in the tough world of criminal law. They all had opinions about how to try cases, having tried hundreds of cases among them. This is a natural and even healthy tension that occurs when these high-powered litigators argue, collaborate, and try to figure out the best strategy for a difficult defense. But it is important to try to keep that tension focused on differences in strategy and not differences in personality.

Like Rosen on the defense, Judge Larry Paul Fidler was born and raised in Los Angeles. After graduating from Loyola University Law School, he became a court clerk in Judge Gordon Ringer's court—a judge who famously subpoenaed President Richard Nixon to testify in a case linked to the Watergate scandal. After clerking for Ringer, Fidler went to work as a criminal defense lawyer for Howard Weitzman, who represented a long list of celebrity clients: John DeLorean, the head of the DeLorean Motor Company, in a drug sting case; Michael Jackson in his first molestation case; and O. J. Simpson. Weitzman was the first attorney that Simpson hired when he flew back from Chicago. Fidler was first appointed to the municipal court by first-time governor Jerry Brown, and was later appointed to the superior court by Governor Pete Wilson. He eventually became the presiding judge of the criminal courts in downtown Los Angeles. He handled his fair share of high-profile matters, including the Reginald Denny case preliminary hearings, involving a truck driver who was pulled from his truck and beaten during the Rodney King riots; the Sara Jane Olson case, an accused member of the infamous Symbionese Liberation Army that had kidnapped Patty Hearst; and the Rampart Division scandal, where officers of the LAPD were accused of planting evidence, racially profiling gang members, and stealing their drugs and money.

Rosen had numerous cases in front of Fidler and had a good relationship with him over the years. He, and most of the defense team, thought because of this relationship and Fidler's former work as a defense lawyer, he would at least give the defense a fair shake in trying their case. They were wrong.

As I have said before, high-profile cases change the way that judges, lawyers, and witnesses act in court. The knowledge that the "world is watching" tends to make them look beyond the evidence and toward how the public will view them in light of rulings, arguments, and testimony. Cameras in the courtroom become mirrors by which judges, lawyers, and witnesses judge themselves through the reflective eyes of the public. This self-reflection creates a projected legacy that makes them mindful of how they themselves will be judged. In essence, each participant in a high-profile trial is a defendant in the public forum, seeking both acquittal and praise for their actions.

Fidler, in a hearing to decide whether to televise the trial against the defense team's objection, set the agenda for media exposure in this case. "We have to get by that case," he said, referring to the Simpson trial. "There's going to come a time that it will be commonplace to televise trials. If it had not been for Simpson, we'd be there now." Fidler added, "You expose yourself as a judge to greater scrutiny."

Judges, no matter how well intentioned they are, are usually not aware of the reverberant impact that "gavel to gavel" coverage of a trial has on witnesses, attorneys, jurors, and the entire process. I have always felt that the judge, the attorneys, and the media should sit down in a pretrial conference and collaboratively discuss their concerns and legal rights in order to establish a set of ground rules for the trial. I feel this is a better way of reconciling the inevitable tension between the press's First Amendment rights and the defendant's Sixth Amendment rights. By granting greater access for the media, you inevitably compromise a defendant's rights to an impartial jury. By restricting media access, you impinge on the press's and the public's First Amendment rights.

It's a tough call for a judge, but in a high-profile trial, the First Amendment wins almost every time.

In keeping with his views about "the public's right to know," Fidler released Spector's grand jury transcript to the public. This is rarely done, but Fidler argued that there had already been so much publicity in the case, the release of the transcripts would not have a prejudicial effect.

This is another disadvantage for a defendant in a high-profile case. The press naturally wants to see the grand jury proceeding. In a grand jury, the defense has absolutely no right to question any of the witnesses. In fact, they're not even present. It is the prosecution's show, and they obviously only put on witnesses and evidence that will support their view that the defendant should be charged with the crime and why he or she is probably guilty. At the end of the process, the grand jury's only job is to decide if there is sufficient evidence to take the case to trial. But for the public, it is a jury that has already ruled that the evidence against the defendant is credible. Thus starts the long parade of guilt conclusions in a media trial before the case actually goes to a jury. The press starts broadcasting evidence that was either contained in the grand jury hearing or that is leaked to them by the prosecution or police, some of which would never see the light of a courtroom. This, coupled with the perp walk, which are staged photos of the arrest, and the booking mug shot all combine to convey the guilt of the defendant before the trial even begins.

The defense can only sit idly by, biding their time while anemically muttering the timeworn trial agitprop, "Keep an open mind. Wait until the evidence is all in. Remember, innocent until proven guilty."

It is at this point where the clients call me. When the perp walks, mug shots, 911 tapes, and security camera footage have been released. When the police or prosecutor's leaks have already poisoned part of the public. When the damage has been done, and the prospect of finding an impartial jury and the likelihood of a fair trial is a question mark, if not a remote possibility. When the scales are tilted and the zeitgeist in the case becomes when, not if, the defendant is convicted.

Linda Kenney Baden, who knew my Chicago partner Paul Lisnek, set up a meeting with Spector and Blasier, whom I knew from the Simpson trial. When I first heard about Spector's case, the facts sounded pretty tough. A guy who owns guns comes out of his house with a gun, saying, "I think I killed somebody." Pretty clear. But when Blasier called me and gave me a quick rundown of the forensics, I was hooked. The thing that intrigued me was the white jacket.

Spector had a habit of wearing long dinner jackets. He wore them during the trial, and he was wearing a long white coat the night Clarkson died. The police found the coat on the floor of his bedroom. According to the police, Spector was wearing the coat when he forced the gun into her mouth and fired. According to the forensic analysis, there were seventeen tiny specks of blood spatter on the coat, almost all on the left-hand side of the coat and very few on the sleeve. My first impression was if Spector had been holding the gun at the time of the discharge, and the gun was in Clarkson's mouth, there should have been a great deal more blood, tissue, GSR, or bone or tooth fragments on the jacket.

To demonstrate this point, I asked a graphics team I knew to create an animation to show that the gunshot in the mouth would create a tremendous amount of physical material to have been lodged on the jacket, especially the right arm, which Spector used as his dominant hand. I wanted to show Spector and the lawyers what I hoped would be a central image in refocusing jurors on the science in the case.

It is always strange when you go to the house and meet a defendant for the first time. Like a juror, you are always comparing the image of the person you see before you to the "monster" the prosecutors are saying committed the alleged crime. And when you meet at the place where the district attorney is saying the crime was committed, you immediately start doing your own investigation, looking for clues to try to figure out what happened on the night where someone lost his or her life.

When I stood looking at "the Castle" from the courtyard, I made a mental note about how loud the fountain was from that vantage point. This would become an issue later in the trial. When the door opened, I walked immediately into the foyer where Clarkson was found, looked at a chair exactly like the one she was sitting in. I took a moment to take it all in. There were the two white chairs. There was the staircase. There was the table next to the chair with the drawer that held an empty holster. There were two silent suits of armor that stood sentry, witnesses to whatever happened that night. There was the white John Lennon piano that he used to record the song "Imagine." There was the living room and the coffee table that held a Jose Cuervo tequila bottle, a Canada Dry Ginger Ale bottle, and brandy snifters. The white jacket, the white chairs, and the white sofas would become grim canvases on which we had to create a picture of the last hours of Clarkson's life.

I sat down with Spector and Blasier. Blasier is a small, crisp man with a thin mouth and sharp mind. I shook Spector's pallid, trembling hand. He had a sadness about him, an aloofness that is the nurtured habit of the disaffected loner. The rebel continually looking for a cause. He learns by challenging. He tests by confronting. He looks not at the center of a picture for answers but at the margins for the boundaries. And no doubt, this is the source of his genius and his grief. For he has pissed off a lot of people.

In a first meeting with clients, I always believe it is best to let them see the case through a juror's eyes. Too often the defense team approaches their cases with an advocate's eye, always looking to shape, argue, and angle the case toward a winning position. However, without the jury view, the defense is looking through the ivory tower of

Century City skyscraper windows. My job is to press the elevator button and bring everyone down to the ground floor, put them in a pickup instead of a BMW, and drive them through the razor wire of South Central and the Asian markets of San Gabriel. To see if they think the case looks like such a winner from a street corner in Pico Rivera or Inglewood instead of a corner table at Spago in Beverly Hills with crisp tablecloths and unctuous waiters.

Some consultants like to curry favor by telling the client what they want to hear. I give the bad news first, the cold water, and the wake-up call. Because everything that follows in terms of developing evidence, themes, and arguments stems from two simple questions: what will make the jury want to convict, and what will make the jury want to acquit? The prosecution goes first, and the jury hears all of the negative evidence in their case. That is where it is important to start. Once you have defined all of the bad stuff the district attorneys will be throwing at your guy, you can start mapping out your countertactics and affirmative strategies.

So I outlined the tough positions for Spector first, most of them obvious. The women that would testify about his penchant for gunplay, the eyewitness account by the limo driver, the alcohol, his house, his gun, blood on his jacket. Then the not so obvious issues. He did not call 911 after the shot. He was inside the house for forty minutes alone before the police showed up. The callous statements to the police. The famous fright wig appearance on May 23, 2005, where he showed up for court with a massive puffy perm. His current gaunt appearance, intense stare, and shaky demeanor. Younger woman and older man. Beauty and the beast. Power and vulnerability. Celebrities use and discard people. Celebrities get away with murder from O. J. to Robert Blake.

Until you can outline all of the issues that the opposing side, the judge, or the jury can use to beat you, you cannot effectively present your case to address the concerns of the jury. You certainly can't pick a jury. Because, in a criminal case, a defendant is defending against the prosecution's case, a judge's attitude or rulings, and all of the loose threads that jurors will use to weave their own tapestry of what happened. Because all criminal defendants live with a juror's double portrait: the image of the kind of person who could have committed the crime, and the demeanor and perceived attitude of the defendant sitting in court. Jurors are constantly comparing these two portraits to ask themselves, "Does he look like he did this?"

At the end of our meeting, Spector looked a little stunned, but he understood. It wasn't just about the evidence. It was also about the atmospherics surrounding the evidence.

The optics and frame of reference for the jury had to be changed. And this is where Baden's, Plourd's, and Blasier's expertise became essential. We would focus on the science and not the story. The prosecution's case was all about the sensationalized Lifetime movie about Spector: abuser, alcoholic, powerful manipulator, and his hapless victim, Lana Clarkson, the happy yet vulnerable actress. The more we focused on refuting these past incidents with women and guns, his drinking, and his overall conduct, the more this played into the prosecution's made-for-TV movie. But the forensic evidence had none of the problematic personality issues. It demanded cold, clear-eyed analysis and not tabloid *TMZ*-style speculation.

Blasier arranged for me to meet with Cutler, lead counsel on the case. I met him for drinks at the Ritz-Carlton hotel in Pasadena, where Spector was putting him up. Cutler had the build of a meat packer and the vocabulary of an English scholar. He loved words and used them as weapons and for wooing judges and juries. He crushed my hand, ate bowls of salted nuts, and discussed his career and thoughts about the case.

Cutler was East Coast and old school in his advocacy style. He was used to pushing and cajoling judges, juries, witnesses, and opposing counsel. It was a persuasion model with the attorney at the center of the case, using their strength, skill, eloquence, and influence as the moving force. It is a style that works well for some juries but not for others. He confessed he had never used a jury consultant and did not necessarily see the need. He trusted his instincts and his experience.

I realized that Cutler was also not a big fan of the forensic evidence in the case. He was Spector's champion—wanting to prove to the jury that his client was a genius, that the women who dared testify against him were opportunists, and the police and prosecutors were just out to besmirch Spector's accomplishments and good name. Spector liked this strategy, of course, because he wanted to restore his reputation. Cutler was enamored of big conspiracy themes and the grandiose character story of Spector's rise as an artist. This story suited Cutler's own character and sensibilities.

Nevertheless, even though Cutler and to a certain extent Spector were skeptical of my work, I persuaded them to conduct a focus group in the case to test evidence, themes, and approaches to the trial. While mock trials are more like full-blown dress rehearsals, focus groups are more like conversations that allow you to dig into a jury's thinking about the case a little deeper, probing into how they use the issues in the case to construct their own narrative.

We did two focus groups, one in the morning and one in the afternoon. We tried two separate strategies. In the morning group, we tried a strategy centered on Cutler's themes: we strongly questioned the motives of the women testifying against Spector and focused on the lack of any real motive or evidence that proved Spector killed Clarkson. In the afternoon group, we tried the science strategy where we focused more on the forensic evidence that actively disproved that Spector was holding the gun at the time, showing that Clarkson was holding the gun, and evidence that indicated Clarkson may have been suicidal.

If you listen to jurors, if you really listen to them, they will not only tell you what they think of your case, but they will also tell you what you've missed. As a group, they can be excellent detectives and scientists. This phenomenon was made popular in a 2004 book by James Surowiecki called *The Wisdom of Crowds*, in which he argues that groups, in certain situations, make better decisions than individuals.

Of our two focus groups, the morning group leaned more toward conviction, and the afternoon leaned more toward acquittal. Neither group was unanimous, and both raised serious questions about the evidence on both sides. This is actually the best possible result in a focus group, because you can learn from the results and refine your case. And despite all of the negative publicity about Spector, both groups of jurors provided hung juries. Although Spector and some of the attorneys were disappointed that we did not get acquittals in these groups, in most criminal defense cases, a hung jury is a huge win.

More importantly, some of the jurors latched on to the forensic evidence as their reasonable-doubt anchor. We needed to do a lot more work to make the science clearer and more understandable, but it got traction. Since Spector's history of using guns around women was so compelling to some jurors, we needed to make sure that the forensic evidence was equally compelling. Since *CSI* was at the height of its popularity, I felt if we could give our jurors virtual lab coats and make them the crime scene investigators and the scientists, we would stand a better chance of them seeing the evidence the way we saw it.

We learned a few additional important points from the focus groups. The more we were able to show through the forensic evidence that Clarkson had been holding the gun, the more jurors were willing to accept that she may have had problems that led to her suicide, or a drunken and reckless handling of the gun, which resulted in an accidental discharge. Additionally, when jurors were able to focus on the forensics that put the gun in Clarkson's hand, they also postulated that she could have gotten the gun out of the holster in the drawer next to the chair in which she was sitting.

Finally, even though the focus groups did not give us a statistically significant profile of pro-prosecution versus pro-defense-leaning jurors, we had an indication of who we wanted on the jury: smart and skeptical jurors.

I also had the good fortune in this next period to get to know two lawyers who would end up taking the leads in the case: Linda Kenney Baden on the science issues, and Roger Rosen on the non science issues. Even though Dame Helen Mirren played her excellently in the David Mamet HBO movie, *Phil Spector*, Baden always reminded me of the first actress who was slated to play her, Bette Midler. Baden was bright, brassy, did not suffer fools, and had a wicked sense of humor. She knew the science, the law, and had the rare ability to make the arcane understandable. Rosen was trim and affable, a gentleman's gentleman, always polite, and carried himself with the kind of integrity you look for in a defense lawyer. And where Cutler was a jackhammer in his advocacy style, Rosen was an ice pick, cool and pointed.

As the trial approached, we tried to forge a unified strategy for presenting tough facts to a tough audience. I met with Cutler again, and it appeared he wanted to pursue his original theme of focusing on Spector's character. Although he was reluctant to disclose his specific strategy, it seemed as if he wanted to portray Spector as a misunderstood romantic regarding his relationship with the five women who were supposed to testify that Spector threatened them with a gun. Cutler's strategy alarmed me, as I knew these five women were the most dangerous aspect of the case. All of them had had some relationship with Spector. All of them would testify that he had pulled a gun on them and threatened them. If Cutler attacked the credibility of these women, jurors could see this as another of Spector's assaults. In a case where the defendant will not testify, the personality of the lawyer becomes the attitude of the defendant.

California's 1101(b) statute regarding witnesses specifically allowed, under a judge's discretion, that the past conduct of a defendant can be admitted for limited purposes: to show that the defendant was in fact at the scene when there is a question about whether he or she was present, to show that the injury or death the defendant caused was not an accident, or to show that the defendant had the intent to commit the crime. The defense lawyers argued to Fidler that the 1101(b) evidence may have been relevant if Spector had previously shot someone. But he never had. This evidence is not supposed to show a pattern of conduct because pattern evidence is prejudicial. It can easily lead a jury to leapfrog the evidentiary necessity of proving the circumstances of the crime and allow them to speculate, "Well, he did it before so of course he did it again."

> 1101. (a) Except as provided in this section . . . *evidence of a person's character or a trait of his or her character (whether in the form of an opinion, evidence of reputation, or evidence of specific instances of his or her conduct) is inadmissible when offered to prove his or her conduct on a specified occasion.*
>
> (b) *Nothing in this section prohibits the admission of evidence that a person committed a crime, civil wrong, or other act when relevant to prove some fact (such as motive, opportunity, intent, preparation, plan, knowledge, identity, absence of mistake or accident . . .*
>
> —California Evidence Code

This highlights another codified contradiction in our criminal justice system. The 1101(a) section says you can't use this evidence to show character. The 1101(b) section says you can use it to show motive and intent. For a jury, character, motive, and intent are inextricably tied together. Juries also love patterns. They use character evidence to search for motive. This prompts them to look at the defendant and evaluate, "Is he the kind of guy who would do something like this?" Despite the law, having five women testify that Spector threatened them with a gun was entirely about character.

So Cutler's "misunderstood romantic" angle concerned me. I saw it potentially as a case killer. Because the more time you spend on this evidence, the more weight you give it in the jury's collective mind. It tells the jury that *you* think it is important. Then the case becomes about Spector's alleged abusive relationship with women instead of what the science says happened that night in that entranceway.

Even if it would be possible to discredit one or two of these women, there is no way a jury would dismiss all five of them testifying about incidences that occurred over a thirty-year period. My thought was to treat these witnesses respectfully and lightly, emphasizing that all of these incidences occurred after they had been in a relationship with Spector. All of these women stayed in contact with him and, although frightened by his behavior, never actually felt in danger of being shot. Jurors can understand that a defendant like Spector can be dysfunctional or even abusive without being a murderer. But it was best to minimize the potential damage of this "character" evidence and get them off the stand as quickly as possible.

This is one of the challenges as a consultant, whether you are working for a criminal defendant or a corporation in a civil lawsuit. Defense attorneys like to defend. They are reactive and are trained to be. But sometimes the vehemence of defending against accusations actually lends greater weight and credibility to the charges themselves. Think about it personally. You hear a crash in the other room in your house, and you walk in to find your seven-year-old daughter staring horrified at the broken pieces of your favorite golfing or fishing trophy. She immediately starts protesting that it's not her fault, starts pointing fingers at her brother, the dog, gremlins, and aliens. The more she protests, the more you are convinced she is guilty. Now think of bank, oil company, automotive company, and tobacco company CEOs in congressional hearings.

Now think of the same crash in the other room. You walk in, and your daughter calmly says she is sorry that your favorite trophy got broken, she knows how important it was to you, and here is what happened. Think of your willingness to listen to what she has to say. You still may be suspicious (given her history of breaking things) but you will be more open to listening to the explanation and less skeptical of her excuses. With a reactive refutation, protests, and blame shifting, it is much easier to come to a simplified guilt conclusion. In accepting even partial responsibility, you have the appropriate tone and context for a plausible defense.

The second challenge you have as a consultant is convincing the client that there are nuances to the story. Remember, prosecution case stories are usually two dimensional in character development—good and evil, Clarkson good, Spector bad. Part of your challenge is bringing dimensionality to the case story so the jury can appreciate the complexity of human behavior. Spector himself has talked about his battles with his demons in the British documentary *The Agony and the Ecstasy of Phil Spector.* "I may not believe in God, but I sure the hell know there's a devil." Clarkson had them as well. But until your client understands the importance of character complexity for the jury, they will always be reactive, protesting that their motives are entirely pure.

Finally, as a consultant, you have an integrity issue. The client ultimately makes the call. And the attorneys are the ones who are ultimately trying the case. But I've worked on a thousand trials, and I've helped pick hundreds of juries. I have to give the client the clear, unvarnished risks and rewards of their chosen strategy. On one hand, I want to honor the experience, instincts, and choices of the attorneys who are on the front line of the case. On the other hand, there are times where I am convinced they are dead wrong and it is my job to push them toward a strategy that *I* am convinced will work, based on my experience, instincts, and research. Sometimes it's a hard choice.

But in a tough fact case, when a man's life is on the line, what I want and even what they want is not important. It's what the jury *needs*.

JURY SELECTION

In a high-profile case where the jury pool has already seen and heard the press coverage about how bad a guy your client is, jury selection is jury de-selection. Michelangelo once said, "I saw the angel in the marble and carved until I set him free." So the art in jury selection is in the carving. You are not picking positive jurors, you are eliminating negative jurors. Hopefully, when the carving is done, you have a receptive audience.

To do this, you have to identify jurors with attitudes that are most harmful to your case. It's not about race, gender, or age. It's all about attitude. These personal experiences and core beliefs control how jurors view the evidence. And unless you know how those experiences and beliefs will interact with the evidence and arguments in the case, you do not have an accurate barometer for the jury's reaction—how warm or chilly they will be to your case. More importantly, jury selection, if done correctly, is a preview of jury deliberations. You are trying to get jurors to speak with you and each other about how they see the issues in the case to gauge their worldview, how they best like to get and use evidence, and, most importantly, how their personalities will interact with you, your client, opposing attorneys, the judge, each other, and ultimately the case. In Spector's case, there were a lot of negative attitudes I saw as important in identifying pro-prosecution jurors. These were:

1. I have heard about the case and I already think he's guilty.
2. I have seen pictures of him and he looks like someone who probably killed her.

3. Celebrities get away with murder (O. J. Simpson, Robert Blake backlash).
4. Celebrities are reckless, entitled, and manipulative.
5. Men are abusive.
6. If Spector has pulled guns on women before, he probably killed her.
7. If someone said he heard Spector confess, he is probably guilty.
8. Gun owners are reckless and more likely to kill someone.
9. If someone has been drinking and they have a gun in the house, they are more likely to kill someone.
10. If someone is shot in a house with the homeowner's gun, the homeowner is responsible, no matter who pulled the trigger.
11. A criminal defendant probably did something wrong, or they wouldn't be charged.
12. A criminal defendant should prove their own innocence.
13. A criminal defendant should have to testify to defend themselves.

So I designed a questionnaire to discover jurors who had these attitudes. Cutler and Spector were horrified when they saw the questionnaire. They did not understand that jury selection is an exercise in masochism, counter to your every instinct as an advocate. The necessity is to get a juror to articulate, first on paper and then in open court, how much they hate your case, your client, and maybe even you. Cutler and Spector's understandable natural instincts were to rehabilitate Spector's image, so they wanted to put only good things about him in the questionnaire. But unfortunately, when you do that, you don't identify your negative jurors. And you can't carve to set the angel free.

But they listened to me. Fidler sent out the questionnaires to prospective jurors, and they filled them out three weeks in advance. The district attorney's office volunteered to copy them and notified us when they were done. I went down to pick up the boxes of questionnaires. Now, even though I have primarily worked for the defense on criminal cases, I have done work on occasion for U.S. attorneys and for prosecutors in other jurisdictions. I had even been hired by Bill Hodgman in the same Los Angeles district attorney's office to help them on a case. No matter who hires me, I always believe in maintaining a civil and friendly relationship with the opposing side in a case. But when I walked into lead attorney Pat Dixon's office to pick up the questionnaires and introduced myself, he refused to shake my hand, gesturing dismissively to the boxes on the floor. It was then that I realized the office had clearly gotten the message to win this case at all costs. Give no ground. And do not give the slightest impression of friendliness. This was war.

The problem with hostile gamesmanship in trials is you motivate the other side. Yes, everyone wants to win. But when the other side talks trash or does the heavyweight stare down, it just makes you want to beat them even more. There are times when the judge in a trial demands cooperation between counsel. Professional courtesy is useful when you have to work out trial issues with your opponents. But when you get the take-no-prisoners approach from the other side, it makes negotiating the smaller concessions that much tougher. However, we soon found out the DA's scorched-earth policy, especially when supported by the judge, gave them a strong strategic advantage in the case.

We read three hundred juror questionnaires and rated them on a one-to-five scale, with one being the worst and five being the best. The jurors rated one you have to get rid of, and the jurors rated five are the ones the prosecutors will strike if they're paying attention. You also make a list of "hardship" and "cause" challenges. Hardships are jurors who say they cannot sit on long cases because they would have extreme financial difficulty in sitting on a case, are taking care of small

children or elderly parents, or have pre-paid travel plans. Cause challenges are jurors who have stated a bias in the questionnaire or in voir
dire questioning that would impair or prevent them from being a fair
and impartial juror in the case. This is why we were careful to include
a number of questions to discern whether jurors had a bias in the
thirteen categories I previously listed. You want to articulate the specific bias that you are asking the judge to excuse the juror for. The judge
can grant unlimited cause challenges, but you have a limited number
of peremptory strikes where you can dismiss jurors without a reason.
The more cause challenges you get granted, the less you have to use
your strikes on the really badly biased jurors. You can then use your
strikes on the more marginally negative jurors, leaving truly neutral,
impartial, or even positive jurors. Again, the art is in the carving.

One of the luxuries we had in the case with a sophisticated judge
like Fidler was our ability to have the questionnaires three weeks before
jury selection in order to fully evaluate them. Most of the time, you
do not get a questionnaire at all and have to make on-the-spot decisions
on jurors that you are hearing from that same day. When you do have
a questionnaire, it's usually very limited, and you only have overnight
or an hour to review and rate the jurors.

We were concerned that there might be "stealth" jurors: prospective
jurors who would give socially acceptable answers about fairness on
their questionnaires, while hiding a true agenda to get on the jury to
convict Spector. Some stealth jurors want the fame from sitting on a
famous case. Some want to write the book and capitalize on the talk
show circuit. Some have a political or social cause they want to advance
and see the case as a platform for that agenda. But most stealth jurors
want to convict the defendant.

California statutes allow you to investigate jurors. However, Fidler,
at the request of the prosecution, did not allow us the names of the
jurors, giving Spector what they call an "anonymous" jury. Anonymous

juries have more typically been used in gang cases where there is fear of jurors being intimidated or tampered with. But some judges are using the anonymous system to prevent the media from obtaining information about jurors. I understand the instinct. However, the media, with its investigative resources, knows who all the jurors are by the end of the case. Without names, it is difficult for us to conduct background checks through Google searches, publicly available Facebook pages, or Twitter feeds. There are strict ethical rules about doing these searches. You may not "friend" a juror on Facebook or follow them on Twitter, as that would constitute contact, no matter how virtual it may be. You may only look at publicly posted information that anyone with public access may obtain. And while jurors these days are pretty savvy with their privacy settings, you can still obtain useful information to help fill in a portrait of a particular juror. You want to have the fullest picture you can of a juror who will ultimately be ruling on the life and future of your client.

Once we had read and rated the questionnaires, we created a comprehensive selection plan. This meant creating summary sheets for each juror based on their questionnaire responses. We then sat down with the attorneys to discuss the plan: here are the jurors we need to develop cause challenges on to save our precious peremptory challenges, here is the profile of jurors whom the prosecution and their consultant will likely try to eliminate, here is the profile of jurors they will want to keep on the jury. Finally, here is the profile of the types of jurors we would ideally like on our final panel. And you also need to look at the sequence of jurors that will be called into the box—where there is a good streak of jurors or a particularly bad streak. This is important so that you do not run out of challenges when there is a particularly bad group of jurors coming up that the prosecution can load onto the panel.

This is where we play jury-selection chess. You plan your moves carefully, also anticipating the prosecution's probable moves, knowing that you will also have to improvise on the fly. I knew the prosecution would have a consultant on their team, given their zeal for a conviction in this case. I also knew it would probably be Howard Varinsky, an excellent consultant from the Bay Area who had handled a number of high-profile jury selections for prosecutors: the cases against Scott Peterson, Michael Jackson, Martha Stewart, and Dr. Jack Kevorkian.

From reading the questionnaires, we also knew we had a very tough panel of jurors. A lot of them had heard about the case. About a quarter already thought he was probably guilty. More than half thought a criminal defendant should prove his or her innocence and should testify to defend themselves. A fair number thought celebrities took advantage of others and got special treatment. Many thought a homeowner who owned a gun should be held responsible for a death, whether they pulled the trigger or not. There were only a few jurors whom we thought would be most receptive to our case, and those could be easily identified by the district attorneys and their consultant and eliminated through peremptory challenges. Jury selection is about reducing the risk you have on the jury. But when you have a tough case and an even tougher jury pool, sometimes you have to play high-stakes poker. That is, you actually have to up the ante and increase the risk for both sides.

The *Los Angeles Times* wrote an article titled "Spector Jury Selection a High-Stakes Battle of Wits" that came out on the first day of jury selection. In it, a Texas consultant was quoted as saying how we were looking for jurors enamored of celebrity and how important opening statements were and how the trial would "be over before one shred of evidence is presented." This was a massive oversimplification of a commonly held myth.

Another phenomenon you have to deal with in high-profile cases is a slew of experts speculating and second-guessing every move you make. It's tough, because the media in these cases covers the horse race—who's winning and losing the case at any given time—instead of the nuances of the justice system. For full disclosure, I am one of those talking heads. However, I have tried to take an educational approach to my commentary, because the public does not have an accurate picture of the complexity and dynamism of these cases.

When we sat down to map out the jury-selection plan, it was decided that Rosen would do a majority of the voir dire, as he had the most experience with Los Angeles juries. Cutler had never tried a case in Los Angeles before, so as lead attorney, he would ask some initial questions to build rapport and get a better feel for L.A. juries.

The district attorney went first with prosecutor Pat Dixon leading off as the senior attorney on the case. He was a thirty-year veteran and head of the major crimes division in the office. He was tall, silver haired, and had a smooth, severe demeanor. However, a majority of the prosecution's voir dire was done by Alan Jackson, a young but experienced district attorney who had finished successfully winning a conviction the previous year of the cold-case murders of racing's Mickey Thompson and his wife. Jackson was charming, quick, and aggressive. A shock of dark hair would flop onto his forehead, creating the impression of a handsome and trim version of Bob's Big Boy. Both of the prosecutors wore the uniform: dark suit, white shirt, striped tie.

Without a hint of an accent, Jackson told jurors to forgive him if he lapsed into his native Texas idiom and uttered "y'all" occasionally. It was the rapport-building phase of voir dire and all attorneys have their shtick—cocktail-party banter that is planned ahead and uttered to juries dozens of times. These are planned and specifically designed stories to let jurors know that the prosecutor is just like them.

The rapport-building phase is part of the mythical Persuasion lore in the Book of Trial Rules—an unspoken set of conduct that all attorneys learn to influence juries. As with all lore, some of these rules are based on survival, some on common sense, and some on pure myth—what one lawyer did a long time ago that has been repeated over the years, whether it worked or not. Some of these commonsense persuasion rules include remembering jurors' names, standing respectfully when they enter the courtroom, and acknowledging their personal struggles if they talk about the loss of family members or medical problems. Most attorneys think of rapport building in terms of telling quaint personal stories to show that they are similar to jurors. "Oh, I see that you went to school at the University of Nebraska. My brother went there. Go Huskers."

Attorneys then turn to the second chapter in their Book of Trial Rules: Indoctrination. Like most myths, indoctrination has a grain of truth. A principle called the *primacy effect* states that jurors are most receptive to information they first hear. And advocates like to start selling their cases early and often. As a result, many attorneys get up and examine jurors like a witness. "Would you have a problem voting to convict Mr. Spector, if we proved our case to you beyond a reasonable doubt?" The myth behind indoctrination is it presumes that jurors are passive, neutral, and compliant. And maybe they are for the short time that the attorneys are talking to them in jury selection. But then jurors are their own dynamos of decision making for the rest of the case.

But the problem with most attorneys in jury selection is that they really don't care about the jurors. They care about *the case*. They feel the facts that they have spent months, if not years, working on will overcome all obstacles—a judge's rulings, a witness's shortcomings, and juror predispositions. It's a useful delusion. But it prevents attorneys from understanding that the facts of their case are only as good as the jury's interpretation of those facts. Their mistaken assumption is that a case presentation is a straight-chute data dump directly into an empty file folder in the jury's collective brain. Not so. As soon as the words leave the attorney's or witness's lips, the information goes through a series of filters, subfilters, chutes, tunnels, and tracks that Rube Goldberg would be proud of. Thus, the check marks on the verdict form are as much a product of the juror's own life experiences and psychological/cognitive processes as the evidence itself.

Treating jury selection as a necessary nuisance results in many a surprise verdict for attorneys and clients. It is a shame, because the jury-selection process is a real opportunity for attorneys to build real credibility and rapport with jurors by actively engaging them in a discussion about the case and the client. If jurors are engaged, they are more tuned in to what the attorneys and the witnesses are trying to communicate, and the attorneys are more tuned in to what the jury wants to hear.

Jackson, in his voir dire, was charming, authoritative, and managed to ask some jurors about the answers in their questionnaire. He then ran through a series of indoctrination questions about burden of proof and circumstantial evidence, all designed to extract a series of promises from them. Some jurors smiled, some nodded. But in the mostly one-way communication, the jury heard *him*, but he did not hear *them*.

Then Cutler, natty in an impeccable suit and pocket square, rose and addressed the jury. In his rapport-building section, he spoke in his native Brooklynese about not understanding Los Angeles: the continuous traffic and the lack of good delicatessens. I could see the jury looking at him quizzically, not understanding why he was vaguely insulting their city. In his indoctrination section, he then spoke about "the deleterious and dangerous rumors" in the press about Spector. He told them they should not automatically conclude Spector killed Clarkson because she was found dead in his home. He finally sat down. And that was it. If you really look, you can see it in the air between the lawyer and the jury. There is either a connection or no connection. Cutler had not flipped the switch.

Luckily, I had been working with Rosen to do the jury-selection work that needed to be done. While much is made of lawyers and consultants rigging a jury to acquit their client, it is a practical impossibility. Most of the time, you are just hopeful that you will be able to get rid of most of the jurors who already think your client is guilty. In most jurisdictions, the conviction rate hovers around the 90 percent mark. Research also shows that jurors who have been exposed to pre-trial publicity are more likely to convict. So you are mainly looking for jurors to just give you a fair listening.

Some say that voir dire means to speak the truth. Some say that it is derived from two French verbs meaning "to see" and "to speak." Despite this debate, good voir dire is where jurors spend most of the time speaking and telling you *their* truth. Great voir dire, if you are really listening to jurors, is a preview of deliberations, where jurors are reenacting, prior to hearing the evidence, how they will ultimately be discussing the case. But you have to ask really good questions and listen carefully to get them to tell you what their truth really is.

Most jury selections unfortunately end up with lawyers telling jurors how they *should* think about the case. They talk *at* the jurors. Jurors will then nod dutifully and parrot back their agreement. "Yes, I can be fair and impartial. Yes, I would be willing to consider circumstantial evidence." When, in the back of their minds, they are really saying, "I'll tell you what you want to hear. And I know what you are trying to get me to do. I will agree with you here in open court in front of all of these people. But, when push comes to shove, I will only do what makes sense to me." Mind you, these are subconscious thoughts. Jurors want to be obedient and deferential to authority so, when confronted with a stern proclamation from an officer of the court, they try to be agreeable. But unless you ask good questions and listen carefully, they will not tell you candidly how they really feel.

Rosen did a masterful job when he got up in front of jurors. He engaged them in a conversation instead of a lecture. He got them talking instead of doing most of the speaking himself. And, most importantly, he did an excellent job of listening to them. For a consultant like me, this is the whole ball game. When jurors feel listened to, they are more likely to express their true feelings and not hide behind socially acceptable answers. And while I am trained and experienced in reading nonverbal behaviors—microexpressions, paralinguistic clues, and vocal idiosyncrasies—the real skill in voir dire is getting jurors to truly express their deepest feelings and experiences, some of which they themselves are not aware of. This is the essence of real rapport, where jurors share something personally meaningful and feel that the attorneys listen, acknowledge, and validate their experience. When you are able to really listen to jurors and find out what is important to them, you are building an audience for your case and understanding how to shape your evidence to meet their expectations.

Rosen's skill also allowed us to get more challenges for cause on jurors by getting them to state they couldn't be fair. Fidler had to excuse them, enabling us to save a number of our peremptory strikes. Additionally, he was able to get jurors to talk to each other, which allowed me to create a projection of how the jury would likely deliberate with each other. Seeing that dynamic was extremely useful in determining what our final jury panel would be.

Given the challenges of the case and the final jury pool, I felt that we had to raise our risk tolerance. Normally, you strike all the strong jurors that you think will go against you. And in truth, your main focus is not on the final twelve but on the two or three jurors that will be opinion leaders in the deliberation room.

Prosecutors need consensus, a get-along jury to render a unanimous verdict. They have traditionally eliminated African Americans and liberals, knowing these demographics are more skeptical of authority and police investigations. Prosecutors typically favor Asians, engineers, and conservatives, thinking them more deferential toward authority, respectful of law enforcement, and suspicious of sneaky defense lawyer tricks. These stereotypes and easy labels often replace meaningful information about juror attitudes toward the specific issues in a case. Jury *feelings* about police investigations and gun ownership are too granola crunchy for hard-evidence prosecutors. But these attitudes are the engine that will drive any verdict.

I knew we needed a strong, skeptical, and very independent jury. Not sheep. Defense lawyers, especially in tough fact cases, are also looking for outlier jurors, lone wolves who might split or hang the jury and take a few jurors with them.

So the peremptory-strike chess match began. Each of us went back and forth a few times, alternately chanting the phrase, "If it would please the court, we would like to thank and excuse . . ." In California, we have a procedure called back strikes. At any point, you can accept the panel of jurors. If the other side accepts as well, you are done and you have a jury. However, if they keep striking jurors, you can go back and start striking additional jurors and you are one strike ahead of them. If you pass twice and they keep striking, you are two strikes up on them. This way, when they are done, you can go back and cherry-pick certain jurors that you then want to take off after they are done, having a better means to shape the final panel. However, there is also a risk to this strategy.

At a key point midway through the strike section, the prosecution passed on the panel and accepted, thinking we would keep striking. In a traditional case, they had good reason to think we would. We had three engineers; a vice president of marketing for New Line Cinema; and an NBC producer who had covered the O. J. Simpson and Michael Jackson cases, and even the Spector case early on. These were traditionally conservative, pro-prosecution jurors. But we were not in a traditional case.

We took a break and went back into the jury room to discuss the panel. The lawyers all wanted to strike the engineers, the executive, and the NBC producer. I told them no. We had to accept the jury that we had, even though we had seven strikes left. They were stunned and started to argue with me. We asked the judge for more time. I explained to them that we had exactly what we needed on this panel. A group of highly intelligent, skeptical, and independent jurors. Jurors who could understand all of the science and forensic evidence that would be the cornerstone of our case. Jurors who would not be cowed or charmed by Alan Jackson and the prosecution. I specifically knew that the NBC producer would have a lot of experience with the forensic evidence and would know the reputations of our experts: Dr. Henry Lee, Dr. Werner Spitz, Dr. Vincent DiMaio, and Dr. Michael Baden. More importantly, he just seemed like a fair guy. While one of the civil engineer jurors who was a Mormon concerned most of the team, he knew about guns, had known friends who had been involved in accidental shootings, and had two co-workers who had committed suicide. More than anything, I wanted to keep this juror. He was smart, and he had a specialty in hydrological engineering, making him more receptive to the blood spatter arguments we would be making. He understood that accidental shootings happened and that people who are suicidal may not show it outwardly. I knew he was foreperson material.

I explained that, while risky, you want jurors who have had tough and even tragic life experiences in defense cases. They understand that sometimes bad things happen to good people. Jurors who are sheltered and have never had a tragedy are more reliant on the police and prosecutors to keep them safe, taking them at their word. I further explained to the team that while one strong juror could bully a group of weaker jurors into a verdict, if you had several, the chances of one juror strongarming the others was minimized. In fact, you increased the chances of disagreement with a number of alpha jurors. I convinced the team to stop and accept the panel, a move I knew would surprise the prosecution. I also had looked ahead and knew that we would run out of strikes just when we got to a very bad group of jurors.

When we went out and accepted the panel of jurors, the prosecution looked astonished. But you could almost hear the jaw of the NBC producer hitting the floor of the jury box. He could not believe it. Never in a million years did he think he would be chosen for *this* jury. Later,

Linda Deutsch, who covers all of the high-profile trials for the Associated Press, came up to me and told me we had made a good choice. She said she knew the producer and said that he was a very fair guy.

OPENING STATEMENTS

Jury selection is a lot like matchmaking. You are not only looking for how jurors will react to the evidence, you are also looking to see how their personalities interact with the attorneys and key witnesses. Given this dynamic, I was concerned after voir dire that Cutler would not be a good match stylistically for the kind of jury we wanted in the case. So I was conflicted. Even if there are differences of opinion on a high-profile team, I always try to arrive at an agreement to meet the wishes of both the client and lead attorneys, but more importantly, to serve the needs of the case. Cutler still voiced his opposition to making the science a key issue in the case. But we had just picked a jury who would be receptive to the science. We were at a crossroads.

I spoke to both Rosen and Linda Kenney Baden about these concerns, and they told me I should speak to Spector. After I did so, Spector made the decision to have Cutler share the opening statement with Baden. During a break in court one day, Cutler came up to me, red in the face, and said, "I'm going to kill you." Even though I knew it was an expression, given Cutler's past representation of Gotti, I did get a little worried.

I knew that Cutler would not be receptive to any of my suggestions, so I started working with Linda on the science side of the case for her portion of the opening statement. I wanted to find a theme that I felt characterized the prosecution's case and focused the jury on the forensic evidence. I came up with the phrase, "Is it story or is it science?" I wanted the jury to understand that the prosecution's case was a contrived story that was dependent on a lot of speculation and bad char-acter evidence about Spector. I wanted to contrast this with the hard science that showed Clarkson was holding the gun when it went off. We wanted to show that the prosecutors had manufactured this soap opera and then tried to make the evidence fit their story of the case.

It is important in an opening statement to organize the important evidence for the jurors in the case. Clear evidence increases the salience of those facts for the jury. We wanted to leave them with ten key sci-entific facts that would show that Clarkson was holding the gun when it went off.

1. The gun angle and the subsequent bullet path in Clarkson's mouth demonstrates an upward trajectory, suggesting Clarkson is holding the gun. Otherwise, Spector would have to be kneeling in front of her, which would have exposed him to more blood spatter, gunshot residue, and other tissue and bone from the explosion of the gunshot.

2. There is a majority of the gunshot residue on the tops of both of her hands, especially thumbs and forefinger, sug-gesting she is holding the gun. There is very little GSR on Spector, and Clarkson's DNA on his hands suggests he did not wash it off.

3. There is none of Spector's DNA on the gun and only another unidentified person's genetic material on a gun cartridge.

4. With no exit wound, all of the gases from the gun explo-sion release blood, tissue, bone, and teeth out of the mouth. There is no tissue, bone, or teeth on Spector's body, hair, or clothing.

5. There is a blood spatter pattern on her hands and dress, showing where her arms and hands held the gun. There is

a lack of blood volume on Spector's clothes and body, which would be more evident if he were holding the gun.

6. Clarkson was six feet tall and Spector is five feet, five inches. She was twenty-four years younger than him, worked out, and was healthier and stronger than him. There was no evidence of a struggle. People do not allow guns to be put in their mouths without a struggle.

7. Blood clotting on a cloth that was found in one of the bathrooms shows that minutes after she is shot, Spector tries to clean her face to help her. No effort is made to cover anything up.

8. There is a tooth fragment on the stairs from the explosion in her mouth. If Spector was in front of her, his body would have blocked the trajectory of the tooth.

9. The gun was not wiped down.

10. There was nothing under Clarkson's nails, suggesting that no struggle occurred between her and Spector.

On the day of opening statements, Jackson's presentation was crisp, animated, and strong. He had a PowerPoint with a black background and Courier font, making it look like a crime novel. He spent a great deal of time on Spector's history of guns and women, his drinking, and the events on the night of the shooting, ending with his statements to the limo driver DeSouza. He made a number of points about Spector's not calling 911 and attempts to cover up his crime. It was short on detail but it was a compelling argument, laying out the challenges I knew we would have in the trial.

When Cutler got up to give his portion of the opening statement, the prosecution told Judge Fidler that they would not be introducing some of the police statements made by both the officers and Spector at the time of his arrest. Because the prosecution did not introduce them, we could not bring them up either. Cutler had apparently based most of his opening statement on these exculpatory statements and was surprised that Fidler was now ruling that he could not use them. Cutler told the judge that he felt "like he had his pants down and was naked before the court," and that it was unfair. Fidler replied that it was the law.

So Cutler got up and, with very dramatic gestures, spoke about Spector's talent and genius and about Clarkson's suicide. He berated the police investigation and exclaimed that they "had murder on their minds." In Shakespeare's words, he "tore a passion to tatters, to very rags, to split the ears of the groundlings." There were a number of sustained objections, and he sat down.

Baden, by contrast, got up and spoke of the forensic evidence and the science in the case. She was pointed, clear, and measured in her opening, laying out the ten points we had outlined in her PowerPoint. The jurors were attentive, even if the press made the most out of the more dramatic prosecution opening and the fireworks between Cutler and Fidler.

Mick Brown from the British newspaper *The Telegraph* was covering the trial and wrote the following day, "Conventional wisdom has it that the job of counsel in any criminal trial is to present the jury with a narrative they can latch onto, and Mrs. Kenney Baden's address was a master class, presenting a series of telling points, helpfully numbered one to ten, describing how the copious amounts of blood-spatter and gun shot residue on Lana Clarkson's hands and dress, and the relatively small amounts of both found on Spector pointed to the fatal wound being self-inflicted."

DEFENSE TEAM ON TRIAL

After opening statements, we learned exactly how desperate the district attorneys were for a win in a big case. Unbeknownst to us, the prosecutors and the judge were investigating evidence tampering on the part of prior attorneys Shapiro, Caplan, and noted forensic experts Dr. Michael Baden and Dr. Henry Lee. Armed with statements by Shapiro's former law clerk Gregory Diamond, who was trying to sell a Hollywood screenplay, and would-be investigator Stanley White, who had accompanied Shapiro and the rest of the experts on the scene, the judge appointed a special master to look into allegations that either Baden or Lee had picked up and taken evidence from the scene.

This investigation was going on without our knowledge when we were in jury selection and preparing for opening statements. Instead of delaying opening statements, holding hearings, and making rulings, Fidler waited until after our opening statements to hold hearings on these issues. By then, we had told the jury that they would hear from the esteemed forensic experts Lee and Baden.

Fidler then held a series of hearings where he forced everyone to testify about what they had allegedly seen during that walk-through. There were conflicting accounts from both of the prosecution's witnesses: White saw Lee pick up something, and Diamond saw Baden pick up something, then recanted and said he did *not* see Baden pick anything up. Defense investigator Bill Pavelic said he didn't see anyone pick up anything. Fidler also forced Spector's former attorney Caplan to testify under threat of contempt, despite ethical rules by an attorney not to compromise the defense of her client, even a former client. She testified she saw Lee pick up something.

Both Baden and Lee testified they did not pick up anything. Both of these men had sterling reputations and had worked with prosecutors (including Los Angeles police and prosecutors) and defense attorneys alike for decades without the hint of impropriety. They had nothing to gain and everything to lose by hiding evidence. More importantly, if they had found something that had been missed by LAPD investigators in their thirty-six hours on the scene, it would have benefited the defense to turn it over.

But despite inconsistent and ambiguous testimony from the witnesses and the inherent credibility of Lee and Baden, Fidler ruled as a matter of fact that Lee had improperly taken evidence from the scene and Baden had not taken anything. This made it impossible for Lee to testify, as the judge would instruct the jury on his finding, and the prosecutors would be able to cross-examine him on this contrived piece of fiction.

In the Simpson case, the experts, including Lee and Baden, had hurt the prosecution badly. They were going to ensure that it didn't happen again.

THE PROSECUTION STORY

Since the prosecution knew the science was their weak suit, they led with emotion. No doubt they had done a focus group and knew, like we did, that jurors would conclude, despite physical evidence, that if Spector had held a gun on women before, he had done it this time as well. If you have one or two witnesses testifying against you, you may be able to discredit one or both of them. But five, no.

Again, it was my feeling that we should get these women on and off the stand as quickly as possible. The more time you spend on certain witnesses, the more important those witnesses become for the jury. Additionally, I felt we needed to treat these women with kid gloves when they were on the stand. Even if there were inconsistencies in their stories or questionable motivations for their testimony, it needed to be done with a light touch. If an attorney beats up a witness on the stand, jurors can easily believe that the defendant beat up the witness on the night in question. The witness's testimony becomes a reenactment of the incident they are testifying about. If they are scared and weeping on the stand, the jurors have a picture of the way they felt that night. If the attorney questioning them is combative and sarcastic, they can easily transfer that behavior to the defendant's conduct that night.

Rosen had prepared to use the softer touch with these women. He planned his questions to be short and to the point, get in and get out. The most recent incident with one of these women was more than a decade before Clarkson had been at the house. Many of these women still maintained relationships with Spector, even after these incidents. Some of them did not actually feel they were in danger, even when Spector had held guns on them. So using a softer touch made sense to bring out these important points.

Cutler was given the cross-examination assignment of one of the women from Spector's past, Dianne Ogden. She seemed like an easy witness because she actually still had feelings for Spector. On the stand, she confessed that she still loved Spector and had never truly feared for her life. But then, for some reason, Cutler decided to aggressively cross-examine Ogden. He started shouting at her, accused her of lying, and then she started to weep. Judge Fidler admonished Cutler twice to "lower his tone." It was a disaster. She appeared victimized by the defense, and by transference, Spector, one more time. It was the last witness Cutler would handle in the trial.

Adriano DeSouza was up next, and he proved to be a good witness for the prosecution. He was clear and consistent in his testimony about the events of the evening. He had driven Spector around that evening and had seen him get progressively drunker and more cantankerous. However, he also testified that Clarkson had willingly agreed to come to Spector's house. As in previous statements, he again clearly stated that he had heard a *pah* sound when he was sitting listening to music in the town car, then Spector had emerged from the house a few seconds later, gun in hand, stating, "I think I killed somebody."

Courts have relied on eyewitness testimony as the main staple of evidence since the onset of trials. Thousands of defendants enter plea deals or are convicted every year based on a witness's assured recollection. It also fits our common sense: if an independent person said they saw someone commit a crime, well, they must be right. Yet the fallibility of eyewitness testimony has been known in the research community for almost forty years. The Innocence Project, headed by Barry Scheck and Peter Neufeld, has calculated that nearly 75 percent of the 301 convictions overturned by DNA evidence have been as a result of mistaken eyewitness identification.

Elizabeth Loftus, a cognitive psychologist, has studied the malleability and fallibility of human memory for thirty years. She has conducted numerous studies that show how memories can be constructed, contaminated, and distorted. In one of her famous studies, participants who saw slides about an automobile accident and were asked how fast the cars were going when they smashed together remember seeing broken glass, even though there was none. In another study, researchers in Canada were successful in planting memories in about half of their subjects that they were attacked by a vicious animal when they were children.

There are five essential areas where eyewitness testimony has been shown to be inaccurate. First, leading questions, suggestive language, or additional information given to the witness affects how they remember an event. Second, inattention blindness suggests that some witnesses who are focused on certain events may completely miss other central aspects of the crime. Third, studies have shown that we are much more mistaken when identifying suspects of a different race or culture. Fourth, lineup misidentification occurs frequently where law enforcement intentionally or subliminally points a witness toward a certain suspect. Fifth, the trauma of a violent crime can profoundly alter the memory of that event.

New Jersey now gives an instruction to jurors about some of the potential problems with human memory. The science is so convincing in this area that other states are considering a similar instruction.

But the law treats the brain like a recording device. If a witness said they saw or heard something, it must be digitally stored on the brain's hard drive with perfect clarity, retrievable at a moment's notice. The law rarely appreciates the myriad of psychological factors that can affect that memory. The brain is actually more like an abstract painting than a photograph, with the witness freely interpreting the colors and shapes on the canvas according to his or her state of mind.

And so it was with Adriano DeSouza. It was hard to conclude from his testimony that he was lying when he saw Spector step out of his house that night. No doubt, he thought he did see Spector with a gun and thought he heard him say, "I think I killed somebody." But defense attorney Brad Brunon cross-examined DeSouza and ably brought up a number of factors that could have affected what he saw and heard: It was after four in the morning and DeSouza had been up for more than twenty-four hours. He had been listening to music in his car with the air running, and had been dozing when he heard the gunshot. The fountain in the courtyard next to the car was very loud, and opera was playing in the house. Spector had been drinking all evening, was slurring his words, and also spoke naturally in a softer tone. Although he spoke English fluently, DeSouza primarily spoke Portuguese at home.

When you play back the 911 recording, the first thing DeSouza says to the 911 operator is, "Yeah, I hear the uh, uh, uh, uh, like a noise, and then he opened the door and I think he—I killed her." Then the operator asks him to clarify. And it is not certain whether *DeSouza* thinks that Spector killed her or he thinks Spector said he killed her and was uncertain about it.

The team never wanted to concede that Spector ever said the words, "I think I killed somebody." However, it was always my belief that any homeowner like Spector would feel a degree of responsibility if a guest has killed themselves with one of the homeowner's guns. This guilt could have led Spector to believe that he himself had killed Clarkson by allowing her access to the gun.

Also, DeSouza said he saw Spector come out of the house with a gun in his right hand. This would have been difficult for Spector, given his shakiness, as he would have had to turn the door handle and, while holding the gun, work the latch with both hands, leaving much more blood evidence than had been found. DeSouza also says he saw the brown handle of the gun grip, despite Spector's hand covering it. Psychologists call this confabulation—a trick of the mind to interpose elements of a crime to help make sense out of it for the witness, whether they actually saw it or not.

Despite these inconsistencies, there was no knockout on cross-examination of DeSouza. He was as strong a witness as we knew he would be. However, we had hoped we had raised a few questions about what DeSouza saw and heard, just to take some of the momentum out of the prosecution's case.

The prosecution then went into its forensic case, conveniently slotted at the end of their emotional evidence. The first part of their case had all been focused on a simple circumstantial equation: Spector, when drinking, used guns to coerce women to do what he wanted. They hoped they had made their case to the jury as they knew they would be playing defense on forensics.

They led off with Dr. Louis Pena, the deputy coroner, followed by Steve Renteria, a criminalist with the Los Angeles County Sheriff's Department, and then went on to Dr. Lynne Herold, the senior criminalist for the sheriff's department. All three testified to support a few main propositions of the prosecution's case: that Clarkson and Spector had struggled, that the gun and bullets belonged to Spector, that blood spatter and gunshot residue showed he was within three feet of her when she was shot, and that he had tried to wipe down the gun and clean up evidence. Most importantly, they testified that Clarkson had not committed suicide.

Although Pena and Herold had only seen one inside-the-mouth gunshot wound between them in their thousands of autopsies and crime scene investigations, they dismissed the statistical evidence that

99 percent of all intraoral gunshot wounds are suicides. They dismissed the evidence that guns are the leading cause of suicide. They also dismissed the fact that women, although less frequently than men, use guns as the leading cause of their suicides. In his testimony, Pena relied on the textbooks of two of our experts, Dr. Spitz, a noted forensic pathologist, and Dr. Vincent DiMaio, a gunshot wound specialist, because of his unfamiliarity with the subject.

They also dismissed the lack of struggle evidence, the angle of the wound, the blood spatter, and the gunshot residue on Clarkson. Instead, these three scientists ventured into the realm of pure speculation, concluding that women don't commit suicides with purses over their shoulders, that women rarely shoot themselves when they commit suicide, and that they never commit suicide in strangers' houses. Pena also said that he relied on an investigator's reports in changing his conclusion from "accidental" to "homicide," rather than his own independent scientific evaluation. Barely a month after Pena had testified that women do not use guns to commit suicide, his boss, Dr. Lakshmanan Sathyavagiswaran, presented a paper discussing fifty women who had committed suicide by gun.

Pena said that he had concluded that Clarkson had "no evidence to indicate depression or any psychiatric disorder for depression." Yet he did not look at any of her computer files or perform a psychological autopsy. So he had no idea of her psychological state at the time he opined that she had no indication of depression.

The political pressure to conform opinions to the prosecution party line is not new. Coroners are elected officials. They have never gotten into trouble for supporting a prosecutor's or police officer's testimony. But they have lost their jobs for going against those they routinely work with. Criminal defense lawyers rarely have political ambitions. But there is a direct line from the district attorney's office to a judgeship, city council, assembly seat, or even higher.

Dr. Michael Baden recalls a story when he was first hired as a medical examiner in New York. On his first day of work, he was greeted by Frank Hogan, then district attorney for New York County, and chief medical examiner at the time, Dr. Milton Helpern. They told him, "Justice is a three-legged stool: the police, the prosecutors, and the medical examiner's office. We are all part of a team." Baden knew at that moment that his medical and scientific objectivity was secondary to the primary goal: to help law enforcement prosecute cases. That pressure becomes especially intense when the autopsy findings don't match the police investigation, for example, when an entrance wound in a suspect's back suddenly looks more like an exit wound. Baden explains that we all want to believe we live in a *High Noon* town, where Gary Cooper is the sheriff, and not an *Unforgiven* town, where Gene Hackman is the sheriff.

This is why, in its 2008 report, the National Academy of Sciences (NAS) criticized most of the forensic labs across the country, stating that there was very little science in forensic science. Bite mark, bullet lead, and microscopic hair analyses were all used and misused. There was vast inconsistency in the use of fingerprints, with some labs using nine points to match the fingerprints of a suspect and some using as little as four. The NAS recommended greater consistency and scientific standards in these labs. But more importantly, it recommended that forensic labs be independent, accessible to both prosecutors and defense attorneys alike to avoid the three-legged stool approach to justice. When we tried to enter the NAS report into evidence, Fidler would not allow it.

Again, to dispel any notion that Clarkson was depressed or suicidal, the prosecution ended their case with a number of witnesses testifying to Clarkson's happiness and hopefulness. Her agent spoke about her talent and promising prospects for her getting work in the future. Michael Bay, director of many blockbuster movies such as the *Trans-formers* series, testified to her talent and prospects of getting work. Her mother spoke about shopping for shoes with her upbeat daughter. A demo reel that she produced highlighting her comedic talents was played for the jury. In one of the skits, she plays a blackface Little Richard selling products on QVC, and in an outtake she is seen peeling off the prosthetic latex of the character. Despite the prosecution's efforts to create the image of happiness and light, cross-examination, done delicately by Rosen and Brunon, started to reveal the woman behind the mask, a darker and more complex picture of the troubled actress, struggling with age, beauty, money, and health.

Lawyers, judges, and legal experts all prefer the comfortable confines of linear reasoning to the complex world of psychology. They render the richly textured portrait of human experience, emotion, and choices into a single still image of that person. They then tell you the photograph is the sum total of that person.

Clarkson was neither "happy-go-lucky" nor was she "suicidally depressed." She may have been both, depending on the day, her mood, and whether an audition had gone well or poorly. These adjective labels merely describe the myriad of moods we all encounter as we live our lives. Spector, when he was interviewed at the police station the morning after the shooting, said, "And I don't know what her fucking problem was, but she certainly had no right to come to my fucking castle and blow her fucking head open." The prosecutors puzzled over this statement, not sure whether to use it as evidence. Was the crudeness of the statement indicative of the callousness of a murderer? Or is it merely an insensitive statement of Spector's innocence?

While both prosecution and defense lawyers struggle to define the characters of both victims and defendants, the real question for jurors is how the full portrait of that person makes them act in a particular way. In many ways, jurors have a much richer appreciation of the often chaotic and contradictory human condition than those in the legal profession. Jurors want to be inside the case, to be a part of it and get to know the real characters so they can make the important decision about guilt or innocence. They want to join Clarkson and Spector as they step from the town car and into the Pyrenees castle on that cool February night. They want to walk with them up the steps, the courtyard fountain rushing in the background, and step inside with them, the front door closing softly behind them.

THE SCIENCE DEFENSE

It was toward the end of the prosecution's case that lead attorney Cutler decided to take a leave to film his short-lived, ironically named television show *Jury Duty*. In it, "Judge" Cutler would preside over a jury of three celebrities who would hear small claims of real cases. In discussing his decision to leave the trial, Cutler reasoned, "Getting away from the pressure cooker is good for me. I can see more clearly." Cutler also stated he would be back in time for closing arguments and would be reading transcripts and watching the trial online. It was stunning and unprecedented that the lead lawyer for a client on trial for murder would leave the trial for weeks to film a television show. But since we knew that Cutler did not have much faith in the scientific evidence, it may have been a blessing.

We led off the case with the two renowned experts, DiMaio and Spitz. Both had virtually "written the book" on their specialties, and the coroner and medical examiner had both relied on DiMaio's and Spitz's texts in conducting their work. Along with James Pex, another forensic scientist, they tried to explain to the jury the scientific basis for the conclusion that Clarkson had been holding the gun when it went off.

First, the prosecution contended there was a struggle between Spector and Clarkson, using some bruising at her wrists as evidence. However, there was no sign of a struggle in the living room or in the foyer where Clarkson was shot. Additionally, there were no other cuts or bruises on her body from a struggle and no tissue, hair, or DNA from Spector under her fingernails. It would be assumed that no one would willingly let a gun be put in their mouth, yet there were no cuts or bruises around her lips and no damage to her teeth or gums from a gun trying to be forced into her mouth. All of the teeth that were broken were from the inside out from the blast of the gun in the mouth. The only bruise was on the tongue, which was again consistent with the blast from the gun as it went off. Then there was the size and age difference. Clarkson had at least seven inches, thirty pounds, and twenty-five years on Spector. Clarkson worked out regularly. Spector did not.

The autopsy also showed a slight upward trajectory to the bullet. This is consistent with the angle of someone who is holding the gun themselves. Spector would have to be kneeling in front of Clarkson in the chair in order to get that same trajectory. Then the expulsion of blood, tissue, gunshot residue, and teeth would have been sprayed over Spector's hair, face, and the upper portion of his jacket.

Which leads us to the cloud. When there is no exit wound, the pressure of gases from a gunshot blast builds up and those gases are expelled out of the only available orifice. That cloud of matter leaves a pattern that can tell forensic scientists much of how the shooting happened. Two of the experts concluded that this cloud of matter can travel up to six feet and even Pena has seen spatter that had covered an entire room. One of Clarkson's teeth ended up on the stairs twelve feet from where she sat, demonstrating the force of this gunshot blast. With that cloud, you would expect to see a volume of blood, tissue, and gunshot residue all over Spector's white coat, especially covering the right arm that Spector would have used to shoot the gun.

Spector's coat became a morbid canvas for the final portrait of Clarkson. Yet there were only sixteen small spatter droplets on the left-hand side of Spector's coat and nothing on the right side or right sleeve of the coat. Nothing except one small spatter on the right triceps side of the arm by the elbow. The laws of physics and gravity apply, even in the lofty heights of the Pyrenees castle. And blood spatter cannot shoot from Clarkson's mouth and then turn a corner to land on the elbow side of the jacket of the extended or bent arm of a shooter.

The spatter did cover the front of Clarkson's dress. But you would expect to see a void or space where Spector's shooting arm had been. There was no such void. Yet there was blood spatter and gunshot residue on Clarkson's hands exactly where you would have expected them if she had been holding the gun.

If Spector were in front of her as the prosecution alleged, he would have not only blocked and been a sponge for this cloud of matter, he would have also blocked the tooth that flew out of Clarkson's mouth and landed twelve feet away on the stairs.

And since the gun was a key piece of evidence for the prosecution, they argued that Spector had wiped it down. Yet there was checkering on the gun grip and crevasses on the gun that would easily have contained Spector's DNA. Yet none was found. The only DNA that was found on either the gun or the bullets was Clarkson's.

Where else did they find Clarkson's DNA? On Spector's hands, showing that he did not wash them. This is especially important, as they only found one particle of gunshot residue on Spector's hands. One. They had discovered many particles on the back of Clarkson's hands, and they did not even swab the palms, as they do in many other state forensic labs.

They also found Clarkson's DNA on Spector's genitals along with another unidentified person's. They found Spector's DNA on her nipple. Since the prosecution's theory is that he forces women at gunpoint to stay to have sex with him, why would Spector have forced the issue if he had already had sexual contact with Clarkson?

Then there were the statistics. Ninety-nine percent of intraoral gunshot wounds are self-inflicted. Pena, the deputy coroner, had never seen an intraoral gunshot wound that was a homicide. Spitz, in his fifty-four professional years of conducting sixty thousand autopsies, had never seen it.

So how did the blood get on Spector's jacket? We will never know for sure, although two theories could explain it. First, Spector could have been within the experts' six-foot spatter zone. He could have been moving to her as she shot. Dr. Baden also proposed a theory that he discovered during the trial. Even with an intraoral wound, she could have exhaled agonal breaths, which are the final breaths of a dying person. As Spector reached her, these agonal breaths could have expelled spatter droplets that could have gotten on the coat as he reached her. In fact, the grand jury was told about these agonal breaths and the possibility of spatter occurring this way. Yet it never made its way into trial.

As Jackson knew that his case could fall on the credibility and opinions of our experts, he took a no-holds-barred approach to them, excoriating them for how much money they had been paid, small inconsistencies in their reports or testimony, or the fact that they had not examined other small elements of the case. Later, in closing arguments, Jackson would call our use of these experts a "checkbook defense." The phrase was immensely ironic when the prosecution themselves have used the same experts on their cases and spent significantly more money prosecuting Spector than he had in defending himself.

While many in the public grouse about inequity of high-profile defendants paying for experts, they often don't consider the personnel, resources, and budget that the prosecution brings to bear in these high-profile cases. If the government decides a case is important, they have virtually unlimited resources to bring to the case. They don't just hire outside experts—they pay the salaries of every single person working in a crime lab, not to mention funding the crime lab itself. Almost all criminal defendants are overwhelmed by these resources and don't have the money to challenge the investigation or evidence against them.

THE JURY VISIT

A picture may be worth a thousand words, but it doesn't tell the whole story. Juries must rely on descriptions and pictures of a scene where the alleged crime happened. But what they want is a fuller, three-dimensional portrait of the scene. The prosecution usually controls the visual evidence in a case because the medical examiner and police control the scene during the investigation—it's incredibly rare for a defense attorney or expert to be present at the scene of an alleged crime during the initial investigation. Thus, the police take pictures of what they deem to be important.

We wanted the jury to have a full picture of the case. We wanted to demystify the Pyrenees Castle, the "crime scene," and let them do a little investigation for themselves. We wanted them to see the foyer, the chair where Clarkson sat, and the drawer that contained the empty holster. We wanted them to have a full view of that entranceway and that living room so they could evaluate the forensic evidence for themselves.

We asked Fidler to allow a jury visit. This would entail a field trip where jurors would be loaded in several vans and would then tour the scene in a highly controlled manner. There would be ground rules about where they would be able to look and how long they would be able to spend at the site. The judge agreed and it was arranged.

I sent a note to the defense team, asking to make sure that the fountain in the courtyard was turned on. I wanted the jurors to hear how loud the fountain was, to understand that it could have interfered with DeSouza's hearing Spector accurately when he came out of the house. Unfortunately, Spector mistakenly copied a disgruntled former employee when forwarding my email. She gave it to the prosecution, and they accused me of trying to manipulate the site visit. The fountain was either on or off. I had just asked that the fountain be turned on to represent what the sound would have been on the night of the shoot-ing. The judge shrugged this off, and the jury visit was on.

On August 9, 2007, the jurors toured Spector's home. They were limited to the courtyard, foyer/entranceway, and living room. They wanted to see other rooms in the house, but the judge denied their request.

Most significantly, the jurors had taken copious notes and had compiled a list of ten questions they wanted answered as a result of their visit. The questions revealed that they had been paying close attention and were tracking some of the forensic issues. Unfortunately, the judge told them that they could not ask questions. But this told me that they were indeed a strong and independent group, intelligently tracking the scientific evidence in the case. The civil engineer who had a specialty in hydrology helped compile the jury questions, another indication that he was a strong candidate as foreperson.

LANA CLARKSON

Depression is the inability to construct a future.
—Rollo May, psychologist

Everyone is afraid of suicide. Nobody wants to accept the possibility that someone they know who can look so normal one day can take their own life the next. It is always sudden, always unexpected. It defies logic and is deeply disturbing, because we all go to bed at night think-ing no matter how bad a day we had, things will somehow turn around.

Even within our team, there was reluctance to present this theory, even with the strength of the forensic evidence. That is why I felt it was important to redefine suicide for the jury. The prosecution had a simplified argument that suicide is always a carefully planned and intentional act. They also presented testimony to the jury that women don't shoot themselves, they don't kill themselves in other people's houses, they don't kill themselves after they have just gone shopping, and they don't kill themselves when they tell people "things are looking up."

Medical examiners and coroners have struggled with this issue. Estimates suggest that there are up to 20 percent of deaths in which the mode of death is undetermined. And yet uncertainty is the bane of a prosecutor's existence. Ambiguity is not tolerated, especially in a big case. It is understandable, this necessity to jump to conclusions. Especially when the medical examiner's job is to create certainty in cases. Things look like they are. Uncertainty for a jury means reasonable doubt and acquittal. And that goes in the loss column. The one-hour TV procedural at ten o'clock is the place for mystery, not a real crime investigation. Because when a woman is dead with the gun of another man at her feet, you want to know. Even if you never really will. You want to feel like you do know.

Except when there are real unanswered questions and a legitimate mystery.

The psychological autopsy was developed in the 1960s in the Los Angeles coroner's office to specifically deal with this kind of uncertainty. It is a medical procedure where, in conjunction with the coroner's officer, professional psychologists, psychiatrists, and other mental health professionals go back and try to discover if there is something in a decedent's background that would explain whether they would have killed themselves, lacking any other mode of death. A psychological autopsy can assist in clarifying this mode.

In March of 2004, when the investigators started looking at Clarkson's computer, these questions must have arisen because Steven Dowell, a criminalist from the coroner's office, suggested that a psychological autopsy should be done. After all, they had a box of letters that spoke to Clarkson's psychological state. However, in two meetings in May of 2004 and March of 2005 when a psychological autopsy was suggested, the district attorney claimed they had never heard of the procedure. Spector had already been indicted and charged, and so what did the district attorneys do? They told Dowell they had already established that Spector was the only one responsible for Clarkson's death. So Pena's superiors locked up all these documents and did not show them to anyone, including Pena.

What did the computer files and this box of letters describe about Clarkson's life? She had had an accident where she had broken both wrists (possibly explaining the wrist bruising), and pharmacy records showed that she had a dependence on Vicodin—at one point up to eighty pills in a month. There were times when she drank so heavily she would black out. The night she died, her blood alcohol content was 0.12.

Clearly dismayed by the lack of career advancement, she also had severe money problems, having to borrow from friends. She had just broken up a month before with a man she had called the "love of her life." In an email, she had said that she had a desire to "chuck it all" because "it was just too much for one girl to bear."

Reflecting these two portraits of Clarkson, her friends had differing things to say about her in court. Her best friend, oddly named Punkin Pie, discussed her depression in court, and Alan Jackson excoriated her for her traitorous, yet true, picture of the friend she loved.

We even had a hearing so that Fidler could decide whether madam Jody "Babydol" Gibson would testify. She had notified the defense that Clarkson had worked for her as an escort from 1992 through 1998 and that Clarkson had even had a gun fetish.

In high-profile cases, you always have witnesses who come out of the woodwork to testify. Many have hidden agendas: aspiring actors, dilettantes with screenplays or books they want to promote, or folks who just want to feel the spotlight warmth of public attention for a few days. Some genuinely want to help. The investigators vet them like senatorial candidates to see where their skeletons hang and how they might be pilloried in cross-examination. Because your case's credibility can hinge on their testimony. Ultimately, the lawyers have to make a call to see whether the witness will add to or detract from the case.

We felt we had to present the evidence to the court on the issue of Clarkson's familiarity with guns. We knew she used to go to the Beverly Hills Gun Club and had trained with guns for acting parts, so she was not afraid of weapons. But "Babydol" was trying to promote a book and had some obvious baggage. The judge ultimately ruled that Gibson's testimony was prejudicial and would not be allowed. We were both disappointed and relieved that this evidence about Clarkson would be excluded.

When we speak about suicide, we are often mistaken from a scientific standpoint. For a forensic pathologist, a suicide is a self-inflicted death, whether intentional, accidental, spur of the moment, or reckless. These pathologists see bodies frequently without notes and without explanations. In fact, one of the coroner's forms in Clarkson's case said "Suicide/Accident" at one point in the investigation. Whether Clarkson found the gun in the drawer in the foyer and decided to handle it, play with it, or was acting out a role, we will never know. Whether she was playing with the gun sexually with Spector and it accidentally went off, we will never know. But the forensic evidence and her own computer files strongly suggested she had the gun in her hand.

CLOSING ARGUMENTS

As the defense case started winding down, we wondered who would be giving the final summation of the case. Cutler was fully expecting, having been absent from the case for most of the trial, to return to give closing arguments. Which was impossible. He had alienated the jury in voir dire, had to punt in opening statements when the judge ruled against him, and had badly scorched a sympathetic witness. And he had also been gone for most of the trial. He couldn't close. He had no rapport with the jury, no on-the-ground knowledge of the infinite subtleties of the day-to-day trial events, and he failed to appreciate the most important evidence in the case, the science.

Finally, Spector decided that Linda Kenney Baden would do the closing arguments.

While many attorneys start writing their closing arguments during the trial, we were given less than two weeks to write a closing argument in a six-month trial. We worked without sleep, me, Michelle Ward, and Jonathan Ross from my office. We reviewed trial transcripts of testimony, organized the evidence, crafted the language, and developed a PowerPoint of images and summary bullets for jurors to note and hopefully use in deliberations.

Some feel closing arguments should be short, an hour at most. But in a long trial, you often need to spend real time in closing to remind the jury of testimony that happened months before, to give the defense weight, to interpret what all that evidence means, and how it all fits into a verdict.

On September 5, 2007, Jackson gave a strong and compelling recap of all the evidence in the case, mirroring his opening statement and emphasizing all of the women that Spector had held a gun to, the testimony of DeSouza, and deriding all of our experts and thus the science as a "checkbook defense."

The following day, Baden spent a day going through all of the evidence in her closing argument: explaining but not excusing Spector's behavior with the women, how DeSouza could have misheard Spector, and extensively going through the science that showed Clarkson holding the gun when it went off.

She also outlined the motivation and the trajectory of the decision to prosecute Spector. Detective Paul Fournier, in his initial communication on the first day of the investigation, stated, "This is going to be a high-profile case, no doubt about it. He's a man with a lot of money, okay, he's wealthy and it's going to be considered high profile, okay? It's going to be in the news and it's gonna be . . . I know, it's going to be a big thing."

The coroner's office put in their business records on that first day that the case involved a celebrity, and the investigator from the crime lab put that the case was going to be high profile in the first line of his report.

And Pena went to Spector's house, unusual for a deputy coroner. Even though Pena could not find the gunshot wound at the scene, he wrote "homicide" on his notes when he returned to the office, even before he performed the autopsy. He testified that he was "hoping" for a gunshot wound outside the mouth because it would have "made things easier."

The prosecutors were so confident in this jury, their evidence, and the court's rulings, Fidler decided to only instruct jurors on a second-degree murder charge. Second-degree murder does not require "express malice" or a deliberate intent to kill, but "implied malice," where the person who kills another shows an abandoned and malignant heart. But most importantly, the person charged with second-degree had to be the one holding the weapon. With the second-degree murder charge, Spector had to have an intent to harm or at least a reckless disregard for human life. A manslaughter charge would have made it much easier for a jury to convict Spector, as they would only have to have found that he had either acted in the heat of passion or failed to act with "due caution."

THE VERDICT

As Tom Petty says, the waiting is the hardest part. It's even harder when what you're waiting for is a life-changing verdict. So you become superstitious. You tip more heavily. You wear your lucky ties. You try to do everything the same lest you jinx the verdict. And you wait. I broke a tooth, which I did not take to be a good sign.

A quick verdict often means an acquittal. A longer verdict usually means the jury is finding a way to convict. And when it drags on too long, it probably means there is a split and maybe a hung jury. But there are no hard-and-fast rules. There's always a chance the jury can go either way no matter how long or short they take.

The jury was out for three days, and then an odd thing happened on the fourth day. There was notice from the court at the end of the day. We were told to come down to Judge Fidler's courtroom. We were not told there was a verdict. Just come down to court. The jurors were gathered, and we were told that there was a question from the jury. They had apparently informed the court the day before that they were hung 7–5 (not saying whether it was for acquittal or conviction) and were confused about one of the instructions.

A 7–5 split is a significant calculus in a criminal verdict, especially for a prosecutor. While they may be able to dismiss one or two holdouts in a hung jury as an anomaly or a glitch in jury selection, a 7–5 split is undeniably a statement about the merits of the case. In a significant split after the jury formally hangs, the prosecutors must think long and hard about re-trying the defendant or about offering a much better plea deal. When only one or two jurors are causing the hung jury, the prosecutors are much more likely to re-try, especially in a high-profile matter.

The court brought the jury in and proceeded to ask them about where they were confused about the instructions. This was highly unusual to do in open court as the deliberation process is sacrosanct, and it is problematic to start asking jurors to openly disclose details about their decision-making process. Instead of just giving what they call an Allen or "dynamite instruction," which basically tells jurors to try harder to come to a verdict, Fidler told them to come back the following day. He then told us he was considering giving the jury a brand-new instruction on a manslaughter charge.

This was stunning to us. On a legal level, prosecutors had tried their case thoroughly as a murder case, including arguing throughout that Spector had acted with malice aforethought, the legal definition of murder. A manslaughter charge, which they had never breathed a word about, would have allowed the jury to find Spector guilty if he acted with a conscious disregard for human life. This would have allowed the jury to reach a compromise in order to find him guilty, with the defense never having had a chance to address the evidence of manslaughter. Fidler instructed us to come back the next day, and the appellate team immediately started their research. Their conclusion was that this would be an unprecedented ruling and probably a slam-dunk appeal to get the verdict overturned if Spector was found guilty.

Obviously, Fidler came to the same conclusion. The next day he informed us that he would not give the manslaughter instruction. Instead, he decided to define the second-degree murder instruction further for the jury. This was also highly unusual, as most judges, when juries have questions about instructions in deliberations, just read them the instruction again and tell them to do their best.

So Fidler brought the jury in and instructed them that they could find Spector guilty under three scenarios: he was guilty if he intentionally killed her, as the prosecutors had alleged; if the gun had gone off accidentally while he was holding it as a result of reckless behavior; or if he had somehow been responsible for the gun going off, even if he were not holding it. Some examples Fidler gave were if Spector had been holding the gun and it had fallen out of his hand and had gone off in her mouth, he would be guilty. Or if Spector had left his gun on a table, and there was an earthquake or a big gust of wind and the gun fell off, discharged, and killed someone, he would be guilty. Even if he forced her to put the gun in her mouth somehow and it had gone off accidentally, he would be guilty.

It was here where we really felt that Fidler had clearly decided he wanted to steer the jury toward a guilty verdict. The last two scenarios had never been put into evidence or argued by the prosecutors. We felt the effect was that it gave jurors the ability to arrive at a pseudo-manslaughter verdict without explicitly instructing them on this inappropriate charge. We made our objections, but the jury was so instructed and retired to deliberate toward what we thought would be a guilty verdict.

But then an amazing thing happened. The jury stayed split. Three of the five jurors moved toward guilt but two jurors remained unconvinced. The foreperson, the hydrological engineer that our team had initially been so worried about, and a court clerk from another courtroom downtown were the holdout jurors. The clerk said finally she would change her vote to guilty but the rest of the jurors, in an extraordinarily respectful gesture, insisted that she vote not guilty if she truly did not feel that the prosecutors had proven their case.

So the jury finally delivered their verdict on September 26, 2007—they had hung. A hung jury is the verdict when twelve people cannot unanimously decide on a verdict. The jury we selected seemed to respond to the scientific issues, yet were conflicted between the natural pull of the testimony of the past women and the limo driver. In essence, this jury reflected exactly what we saw in our focus groups before the trial.

Spector was released later that day, and news helicopters caught him dancing with his young wife next to the fountain by his front door where he had emerged one cool February morning.

AFTERMATH

As Spector danced in his driveway, prosecutors vowed to re-try him. The public was outraged that the jury would not convict. Court TV hosts Nancy Grace and Ashleigh Banfield excoriated the jury foreperson, a most principled and conscientious man, on their shows. Both he and his children received death threats. Even Spector's family was divided, with his daughter believing in her father's innocence during the trial and his son voicing a belief in his guilt.

The second trial started close to a year after the first one concluded, with a few cast changes. The entire defense trial team was replaced by Doron Weinberg, an experienced Bay Area lawyer who specialized in retrials. Jackson returned to re-try Spector, but Dixon was replaced by Truc Do, a female lawyer who eventually became a white-collar criminal defense attorney. The evidence played out similarly to the first trial, with significantly less public interest. Although the defense asked Fidler to recuse himself for bias, he refused and conducted the second trial, including making sure that the jury received a manslaughter instruction.

This time, the prosecution knew the defense game plan. They tried a shorter, more streamlined case. I consulted with Weinberg on jury selection, and during the case he ably tried the defense's theory of Clarkson's final moments. This time, the jury finally convicted Spector after a week of deliberations. In post-trial interviews with jurors after the second trial, they described the prosecution's version of events to be "more likely" to have happened than the defense's version.

"More likely to have happened" is a civil standard of proof called "preponderance of evidence," which is not the standard in a criminal trial. In a criminal trial, as most people know, a jury must find a defendant guilty "beyond a reasonable doubt." However, there are no hard-and-fast rules to what a reasonable doubt is. Each juror brings his or her own unique definition of what a reasonable doubt is.

Despite the appellate issues regarding the legality of the testimony of the numerous women who testified about Spector's penchant for guns, and Fidler's conduct in the two trials, the California appellate court refused to overturn the verdict. It is now on its way up to the U.S. Supreme Court on the issue that Fidler made himself a witness during the second trial when he concluded for the jury that a waffling coroner's assistant was pointing to a particular part of her hand where she saw Clarkson's blood spatter. Jackson used the tape of Fidler's conclusion in his closing argument.

Despite years of trials, millions of dollars, and thousands of hours of research and analysis, only Spector will ever know what really happened that night. The trial revealed the loneliness, desperation, and dark sides of both Spector and Clarkson. We all have our demons, specters we try to shake—outrun, outwit, outdrink. But these ghosts catch us in our darkest hours. Maybe the ghosts of John Lennon and Spector's father and son visited Spector early that morning on February 3, 2003.

People of the State of Florida
v. Casey Anthony

| | | | | | | | | | TWO JURIES AND TWO VERDICTS | | | | | | | | | |

Sometimes the smallest things take up the most room in your heart.

—A. A. Milne

Reconciliation of realities is one of the paradoxes of high-profile trials. There is the prosecution's reality, the defense's reality, the media's reality, and ultimately the jury's reality. While the public commonly thinks of *justice* as a fixed result, justice is actually the process whereby the jury merges and reconciles these realities.

On an unseasonably warm November day in 2008, I met Jose Baez for the first time at the Essex House Hotel, off Central Park. He had heard of me, and we had arranged to meet in New York to discuss how to handle the avalanche of publicity inundating his case. Nancy Grace had already done more than a hundred shows on the case, turning her astringently prosecutorial eye to any detail that might prove Casey Anthony's guilt. And she had plenty of details.

Casey Anthony was a young single mother who lived with her two-year-old daughter Caylee and her parents George and Cindy Anthony in an Orlando, Florida, suburb. For thirty-one days in 2008, the young child was not seen, and when asked by her parents about their granddaughter, Casey would say that her nanny, Zenaida Gonzalez, had the child while Casey was at work at Universal Studios. After Casey's car had been towed and her father smelled a strong odor in the trunk when he picked it up, her parents confronted Casey about their granddaughter. Casey tearfully told them that Gonzalez had Caylee, and that she had not seen her for a month. The police were called and while investigating the young girl's disappearance, they learned that Casey had not worked at Universal Studios for years, and that the nanny had never existed. They uncovered many other lies that Casey had told. Most damaging was the fact that Casey had seemed carefree to friends and family during the thirty-one days, attending parties and getting a tattoo inscribed on her shoulder, *Bella Vita*, or "beautiful life" in Italian. The body of Caylee Anthony was discovered five months later in a wooded area within a quarter mile of the Anthony home, wrapped in a black plastic trash bag. Duct tape had been found attached to the skull. Casey was arrested and charged with the murder of her daughter.

The Sunshine Law in Florida makes every single document exchanged between the prosecution and defense a public record, press-ready to be posted on any news site. There would be a court filing and a new round of documents would blaze across the Internet, without explanation or context, showing Casey's text messages, phone calls, visited websites, and photos, all taken from the Anthonys' shared computer. The contrasting photos of Casey drinking and partying while her daughter was missing filled millions of viewers with howls of rage and indignation at the seemingly brazen, uncaring evil embodied by this petite, twenty-three-year-old mother. Baez asked me how all of the shows, stories, and photographs would affect our ability to pick jurors when the trial began. I calmly looked at him and told him that the trial had already begun.

All missing children become our children. We temporarily adopt them. Perhaps we feel that rush of panic when we momentarily lose our own kids in a park or a store. Perhaps it is a child's unfulfilled promise. Perhaps it reminds us of innocence we have lost. But there is something about the purity of a child that breaks all hardened barriers of cynicism and resigned aphorisms about the "cruel world." Caylee's smiling pictures and videos reached out, compelling a city, a state, and then a country to say, "No. We will find you." It prompted everyone who saw her to believe they could protect her.

Thus, the public became de facto investigators, searching for clues to the missing Caylee. Prompted by pleas from George and Cindy, who seemed to become adoptive parents while Casey was in jail during the search for Caylee, nearly two thousand volunteers in the summer and fall of 2008 combed miles of wilderness and swamps to locate this beautiful little girl, hoping against hope. Texas EquuSearch, a large search and recovery organization that coordinated volunteers to look for missing persons, led the effort. Millions watched daily for a promising sign, a fleeting whisper of a miracle. Others donated thousands of dollars of their own money to support the search effort. They pored over the documents already available on the case. In water cooler conversations, they mapped out clues to the girl's whereabouts the way they had seen it done on the many police procedurals they'd watched over the years. They held candlelight vigils. They prayed. And then they were betrayed.

On December 11, 2008, after five months of searches, Caylee's body was found a quarter mile from her own home, nineteen feet from the road. Hope dashed and doubt gone, millions sought an explanation for how this could have happened. How could a woman not report her own child missing after thirty-one days? How could she go to clubs, drink, laugh, and carry on as if nothing had happened? The public couldn't get this explanation from Casey. They had already heard of her lies to the police and her parents. The 911 calls of her mother and her interview with the detectives where she spoke of the fictional nanny were available to anyone to listen to at the touch of a mouse click.

So they turned to those they trusted to help them understand this bizarre behavior. They turned to Nancy Grace, the matron saint of prosecutors and platitudes. And Saint Grace gave them the answer: Casey Anthony, the now infamous "tot mom," was guilty of killing her own child—the most reviled and primal crime a parent could commit. More disquieting, Casey appeared to almost celebrate her daughter's death in the thirty-one days before her body was found.

And so, in December of 2008, the public's role shifted from investigator to prosecutor. As the press and the Orange County district attorneys dug into Casey's life, they revealed more details to fuel the public's ire. She was a young, promiscuous single mother. She exposed her daughter to multiple boyfriends. She lied. She would leave her daughter to go and party. She did not report her own child missing. These behaviors violate puritanically rooted social norms and deeply held moral values. And while they may be tolerated in a normal young woman, these violations become fatal character flaws when that woman's child dies unexpectedly, especially under suspicious circumstances.

Those who might have believed that the child had somehow been abducted now became convinced that there was only one person who could be responsible for the child's death—her mother. In the iconography of women criminal defendants accused of killing their children, such as Andrea Yates or Susan Smith, Casey Anthony did not appear to be crazy, therefore she must be evil.

Baez called me as soon as Caylee's body was found. There were news helicopters, news vans, and wall-to-wall media coverage. It was on every local station in Orlando. But Casey didn't know. They didn't tell her. The sheriffs brought her into a holding cell under some pretense, left a television on with the news coverage, and then filmed her as she realized what she was watching. In the tape, you see her bent over in her chair, crying with her head in her hands as she realizes that the news footage is the discovery of her dead child. Prosecutors set up this theater, thinking they could catch Casey unguarded, cold and unemotional, to demonstrate to the jury her callous disregard for Caylee's life. But they captured her grief instead.

The police were already focusing on the forensic evidence from the trunk of Casey's car. Dr. Henry Lee, the renowned forensic scientist, had already volunteered to examine this evidence, but Baez needed an expert to examine the remains for the cause of death. Knowing that I had worked with Linda Kenney Baden and Dr. Michael Baden on the Spector case, he asked about them and we all had dinner when we met in New York. Linda's reputation as one of the preeminent attorneys on criminal forensic evidence had only grown since her work on the Spector case. Michael Baden was the most renowned forensic pathologist in the country, appearing in his own show, *Autopsy*, on HBO as well as working on the Claus von Bülow and Byron De La Beckwith trials and conducting examinations into the deaths of President John F. Kennedy, Sid Vicious, John Belushi, and many others. Linda flew down to Florida and started working with Baez in December 2008 on the forensic evidence.

As there were numerous misassumptions and errors that were being dispersed into the mainstream media by pundits and personalities, we had to make some key strategic decisions in the case. Do we speak out to counter the negative publicity in the case or stay silent? Do we affirmatively put out a defense theory, or just give the press enough information to actively question the prosecution's emerging story of the "crime"? The story of Casey's guilt had already gained tremendous momentum, becoming the media's reality of the case. It was my belief that not only would it be futile to try to turn the tide, but that we may actually be able to harness the hysteria and use it to our advantage.

The more the actual evidence mingled with psychics, screaming mobs, former boyfriends, salacious sex, and death threats, the better. The harder it would be for a jury to tell what was real versus what was *tabloid* real. The risk, of course, was that tabloid real would become the only reality for the jury.

I advised Baez that no one wins these trials by playing it safe. We needed to let the press and the prosecutors build their case while we patiently prepared. I thought, at some point, the press would tire of their relentless criticism of Casey and the defense team, and would turn their skeptical eye to the prosecution's theories, evidence, and strategies. But I was wrong.

In monitoring the press coverage on television, print, radio, and the Internet, not only was the public outraged by Casey's behavior, but the journalists were as well. I underestimated the emotional investment that both the public and the press had in Casey's guilt. On February 10, 2009, a memorial was held for Caylee Anthony, arranged by Casey's parents, Cindy and George. An estimated audience of 1,100 attended, including strangers who drove hundreds of miles to pay their respects. Casey could not attend as she was in the Orange County Jail. But the public expected her to watch, and they watched her reaction to see if it fulfilled their expectation of a grieving mother or a cold killer. Since we knew that having no reaction to her own daughter's memorial would surely cause a public outrage, she was forced to make a public statement.

> *I miss Caylee every day and every minute of every day. I can't be there for Caylee's funeral, but someday I want to go and visit her grave and tell her how much I miss her.*
>
> *I allowed my parents to be in charge for the funeral for Caylee. I told them I wanted her buried in a casket and I wanted there to be a gravestone so I could go and visit her. I asked them if there could only be a private funeral for just the family.*

I know they cremated her. I still don't want a public event with cameras and everybody around for Caylee's service, but I can't stop my parents from doing what they want. I truly hope that it will help them.

—Casey Anthony response to Caylee memorial
read by Jose Baez

At this point, the adoption was nearly complete. Caylee seemed to belong more to George, Cindy, and Casey's brother, Lee, than to Casey. She seemed to belong to millions who had watched and prayed for her return. And they were angry with Casey for killing *their* child. Although I have worked in numerous high-profile cases where the public's distaste was apparent, I have never run across a stronger or more palpable anger than I encountered in this case. Not in tragic death civil cases, not even in other death penalty cases. There is frustration anger and there is betrayal anger. This was an anger born of deep hurt. It was personal.

As the months rolled on, the stories rolled on as well. The tapes of jail visits between Casey and her parents were released, scrutinized, and posted on YouTube. When there was nothing new, the press reported on Casey's jail allowance and her junk food purchases. Helicopters followed Baez to report on his alleged mortgage problems. And the audience built. Social media lit up with constant blog posts on the case. The Caylee Daily, a site started during the case, posted eight million hits by the time the trial started. Justice4Caylee as well as numerous other blogs and newly created websites openly pursued a pro-prosecution editorial bent, calling into question every defense move and lauding every minute detail that could implicate Casey in her daughter's death.

Scot Safon, the executive vice president of programming for

Headline News Network, gave an interview where he openly stated how important the Anthony trial was to HLN. "It's a gigantic deal for us . . . It speaks to so many issues, to the responsibility parents have, to the responsibility grandparents have, to the vulnerability of children, to the fact that this could play out in the midst of what might seem a normal family." He went on to discuss how audiences across the country felt they could relate to the people in this "story." This is the same chord that entertainment executives look for in both fictional and reality television: that the audience feels like they know the Anthonys. "Based on what we hear, the audience says it's outraged, but there's an undertone of identification with the anxieties that a story like this points out."

And it is at the intersection of the two highways, justice and journalism, that the First and Sixth Amendments again collide. The First Amendment guarantees the right to free speech, and the Sixth Amendment guarantees the rights of a defendant to due process and an impartial jury. There is nothing in the Constitution about fairness. However, the founders did understand the importance of impartiality. Our first trials in this country were tried by local juries—those familiar with the parties in the case and the matter being tried. However, in 1807, this changed with a case of some notoriety at the time.

On February 20, 1807, Aaron Burr, former vice president of the United States, sat and played chess in Fort Stoddert with the daughter of the judge who was responsible for his arrest on the charge of treason. Burr was known as one of the founding fathers of political campaigning, wooing the members of Tammany Hall, a New York City political organization, to win over members of the newly formed delegates of the Electoral College in presidential campaigns. Thomas Jefferson and Burr tied in electoral votes for the 1800 presidential campaign before Alexander Hamilton, a former law partner of Burr, swung the election in Jefferson's favor. Later, Burr and Hamilton exchanged accusations after a heated election in which Burr had lost the New York governorship. Burr demanded a retraction by Hamilton of supposed assertions against Burr's character. When Hamilton refused, he was challenged to a duel. In a field in Weehawken, New Jersey, Burr shot and killed Hamilton in a duel in 1804. In 1805, Burr foresaw a war with Spain. With the help of General James Wilkinson, he gathered a group of about eighty men to train and outfit them for the exploration and claiming of territory prior to this conflict. Wilkinson turned Burr's plans in to Jefferson, who promptly had Burr arrested for treason. The animus between Burr and Jefferson was well known, and the newspaper accounts of the treason charges against the former vice president were voluminous and highly inflammatory.

When jury selection for his trial began on August 3, 1807, Burr's lawyers argued that "the public mind has been so filled with prejudice that there was some difficulty in finding impartial jurors." Only four of the forty-eight jurors questioned that first day could be seated, most admitting that they had been predisposed toward Burr's guilt by what they had read in the newspapers. While many were eliminated from serving, a few jurors who had expressed negative views of Burr and the alleged treason were still seated on the jury. On September 1, 1807, the jury acquitted the former vice president, setting up the long battle between the First and Sixth Amendments. From that point on, the courts decided that a jury should be an "indifferent" group of citizens that had no knowledge of the case or interest in the outcome. This battle rages today in courtrooms, and on televisions, computers, and iPhones across this country.

While the jurors in the Burr treason trial had been exposed to many newspaper accounts of the charges, they did not have the electronic media or the journalism standards that we now face today. In today's journalism model, the media are the masses with Twitter feeds, Facebook, and blog posts feeding mainstream news sources. In turn, mainstream media must feed the public's 24/7 news hunger with a steady diet of hard news stories, rumors, speculation, and opinions redigested across media platforms.

The Sixth Amendment of the United States Constitution reads, "In all criminal prosecutions, the accused shall enjoy the right to a speedy and public trial, by an *impartial jury of the State and district wherein the crime shall have been committed*, which district shall have been previously ascertained by law . . ." But when you have more than 75 percent of the American population who use the Internet and television for their news, you have a much more indistinguishable district. In fact, the venue for a court case is subjected to more national news and opinions than in the past, making a "district" in the constitutional sense much more national.

And this is where the battle between the First and Sixth Amendments became a full war during the Anthony trial, challenging the very foundation of our criminal justice system and raising troubling questions. Should the public be able to vote on a defendant's guilt? How does one seat an impartial jury when 90 percent of the jury pool knows a great deal about a case and already believes the defendant to be guilty? If the public already believes the defendant to be guilty, should a defendant have to prove their innocence?

This was especially problematic in our case, where jurors who watched numerous television shows or read about the actual evidence on the Internet would be instructed to only consider evidence from the witness stand and law from the bench. In 2011, the term *Casey Anthony* was the fourth most searched Google term. The courts typically deal with this prickly issue by blithely turning a blind eye to the problem. Judges across the country routinely ask jurors *if* they can "set aside" all that they have seen and heard about a case or opinions they have of the guilt of the defendant. Asked this question by the robe of authority, jurors with all good intentions obligingly answer "yes." No one wants to leave the impression that they are an unfair person. Actually setting aside all previous information, especially with strong emotional content, is of course a psychological impossibility.

The Supreme Court has dealt with this issue a number of times, the most recent being the decision they made upholding some of the convictions of Jeffrey Skilling in one of the Enron trials. While the Court has typically recognized that pretrial publicity can have a prejudicial effect, they have ruled that there are numerous ways to cure this effect. Previously, the justices ruled that jurors are not required to be "totally ignorant of the facts and issues involved." However, the courts have been pretty antiquated in their view of the media, let alone the Internet, usually considering only newspaper or television stories to constitute publicity exposure while ignoring Internet stories or social media. "Not totally ignorant" leaves a lot of room for a juror who has seen dozens of negative stories about Casey.

At the end of 2010, I wrote a memo to the defense team asking them to consider making a motion to dismiss the whole case, as I believed Casey's due process rights had been so compromised that she could not get a fair trial. For this, I referred them to the Sheppard v. Maxwell Supreme Court case involving the trial of Dr. Sam Sheppard that I discussed in the Simpson chapter. Justice Black's sharply worded opinion stated numerous similarities to the Casey Anthony case, including the "circuslike" atmosphere of the trial: "Throughout this period the newspapers emphasized evidence that tended to incriminate Sheppard and pointed out discrepancies in his statements to authorities."

Since it was not realistic to expect the court to dismiss the case, I had hoped that such a motion would push the judge to control some of the media and set some ground rules (or at least some suggestions) for the media's coverage of the trial. Baez had repeatedly asked the court to seal documents in the case. Judge Stan Strickland (and later Judge Belvin Perry) refused to seal any documents aside from Caylee's remains, citing First Amendment issues. And here lay my greatest concern for my client—that the public's "right to know" outweighed

Casey's individual right to a fair trial. In their rulings, Judges Strickland and Perry clearly chose the press's and public's rights over the defendant's rights. The Sunshine Law made it difficult for them to shut down the media machine. However, I wish we could have had an open and candid discussion with the judges, the press, and the prosecution to discuss solutions to manage the onslaught of coverage. The Orange County Sheriff's Office and the county prosecutors had to spend countless hours fielding calls from both concerned citizens and crackpots, following empty leads and wild speculations. At the height of the 2008 to 2009 recession and during huge Florida budget deficits, the total tab for both of these offices had to run into the millions in costs and allocation of scarce resources.

There is a type of practiced denial that operates as a survival mechanism in high-profile cases. Judges and even the lawyers like to pretend they are just trying a case like any other case. In refusing Baez's request to seal documents, both Strickland and Perry shrugged off the potentially prejudicial effect this might have on the jury pool in favor of the free speech arguments. Strickland soon became a casualty after he spent time privately discussing matters with a pro-prosecution blogger. Judges must avoid even the *appearance* of impropriety, and his conversations brought on a defense motion for recusal. In granting this motion and recusing himself, Judge Strickland made biting comments about the defense, stating that he felt it ironic that defense counsel was accusing him of behavior that the defense had engaged in. However, a defense attorney is by definition partisan, while a judge must avoid even the impression of favoritism.

One of the first orders of business was to file a motion for change of venue. Orlando had been permeated with stories about the case, and many in the community had direct participation in looking for Caylee and memorializing her. Because of this exposure and involvement, we needed to look for another place for the trial. However, there were only a small handful of venues in the state that were considered to be neutral enough to give a defendant a fair shot in a capital case. We felt that if we could get the trial moved farther south to Miami or another southern district, it would be less likely that the jury there would have had the same degree of press exposure.

I wanted to conduct some community attitude surveys—normal in these high-profile trials—to demonstrate the bias in Orlando. However, since Casey and her family had no money to pay for the surveys or my services, we petitioned the court for funds to conduct the surveys and to help with jury selection. The court refused. Since the prosecutors were now asking for the death penalty, I chose to continue working pro bono for the remainder of the case.

Linda Kenney Baden also could not get court funds and could not afford to pay her own travel and lodging for months of the trial. She had to withdraw from the case but laid a strong foundation for the forensic challenges to the prosecution's case, staying on to advise Baez for the duration of the trial. Andrea Lyon, a noted death penalty lawyer from Chicago, had to withdraw from the case because of similar circumstances. J. Cheney Mason, an extremely experienced Florida criminal defense attorney with death penalty experience, along with Dorothy Clay Sims, a civil litigation lawyer, also joined the team to help focus on the prosecution's dubious forensic case and their "expert" witnesses.

I provided Baez with an affidavit to submit to the court as to my belief that a change of venue was necessary to provide Casey with a fair trial. We completed as much of a media analysis as we could to study the relative exposure of different communities in Florida to press coverage of the case. In the end, both the prosecutors and the judge agreed that the pervasive bias in the Orlando community made it necessary to change venues. The question became where to go. There were extensive negotiations between the prosecution, the judge, and the defense about an appropriate venue.

The judge then made an unusual ruling. Perry said that he would import a jury from another venue to Orlando, where he would sequester them in an undisclosed location for the duration of the trial. This meant that we would travel to another community, pick a jury there, and then bring them back to Orlando to hear the case. This is unusual but not unheard of in Florida. What was unusual was that Perry refused to let us know where we would be picking a jury. We had no idea where in Florida we would be going.

This posed a couple of problems for us. First, based on our research, there had been thousands of stories all over Florida. Therefore, we had no confidence that the rest of the state would be able to give her a fair trial. We should have been able to look at the new community, study it, and decide whether that venue could impartially listen to the case. However, with Perry's order, we would not know where we were going until the eve of trial. This would be too late to study the new venue to determine whether it would be an appropriate place for the jury selection. Second, the imported jury would be sequestered in Orlando, a mixed bag for a defendant. While the jurors would be protected from inflammatory publicity during the trial, they would have to pass the protestors entering the court every day, feeling the tension in the Orlando community and the desire for the conviction. We were also concerned that the Orange County sheriffs, who would be caring for the jurors, would make them identify more with law enforcement in the case. With these concerns, I flew out to Florida to meet with the defense team.

ORLANDO

The origin of the city's name is uncertain, some claiming it comes from the character Orlando in Shakespeare's *As You Like It* who escapes into the Forest of Arden. Some claim the name comes from a fictitious story of a soldier named Orlando Reeves. In Orlando you are never far from water, the wetlands dotted with hundreds of lakes and swamps.

The bedrock is made of porous limestone, and in 1981 a massive sink-hole over three hundred feet wide and ninety feet deep opened up outside Orlando, swallowing businesses and homes. On top of this wet, uncertain landscape, the largest tourist attractions in the world are built. Walt Disney World brings in an estimated forty-seven million people every year. Orlando likes its theatricality and it likes its rides. And from 2008 to 2011, the biggest ride in Orlando was the Casey Anthony case.

Baez, Sims, and I checked in at the Orange County Jail facility and made the long, slow walk through the multiple gates to the inner lockdown part of the jail. There, we waited about half an hour while dull-eyed friends and crisp nuns checked in as the inmates stared and shuffled behind the wired glass, shackled as they were ushered to their visitations.

When I met Casey Anthony, I was struck by how young and energetic she was. Unusual for a woman incarcerated for two years and being tried in a death penalty case. Usually, the inmates become hardened in their attitudes and the way they stare at you, nodding absently as you talk to them about the jury and the trial.

But here she was, handcuffed and eager to talk, engaged, absorbing the advice and strategy we discussed. More than anything, I wanted to help her understand the strange and convoluted way a jury would be selected in a case like this and what the jury would expect from a defendant in a case like this. Of course, you always want the defendant to have a realistic picture of the trial. You don't want to depress them or dash their hopes. But more importantly, you do not want to create false expectations.

And it is strange when you are in front of her. The knowledge that the state is trying to put this petite young woman to death. It is easier when you are distant and it is a news story. Easier when you are just meeting with the lawyers. But when you are in front of your client, especially a young woman, and know that you are trying to save her from death, it is more immediate. More urgent. You feel more, a greater responsibility. It is harder to make the excuses you sometimes make when your client is convicted. Because you know this is it. They do not just disappear into the system. They will reemerge just in time for their death. Not now. Not for years. But they do emerge, a chrysalis of death. And it does not fit our archetype—a woman on death row. Maybe that is why less than 2 percent of death row inmates are women.

In order to get the full picture of this family, I knew I had to see the house and meet the Anthonys. Their home sits on Hopespring Drive, just down the road from Suburban Drive, paradoxical names for such a gothic tale. When you step into her small bedroom, you see a teenager's room: light blue paint, frilly bedspread, posters. There is a sense that Casey emotionally stopped developing sometime in adolescence. What strikes you as you look around are the dozens upon dozens of individual and montage photographs of Caylee spread over all available surfaces. These photographs were there from before the time that Caylee went missing. This room starkly contrasts with the rest of the furnishings of the small home with its black lacquer Japanese furniture and running bamboo in the yard. One is struck by how close and compressed the house is, how near the pool is to the living room, and how close to the site where Caylee's remains were found.

We sat down to speak with George, Cindy, Lee and his fiancée, and their attorney at the time, Brad Conway. There was a palpable tension in the room. We were aware that Casey had made allegations of abuse against her father George and her brother, Lee. We also had heard about George's alleged mistress, Krystal Holloway, and her assertions that George had told her that Caylee's death "was an accident that snowballed out of control." We were aware that George had tried to commit suicide by taking sleeping pills in a Daytona Beach hotel. But George had also given a damning interview to the FBI against Casey. Baez also believed that Brad Conway had reviewed the records for

Texas EquuSearch, the search and recovery organization, while Baez had not been given the same opportunity. Texas EquuSearch was now represented by Mark NeJame, who had previously represented George and Cindy, and there was no love lost between NeJame and Baez. So, at the time, Baez and the team did not know whether George and the attorneys really did support Casey or whether George would implicate her at trial, as he did in later statements. George had been a deputy sheriff in Warren, Ohio, and a detective investigator, and we did not know how closely he identified with and would align with law enforcement in this case. All of his records from Ohio were destroyed in a fire, so we did not know details about his background in law enforcement but, having worked closely with law enforcement in other cases, it has been my observation that the color blue runs deep in the police community.

Secrets can also run deep in families. There is a hidden code—things that are done that should not be done. Things that are said that should not be said. And things that are never spoken of because they are too painful. Too laden with shame and guilt to be uttered. In these cases where you are dealing with terrible tragedy in a family, you wonder what really happened here, knowing that you will never truly know. Never truly understand those secrets. As a trial consultant, you walk into those shadows and try to light the darkness with your own experience, to understand this family, to make sense of them. You do this because, ultimately, you need the jury to understand who these people are and to translate the deep emotions, motivations, and mysteries into a true story for these twelve jurors. But you struggle because this family is different, confounding conventional customs and mores.

As a trial consultant, this struggle, this inward turn of introspection, is important in representing your client. You do not have the luxury of the sole role of advocate. You must speak with the prosecutor's and the jury's voice to the attorneys and your client. They need to clearly hear those voices. Because any trial-strategy or jury-selection decisions must take into account how the jury will hear both sides of the case. You need to know the prosecution's opening statements, their closing arguments, their direct and cross-examinations, their order of witnesses, their demonstrative evidence, and their themes. You need to know how jurors will talk about their case compared to yours in deliberations. So it is your job to be the pessimist, to push your clients to think harder and deeper about the case and to explore *any* avenue that either the state or the jurors may use to convict your client.

Just like everyone else, you want to solve the mystery. You look for the clues to help you find out what really happened: that hidden piece of evidence, that document, that revealing mannerism to provide you with that TV show "Aha!" revelation, when all becomes clear and the pieces fall into place. But it doesn't come. You don't find them. In actuality, the deeper you dig, the more complicated, confusing, and contradictory this world becomes. With discomfort, you slowly realize you will never know what happened. Because the truth lies in the past, on June 16, 2008. It lies in a house on Hopespring Drive. And only those that were there really know. Because this is real life. And real life is messy, incomplete, unknowable. And that is a problem. Because trials are about trying to know the unknowable.

Law enforcement tries to piece together a criminal portrait of the defendant to at least partially explain the unexplainable. Prosecutors try to complete that picture. To make the incomprehensible understandable. They want the jury to have a black-and-white, simplified picture of this world, because they need certainty to eliminate doubt. The prosecution looks for simple equations to make it easy for jurors. Casey lied equals consciousness of guilt equals killed her daughter. Casey went to parties and did not grieve for her daughter equals motivation to be rid of her child equals killed her daughter. Defense attorneys usually present more complex, chaotic, and uncertain portraits of their clients. Ultimately, you are trying to grapple with the same questions that a jury will grapple with. Did she? How? Why? You struggle with these questions to place yourself in the deliberation room. You have to examine your own feelings. Because you want to know how a jury can convict your client. You want to know how they will sentence her to die.

THE FOCUS GROUP

As the trial approached, a unique opportunity presented itself. Linda Kenney Baden introduced me to Ira Sutow, a producer from CBS who was interested in doing a different story on the case. He had seen that the prolonged and negative media coverage had truly created an issue with Casey getting a fair trial. He wanted to do a piece for *48 Hours* on the unprecedented effect of the coverage. I asked him if he would be interested in filming a focus group in which we would recruit a group of Orlando residents that were jury qualified, talk to them about the case, present evidence that had already been in the public forum, and ask them how they would vote. Since we had no money to conduct the focus group and I was working for free on the case, CBS offered to pay for the hiring of our mock jurors and the facility where the focus group would be held in exchange for the ability to film the group. I was not paid for conducting the project. Baez said that CBS had been balanced in their past coverage, and he approved the project. Although we knew we would not be picking a jury in Orlando, we truly wanted to learn how jurors looked at the case, especially the major evidence. Focus groups and mock trials allow the attorneys in the case to understand how jurors interpret the evidence in the case, how they apply their own life experiences and beliefs, and how they grapple with the verdict questions. They are invaluable in developing themes, demonstrative evidence to illustrate your main points, issues to emphasize and ignore, and types of jurors to select or avoid. Most importantly, jury research tells you where your land mines are, the problems you most need to address in order to persuade a jury to vote not guilty.

We selected a random group of Orange County citizens to be representative of the types of jurors you would see in an Orlando courtroom. At the beginning of the group, I spent about an hour with the "jurors," discussing all of the pretrial publicity they had seen. Most of our jurors said they believed Casey to be probably or definitely guilty based on the pretrial publicity. They agreed she could not get a fair trial in Orlando and probably could not get a fair trial anywhere in Florida. They mostly blamed the media for oversaturating the case with so many stories. Based on this publicity, they thought that Casey was a terrible person, had mostly a positive impression of Cindy, and had some real questions about George. Although Baez had garnered almost universally negative press, the jurors believed him to be doing his job and diligently defending his client.

So I took the jurors through the case, asking what they thought of the evidence. I kept the presentation neutral, avoiding both prosecution and defense arguments. I started with a timeline of events, highlighting the thirty-one days that Caylee was missing. Predictably, this was where jurors had the most problems with Casey's conduct, finding it inconceivable that a concerned mother would not report her own child missing, opting to go to parties and happily spend time with friends and family. I then took jurors through the 911 calls, Casey's arrest, and the recorded interrogation by Detective Yuri Melich in which Casey is caught in numerous lies. Again, jurors saw this evidence as damning. And then a curious thing happened.

As I went through the car evidence that we knew the prosecution would use to show that Casey had kept Caylee's body in the trunk, the jurors started having problems with the prosecution's forensic conclusions. Since most of this evidence was introduced through air sampling, jurors questioned the relatively new science and the ability of investigators to discern anything at all, given that the car had sat in the summer Orlando sun with a bag of food and other trash. And even though a neighbor testified about Casey borrowing a shovel two days after Caylee allegedly died, our jurors questioned why she would wait and drive Caylee around for two days without burying her. And when asked about the chloroform searches Casey had allegedly done on the family computer in March 2008 to plan the murder, jurors simply did not feel this was enough to show motive. Moreover, they questioned why she would wait until June of that year to carry out this premeditated plan.

I then discussed the discovery of Caylee's body. The jurors had more problems with this evidence. First, the timeline of the search raised questions about why the body was not discovered earlier. Meter reader Roy Kronk had reported finding a skull in the Suburban Drive location to the police on August 11, 2008, and they had come out to investigate on August 12 and 13. Additionally, one hundred volunteers from Texas EquuSearch combed the area in early September. With all of this activity, jurors found it difficult to believe that no one would have seen the bag containing Caylee's remains, especially since the final placement of the body was only nineteen feet from the road. There was inconsistent evidence that this area was submerged under water at the time of the searches, giving rise to juror belief that the body could have been seen if it had indeed been in the area.

Jurors were further troubled by the lack of DNA evidence, especially on the tape that supposedly covered Caylee's mouth. Even when I explained that DNA easily degrades over time, especially in a wet environment, jurors still believed there should have been more concrete forensic evidence to show that the tape had indeed been placed over the child's mouth or some other evidence from Casey that she had intentionally murdered her child. Jurors look for consistency in evidence. It is difficult to ask them to believe that you can pull air-sample evidence from the trunk of a car, preserve it for months, and draw conclusions about its origin, yet tell them you have no DNA or evidence of chloroform from the child's body.

I concluded the evidence presentation by playing the jurors tapes of the jailhouse visits between Casey, Cindy, and George.

And then, the most surprising revelation occurred. At the end of the group, I asked these twelve jurors, who had previously concluded that Casey Anthony was guilty, which of them would convict her of first-degree murder. Only three jurors raised their hands. More said they *wanted* to convict her but just did not feel that the evidence pointed in the direction of premeditation. I pushed the jurors to articulate what they thought happened on June 16, 2008. Many felt it was an accident—Caylee had drowned in the pool, and the rest had "snowballed out of control," to quote George's supposed mistress, Krystal Holloway. I asked them why Casey would not have just claimed it was an accident and spared herself these accusations. A few of the jurors felt there was a strange family dynamic that prevented Casey from admitting to her parents that her daughter had drowned on her watch. One juror stated that she felt Casey was a narcissist, and people that self-centered would never admit they were wrong. A number of jurors felt that George was involved in some way. When I asked them why, many felt that his statements to his mistress and suicide attempt indicated more than just grief over the death of his granddaughter.

It was evident from the focus group that jurors had a hard time with motive and with the forensic evidence in the case. Without knowing why she would want to kill her own daughter and with uncertainty about how the murder had occurred, jurors were not willing to convict Casey Anthony, despite their initial predisposition toward guilt and their reaction to her lies and behavior in the thirty-one days. Their reactions gave us a clear road map for the trial.

When the *48 Hours* episode aired, and CBS showed the jurors' reaction to the case, the network endured its own firestorm of outrage from the public, with hundreds of emails and blog posts criticizing CBS for supposedly supporting the defense. Also in the show was footage of Florida attorney general Pam Bondi talking about how the prosecution had a "mountain of evidence" and laying out the prosecution's case. The attorney general of the state is the chief law enforcement officer and is the credible authority on crime for most people in the state. When she speaks, people listen. So when she says a defendant is guilty, most people believe her. The only problem is that she is Casey Anthony's attorney general as well, since Casey was a resident of the state and is presumed innocent until proven guilty. So when the attorney general goes on national television and proclaims one of her citizens guilty, it can be viewed as an attempt to prejudice the jury pool, which could be considered jury tampering. It raises more questions about how political interests influence how cases are investigated, charged, and prosecuted in a high-profile media trial.

THE JURY SELECTION

Once we knew a clearer path to defending this case, we still needed a jury that could also deliver the same verdict as our focus group respondents. It is one thing to sit in a room for four hours and give your opinions on a case where there is no consequence to your final judgment. It is quite another to be pulled from your home, moved eighty-five miles, and sequestered for six weeks during a nationally covered trial, where you know the public and the pundits are clamoring for one result.

A jury questionnaire is one of the easiest ways to discern whether a jury has been prejudiced by pretrial publicity or has any other biases that would impair their ability to be fair and impartial. Jurors can fill it out and give voice to their candid attitudes without the pressure of a robed authority and strangers judging their responses. A questionnaire is used frequently in both civil and criminal trials and almost always in high-profile trials. Perry refused our request for a questionnaire and laid out his jury-selection plan. He would reveal the location of the jury selection to selected lawyers on the trial teams a few days before trial. They could not disclose the location even to members of their own team until the day of selection. With only hours of notice, they would then have to scurry to the location where Perry would pick a jury in five days. There would be no questionnaire and the attorneys would be limited to questions about the death penalty, pretrial publicity, and whether jurors could move to Orlando and sit as a juror on a six-week trial. The jury selection would be broadcast live. I told Baez that this plan was problematic not only for us but also for the prosecution and the court itself. Jury selection in high-profile cases has numerous potential snags that can derail the whole process unless you carefully plan it out. I urged him to have a conference call with the court to make a cooperative plan so that all parties could be better prepared for what was sure to be a unique and challenging jury-selection process.

But the judge was determined to pursue his course. We knew that even Perry was having problems, because he stated at one point that if we could not pick a jury in five days, we would have to come back to Orlando and pick a jury. This was absurd, as he had ruled that Orlando had been prejudiced by the publicity in the case, therefore making it impossible to pick a fair jury in the venue. He could not then rule that it had magically become fair and impartial. The judge relented on moving the selection back to Orlando, but still insisted he would pick a jury in five days. I knew this to be a fantasy. Jury selection in death penalty cases with little or no publicity can easily take two weeks. The media exposure and sequestration issues could have easily pushed this selection to a month. In any case, this unilateral plan created a number of problems.

First, I felt that the entire state had been prejudiced by the pretrial publicity and that we were entitled to make a change of venue motion in whatever venue we were going for appellate purposes. If we didn't know where we were going, we couldn't study the venue or make the motion. Second, while judges may make the decision to broadcast the trial live, jury selection is almost never broadcast. Juror privacy is critical to giving them a sheltered forum to disclose their true feelings on a range of subjects and to allow them to focus on the evidence rather than how the public may perceive their verdict. That they would have to disclose their opinions and personal experiences in front of the whole nation was sure to inhibit their candor and increase the chances that a stealth juror would try to make their way onto the jury. Finally, this plan made it almost impossible for me to attend the jury selection. I had told Baez and the team early on that I wanted to bring another consultant on to lend their local knowledge of jurors in Florida and to provide coverage during the trial since my pro bono involvement limited my ability to participate in a potentially multiweek process in Florida. We had discussed the profile of jurors we were looking for and the types of questions we needed to ask to eliminate the riskiest and most problematic jurors. We had discussed a couple of consultants, and I urged that they be contacted. As the trial approached and the judge was unyielding in disclosing the location, I told Baez I simply could not afford to fly at the last minute to an undisclosed location for an indefinite period of time. We had to scramble to find a consultant at the last minute. To compound matters, one of the contacted consultants then went to the media and announced with outrage that I had "quit" the defense team. This caused more headaches as Baez and I had to try to dispel these rumors and to prepare for the selection.

To reinforce my belief that the entire state of Florida had been polluted by the media coverage of the case, WFTV released a series of polls on the eve of trial. These polls demonstrated that in Orlando, Jacksonville, Pensacola, West Palm Beach, and Tampa, 80–90 percent of jurors knew about the case from multiple media sources and believed Casey to be already guilty. Ironically, about 50 percent said that even though they thought she was probably guilty, they could still reach a verdict in the case. Would that jury still be considered to be fair, impartial, and open-minded?

In the same poll, approximately 50 percent of Floridians supported the death penalty for *all* first-degree murders, meaning they thought anyone convicted of first-degree murder should automatically get the death penalty, disregarding any evidence that might make that person's life redeemable. However, in a death penalty trial, there are two phases: a guilt phase and a penalty phase. Most are familiar with the guilt phase of a trial. Only after a jury has found a defendant guilty of a crime where a special circumstance applies that qualifies them for the death penalty do they move on to the penalty phase. In a penalty phase, the prosecution presents "aggravation" evidence or evidence that suggests the defendant is so bad, he or she deserves the death penalty. In this phase, the defense also presents "mitigation" evidence, or evidence that suggests that the defendant has redeemable qualities and should be given life in prison without the possibility of parole.

The specter of finality always hangs over a death penalty case. You sleep less and worry more. And prosecutors know that when the death penalty is on the table, they have a strong guilt case, preoccupying the defense with preparing evidence to save the defendant's life. But when you are asking a jury to kill someone, you had better make it as easy as possible for them. Because killing is hard. Despite the body count on TV, in movies, and in gaming, a juror sitting in a courtroom is looking at a real person.

And that is why jury selection in a death penalty case is different. Prosecutors are looking at jurors who will make it easy on themselves. An "eye for an eye," they say, quoting scripture and dissociating from the defendant they are looking at. Prosecutors look for jurors who strongly operate under the "just world" hypothesis, an opaque psychological term that becomes vividly colorful in a death penalty case. These people emphatically believe that the world has order and rules and those that break them will suffer the consequences.

And that is when you look hard at a juror in the moment when they are asked whether they would be willing to vote for someone's death. The too quick, too eager "yes" demarks the avenger or calculating ("premeditation equals death") types. Do they believe in a controlled, certain, and just world or a world filled with uncertainty, ambiguity, and unexplained mystery? You look for jurors who will struggle, be uneasy, and can reconcile themselves with unsettling contradiction. For in a death penalty case, you are asking twelve jurors to define justice in the most final terms.

But it is ultimately unfair to jurors. We forbid them from considering punishment in any other case, whether it is shoplifting or a DUI. Yet we ask them to make a literal life-or-death decision involving the most serious of charges. And judges expect jurors to do it easily. "Can you follow the law and impose death?" they ask the juror. And if he or she hesitates, the judge dismisses them for their inability to follow the law. This is why death penalty research shows that jury selection in these cases preloads a jury more likely to convict a defendant in the guilt phase and impose the death penalty. Prosecutors know this. When you ask every juror if they can impose the death penalty, you have subconsciously already asked them to vote on your case. Since you spend time asking "hypothetically" what they would do if they did get to that phase, jurors presuppose they probably will get there.

Florida and Texas have been in competition for the death penalty championship for years. Texas executes more death row inmates, and Florida has more exonerations where the death penalty is overturned. Florida's death sentences have also been marked by horrific, botched executions. Until they made lethal injection an option, Florida called its electric chair "Old Sparky," a three-legged wooden contraption made by inmates, which would periodically set the sentenced man on fire. Florida also has a unique distinction—they are the only state in the union where a defendant can be sentenced to death by a simple majority vote. They have to be convicted of the crime unanimously, but they can be sentenced to death by only seven out of twelve jurors.

These challenges make jury selection in a death penalty case much harder for a defendant. Sometimes a good guilt juror is a bad penalty-phase juror, or vice versa. So you need to decide where to play your cards. Because jury selection is part poker, part chess, and part roulette. You need a strategy, and you need luck.

Perry did not allow us to know where he was picking a jury until the day selection was scheduled to start. Since we all knew this would make attendance unworkable, a team of consultants arranged to monitor the jury selection via the live web feeds and to send emails and texts to the team about questions to ask and thoughts on the individual jurors. At the end of each day, we would look at the jurors and their responses, and consultants who were monitoring the selection in Florida, Texas, and California would have an online discussion about which jurors to keep or kick. But the team on the ground, Baez, Mason, Sims, Ann Finnell, and Casey, had to make the final calls.

As I have said, jury selection is really jury de-selection. You try to identify your highest-risk jurors and to eliminate them by exercising cause or peremptory challenges. You invite jurors to voice their skepticism, hatred, and outright conclusions about your client's guilt. And you only have ten strikes to eliminate those jurors who are most problematic. So you have to target jurors with the worst attitudes toward your client and the highest leadership potential. You are selecting not only individual jurors for the case but also a group to decide your client's fate. And you are most carefully looking at who will lead that group. Both attorneys and the media always ask about the demographic labels of our most desired jurors: men or women, old or young. In Casey's case, the question is whether we wanted single people, or mothers and fathers with young children. But the real truth is you look for an attitude, a mind-set, a worldview, and a temperament that fits the case. In this case, like with a number of other cases I have written about in this book, I again knew we wanted smart, skeptical, and independent jurors. And I needed more than one, because we would need several if we got to the death penalty phase.

The actual jury selection took eleven long days, marred by a series of incidents. At one point a Texas EquuSearch volunteer who had searched for Caylee was called as a juror and discussed the search freely with all of the other assembled jurors. All fifty of those jurors had to be dismissed. At one point, a spectator called out, "She killed someone anyway!" during jury selection, prompting the dismissal of that juror. And Perry almost ran out of jurors, threatening to empanel jurors from the homeless shelter next door.

When you pick juries, you train yourself to hear voices. You sit and listen to prospective jurors, and then you project what their voices will sound like in deliberations. And you listen to those voices to try to match them to the verdict you want. They whisper in your ear during opening statements, when witnesses are on the stand, when you are giving closing arguments, and when the judge finally instructs them on the law. These jurors that spoke to us and sat in judgment of Casey were ordinary people: a gym teacher, a retired nurse's aide, two people who worked for Verizon, an IT worker, a salesman, a secretary, a handyman, a cook. One was a policeman's daughter, one was a lawyer's daughter. Two had difficulty with the death penalty, and two previously thought Casey to be guilty. All would unanimously make one of the most difficult decisions they had made in their lives.

THE TRIAL

I tape every episode.
—Observer at Casey Anthony trial

Our family is at Disney World, but this is more exciting for me.
—Another observer at Casey Anthony trial

The jury was sworn and seated in an Orlando courtroom on May 20, 2011, while another jury had been seated at home for more than two years. The jury in Orlando was charged with keeping an open mind, only considering evidence from the witness stand, and not discussing the case or doing any independent investigation. The jury at home did not have any of these rules. And they had already made up their minds.

Trial strategy is often about leverage and weight—both the type and amount of evidence that gradually moves a jury to the decision you want them to reach. The defense's main leverage in the Anthony case lay primarily in four areas: attacking the prosecution's "fantasy forensics," the Anthony family dynamic, the severity of the death penalty, and the pretrial publicity. Since doubt is a defense attorney's primary tool, our main goal was to create uncertainty and to make the jury question the prosecution's case in all of these primary areas.

Although there was much discussion in the press about Casey's lying, no one can sit and pretend for six weeks without revealing their true character. We knew the jury would be watching her in the small moments before testimony and on breaks to see whether the true Casey would reveal herself. We knew they would watch her reaction to her parents and to the testimony about the discovery of Caylee's body. The jury would be comparing her demeanor in court to the interrogation tapes, to the jailhouse interviews, and to the bar pictures of her infamous "hot body" competition. In essence, she would be testifying in trial through all of these images. This made our preparation easy. She needed to be genuine in her emotional reactions in court. She had to dress appropriately. Anything tight or low cut would emphasize negative impressions of her sexuality and make her seem less like a mother and more like the careless tramp the prosecution was making her out to be. The fit had to be loose and the colors generally light. It was inevitable in a six-week trial that she would relax and smile at some points, joke with attorneys at the table, which would be interpreted in the press. But she needed to be serious and engaged in the trial.

Because the pretrial publicity had been so pervasive, I was concerned that the burden of proof had shifted to the defense proving Casey innocent. While jurors do often hold prosecutors to the "reasonable doubt" standard, it is counter intuitive—we expect the accused to explain why they didn't do what they are accused of doing. This has become more pronounced in a post-9/11, pro-prosecution era where we have regularly suspended the Bill of Rights for criminal defendants under the label of "terrorists" and "enemy combatants." Baez had managed to hold off for nearly three years. Now it was time to tell the story of what happened in his opening statement.

Baez knew that jurors would want to hear from Casey, especially to explain how she lost her daughter, and the thirty-one days she did not tell anyone about her disappearance—our greatest weakness in the case. For that, Casey would have to take the stand, a rarity for a criminal defendant. If she were to testify, Baez would have to introduce jurors to her testimony in the opening statement, including her account of the accident and her allegations of abuse against George and Lee. While there has been much criticism of the lawyers' decision to introduce those allegations, it was ultimately Casey's decision whether she wanted to testify about what happened that June day and what happened on Hopespring Drive when she was growing up.

Baez's opening statement, which discussed the drowning accident and the abuse allegations against George and Lee, created a stunned reaction in the press and the public. But it provided an important framework for the jury in dismissing key pieces of forensic evidence and explaining motive. The drowning accident made the car evidence extraneous to motive. Even though Baez, Mason, and especially Sims, whose specialty was in holding expert witnesses accountable, were planning on attacking the evidence from the car, the accident made this evidence irrelevant to the murder charge. The abuse allegations against George and Lee started to explain the Anthony family dynamic and why Casey or George would have tried to cover up the drowning.

Prosecutors sometimes make the mistake of believing that more evidence builds a better case. They often use the phrase a "mountain of evidence" to describe what the defense has to climb. But more evidence also can mean more questions and ultimately more doubt. In the prosecution's case, they called Casey's family and friends to describe her deception and lack of grieving in the thirty-one days before Cindy confronted her about Caylee. But these same witnesses, on cross-examination, described a remarkable and loving relationship between the mother and daughter, confounding the prosecution's theory that Casey had wanted to be rid of Caylee to live a freer life.

A great deal of the case then turned to the experts. Linda Kenney Baden had laid a solid foundation for the defense in taking the depositions of a number of the state's experts, and the attorneys did an excellent job of questioning the agenda and credibility of the state's forensic experts. They were relying on new science involving captured air samples, a dubious stain on the trunk mat, along with testimony about the horrible smell of Casey's car. The new science had no peer review and had never been previously allowed in a court of law. Moreover, this evidence was being used to bolster the state's claim that Casey had used chloroform to kill Caylee. However, the chloroform "signature" could have come from other sources, and no chloroform had ever been bought by Casey or recovered from the house.

The state also had their own TV star, coroner Dr. Jan Garavaglia, or "Dr. G.," who had her own reality show and testified to her conclusions in labeling the death a homicide. However, she could not conclude the cause of death, relying only on the tape around the jaw and mouth area. In an attempt to tie the body to Casey, an FBI forensic expert also testified to the outline of a heart-shaped sticker, which magically disappeared before it could be photographed. Earlier in the case, Nancy Grace and numerous other commentators had spent countless hours opining on the implications of Casey placing a heart-shaped sticker on the duct tape covering her child's mouth. But testimony also showed that George primarily used the duct tape, and he had discarded deceased family pets in trash bags. All of these inconsistencies created uncertainty about the time and cause of death. The questions were made more glaring by the hype and expectations driven by the media coverage.

And it was here, at the conclusion of the prosecution's evidence, where the pretrial publicity did the most damage to the state's case. Because when prosecutors Jeff Ashton and Linda Burdick rested, there was a palpable disappointment. There was no new evidence, no smoking gun, no new revelations. The public and perhaps the jury had already heard this evidence for nearly three years. It did not have the emotional impact of freshly heard evidence. From an objective standpoint, the state put on a decent circumstantial evidence case. But the Sunshine Law and pervasive coverage of the case had deprived the jury of the weight and heft of their case, making it seem slight, barely able to tilt the scales.

In putting on the defense case, I considered what jurors still needed to hear to answer their questions and their concerns about our case. It was my belief that the jury needed to understand *how* the accident could have happened: the layout of the house and access to the pool. The jury also needed someone to testify about the different ways that people grieve. Since Casey's behavior was so aberrant, so unusual, the jurors needed to understand that people's reactions to loss take many forms, including inappropriate behavior.

When they were on the stand, defense experts addressed and reinforced the questions, inconsistencies, and omissions in the state's case. Significantly, testimony about the discovery of the body raised questions about the very basis of the prosecution's theory. Ashton had continuously said that the tape on the skull told the story about Casey's premeditated murder of Caylee and was the basis for the capital charge. But meter reader Kronk's testimony raised serious questions about when he and the Orange County sheriffs had discovered the body or whether the body had even been in the final location the entire time prior to discovery. More importantly, since the bag had been handled and the skull had dropped out and rolled, questions remained about whether the tape across the skull was there in the first place.

Most importantly, jurors spent time with the Anthonys. George Anthony denied his affair with Holloway and denied telling her the drowning was an accident "that snowballed out of control." He testified about his suicide attempt and denied abusing Casey. Cindy testified that she had done the computer searches that resulted in chloroform appearing in the search history. The prosecution tried to impeach her by showing she was at work at the time the searches were done. Casey's brother Lee testified about the stain in the trunk of the car and about feeling left out of Caylee's birth. They all wept openly in court, joined by Casey at the defense table. The Anthonys became a dysfunctional family for the country. In this live reality show, jurors were left to wonder why Cindy and Lee would clearly try to help Casey with their testimony while George, given numerous opportunities, would not, knowing his daughter faced the death penalty. And if, as the prosecution was claiming, Casey was a cold-blooded killer of her own daughter, what made her that way?

> *Cynthia Marie,*
>
> *As you get this letter, this should be no surprise that I have decided to leave the earth, because I need to be with Caylee Marie.*
>
> *I cannot keep on going because it should be me that is gone from this earth, not her.*
>
> *I have lived many years, I am satisfied with my decision because I have never been the man you, Lee, Casey & especially Caylee Marie deserved.*
>
> *I have never been the man any of you could count on. I have always let each of you down in more ways than I could remem-*

ber. I do not feel sorry for myself, I am just sorry I burden all of you the way I have.

My loss of life is meaningless. . . . I cannot be strong anymore. Caylee Marie, our granddaughter, I miss her, I miss her so much. I know you do too. You were always the one that provided for her. What did I provide?

I blame myself for her being gone! You know for months, as a matter of fact, for a year or so I brought stuff up, only to be told not to be negative. . . . I sit here, falling apart, because I should have done more. She was so close to home, why was she there? Who placed her there? Why is she gone? Why? For months, you & I, especially you always questioned, why?

I want this to go away for Casey! What happened? Why could she not come to us? Especially you, why not Lee?

Who is involved with this stuff for Caylee?

I am going [crazy] because I want to go after these people Casey hung with prior to Caylee being gone.

That is why I got that gun. I wanted to scare these people. You know! They know more than they have stated. You cannot sugar coat, kidglove these people. They need hard knocks to get info from.

Sure that will not bring Caylee Marie back, but was Casey threatened? You know, Casey does not deserve to be where she is!

I miss her, I miss her so much. I am worried for her. Her personal safety is always on my mind. . . . I cannot function knowing our granddaughter is gone. Caylee Marie never had a chance to grow. . . . I have taken what meds was given to me with alcohol & I am ready to give up.

As I can tell by my writing & thinking I am getting very stupid. Wow, what a word STUPID. Yes, I am. Again, I do not feel sorry for myself, but yes I am STUPID. Cannot deal with stuff anymore. The loss of Caylee Marie. The loss of Casey. The loss of us, Cynthia Marie, the meds, I am ready.

Saying good bye, please understand it is for the best. I do not deserve life anymore. Anymore us. . . . You know I never got to say good bye. I am at this place & all is getting fuzzy & my writing is all over the place. I love you, I love you, I hope you get to see Casey soon. All the people we met, wow the writing is getting weird, I love you, I am sorry—I will take care of Caylee—once I get to God. . . . I am so tired, at least I shaved today, Wow—I'm tripping out, I am sorry. I love you—Cynthia Marie. Caylee here I come.

—George Anthony's suicide note

In closing argument, Baez drove home the problems with the discovery of the body and the state's forensic case as well as inconsistencies with their theory of Casey's premeditation. He kept reiterating the holes and the uncertainty in their case, stressing that the state could not prove when, where, or concretely how Casey had murdered Caylee. More importantly, I wanted the jury to know about the hidden assumptions in the prosecution's case. That the state, the prosecution team, the media, and the public all wanted, indeed expected, a conviction. That they were relying on fundamental biases, speculation, and rumor in place of real evidence. They wanted the jury to believe that she was a bad mother, a whore, and a liar. That she did not behave the way we expect a grieving mother to behave. And because of these fundamental assumptions, she must have killed her child. I wanted the jury to know the state was really asking only for the death penalty and that this was really the only charge that they had taken any effort to prove. Since jurors can easily decide on a lower count if they feel the prosecutors have not fully proven their case, I wanted to reduce the chance of this kind of compromise. I wanted them to know the law and their duty as jurors. That it would take diligence to discern the real evidence from all of the publicity. And that it would take courage to resist the public pressure to convict.

THE VERDICT

On a hot Fourth of July weekend, people across the country barbequed and watched closing arguments in the case. And on July 5, after eleven hours of deliberation, the jury in an Orlando courtroom acquitted Casey of first- and second-degree murder, aggravated child abuse, and aggravated manslaughter of a child. They convicted her of four counts of lying to the police. Their first vote was 10–2 for acquittal on the most serious counts, almost the same as our focus group in Orlando. More than 5 million people watched the verdict on HLN, more than watched the catastrophic events of 9/11 unfold. CNN had 2.3 million viewers. Fox had 2.9 million viewers, and MSNBC had nearly a million viewers. Grace's show had 2.9 million that evening, the biggest spike in the history of her show. The outcry was instantaneous, and the comparisons to the O. J. Simpson verdict immediate. And while Simpson was a Jacobean tragedy, bloody with tones of vengeance and sexual jealousy, Anthony was a mythical Greek tragedy, familial, secretive, with fatal flaws and mistakes leading to an irrevocable and deadly crisis.

The jurors were vilified and their decision condemned, evidence of the investment that the public had in one outcome to the case. They received death threats, one left the state, and the rest went into hiding. Perry would later go on *The Today Show* and speak about his "surprise, shock, and disbelief," stating that he thought the "prosecutors had proved a great case" and comparing Baez to a used car salesman, belying his own leanings in the case.

But if Perry, the pundits, and the public listen to what the jurors said, they followed the law, their interpretation of the evidence, and their own common sense. One juror discussed how the legal premeditation instruction requires the defendant's contemplation of the murder before the actual act. Since the prosecution did not prove the time of the murder, he felt the prosecution could not meet this premeditation requirement. Another two jurors discussed the inability of the prosecution to concretely show when, where, and how the murder occurred, leading them to vote for acquittal. These two found credibility problems with George but said they had no evidence of the abuse, so did not consider it. Many of their comments echoed those of the focus group we held in Orlando.

Independent juries are the cornerstones of the justice system. They are chosen by both the prosecution and the defense. They trust that a group of twelve citizens, brave and true, working together to interpret the evidence and the law, will use their independent judgment to arrive at a just verdict. There is no formula, no predictable result. Each jury has its own way of piecing together the evidence in the case and applying the law. We rely on that individuality as the hallmark of citizen juries. Our founders wisely felt this independence was the best safeguard against a state's unchecked power to seize the life or property of a citizen.

Real trials, like real life, are complicated, sad, confusing, and sometimes inexplicable. They do not fit into an hour-long news show or detective drama. American justice is not *American Idol*. It is a process. A messy, frustrating process. And it is one of the prices of unfettered democracy.

I was on a dock in Lake Arrowhead with my daughter when I heard about the verdict. I was relieved but not happy. I did not celebrate. Whatever happened on June 16, 2008, a small but bright light was gone from the world. I paddled out with my daughter into the lake.

Index